AMERICAN
BUSINESS
VALUES

Second Edition

GERALD F. CAVANAGH
University of Detroit

Prentice-Hall, Inc., Englewood Cliffs, New Jersey 07632

Library of Congress Cataloging in Publication Data

CAVANAGH, GERALD F.
   American business values.

Rev. ed. of: American business values in transition.
c1976.
   Includes bibliographical references and index.
   1. United States—Commerce.   2. Industry—Social
aspects—United States.   3. Business ethics.   I. Cavanagh,
Gerald F.   American business values in transition.
II. Title.
HF5343.C38 1984   338.0973   83-21296
ISBN 0-13-024159-8

Editorial/production supervision: Kim Gueterman
Cover design: Ben Santora
Manufacturing buyer: Ed O'Dougherty

Previous edition published under the title of *American Business Values in Transition.*

Printed in the United States of America

10 9 8 7 6 5 4 3 2

ISBN 0-13-024159-8

PRENTICE-HALL INTERNATIONAL, INC., *London*
PRENTICE-HALL OF AUSTRALIA PTY. LIMITED, *Sydney*
EDITORA PRENTICE-HALL DO BRASIL, LTDA., *Rio de Janeiro*
PRENTICE-HALL CANADA INC., *Toronto*
PRENTICE-HALL OF INDIA PRIVATE LIMITED, *New Delhi*
PRENTICE-HALL OF JAPAN, INC., *Tokyo*
PRENTICE-HALL OF SOUTHEAST ASIA PTE. LTD., *Singapore*
WHITEHALL BOOKS LIMITED, *Wellington, New Zealand*

CONTENTS

5 ETHICS IN BUSINESS   126

6 FREE ENTERPRISE AND THE CORPORATION: PEOPLE AND POLICIES   162

FOREWORD

After having been a part of the curriculum in many schools of business for twenty years or more, the field now vaguely described as "business and society" seems at last to be coming into focus. A common core of interest has begun to evolve and to give promise of providing the integrating concepts of teaching and research that have been so conspicuous by their absence in the past. Evidence of this long delayed crystallization can be found in new course descriptions and outlines, in the research interests of those working in the field, and in the proceedings of conferences convened for the purpose of examining the proper content and parameters of this important area of practical, as well as academic, concern. The field and its integrating theme appear very clearly, as suggested above, to be the complex, dynamic, two-way relationship between the economic institutions of our society, with which most schools of business are primarily concerned, and the social systems in which those institutions now operate and are likely to operate in the future.

It would be incorrect and misleading to suggest that the interaction between business and society has not been part of the business school curriculum in the past. In one form or another, this interaction has played an important role in business and society courses for many years. There are, however, several basic differences between what has been done in the past and the new rallying point we now see evolving. The old, and still dominant, approach has been very narrow in its emphasis and in its boundaries and has all too often been limited to little more than an instructor's own specialty in such areas as social control, business and government, or antitrust. Even where an instructor's narrow predispositions are not present, the "social" side of the relationship is often viewed as being static, or relatively so, and external to the current decision or situational context; and the primary goals of the course are those of explaining the phenomenon of business to the students and of analyzing the requirements of business-like, efficient, or responsible behavior in a rather loose social sense. Furthermore, the emphasis is almost wholly the private, large, and industrial aspects of the economic sector, with little, if any, attention devoted to the public, small, or nonindustrial variables.

The flaws in the approach are obvious, and changes are already beginning to take place. What appears to be evolving, and what we believe should be evolving, is a much greater interest in the dynamics of the whole system. What is needed is a systematic analysis of the effects (noneconomic as well as economic) of business on other institutions and on the social system, and of the effects of changes in other institutions and in the social system on the economic sector. Most important, perhaps, the stage should be set for an understanding of the basic assumptions, attitudes, values, concepts, and ideologies that underlie a particular arrangement of economic institutions and social systems and of how changes in these assumptions affect the arrangements and the interactions among the various parts of the whole system.

Two other points ought also to be made here. *First*, although most schools of business do not behave as though it were so, they are actually engaged in training the managers of tomorrow and not the managers of today. As the relationships between economic institutions and their social environment become more intimate, and as each part of the whole system becomes more sensitive and more responsive to changes in the other parts, how much more important it is going to be for the manager to understand the dynamics of the system as a whole than it is for him to know what the momentary conformation happened to be when he was in school. It seems to us, further, that one of the manifestations of an industrially mature society will be the economic sector's diminishing importance and, as a consequence, a reversal of the flow of influence from the economic sector to society as a whole. The manager of the future will need to be more sensitive to changes in society than he ever was in the past. His training will have to include a very different congeries of tools and ingredients than it now does.

Second, we think note should be taken of some evidence now beginning to accumulate that suggests that in the future schools of business may come to play the same sort of influential role in the profession of management that schools of law and medicine now play in theirs. If this change should come about, it will become ever more important that managers, during their period of formal education, be provided with those conceptual and analytical tools that best meet the needs of their profession and of the society as a whole. If present forecasts prove to be accurate and "continuing education" becomes a much more important aspect of higher education than it is now, among the first academic institutions to be profoundly affected will be the schools of business. The influence of the schools upon the profession of management will become more immediate and the need for pragmatic training in the interactions between economic institutions and social systems greatly enhanced.

While there is no great disagreement on these general issues, it would be a mistake to assume that there is consensus on the details. We believe that this series takes into account both the agreement on some of the broader points and the lack of consensus on many of the more specific aspects of the changes taking place in the environmental field. For example, there are people who believe that comments like those made above dictate the integration of social materials in all parts of the business curriculum rather than their use in specialized courses devoted to the field; there are many who feel that the bulk of such work should be done in specialized courses; there are many views in the area between these two extremes. We feel that this series is designed in such a way that it can cater to business school curricula of all varieties.

We visualize this series evolving in a set of concentric circles starting at the core and expanding outward. The innermost circle consists of those books that provide much of the basic material that is usually included in the introductory courses in "business and society," including the institutional role of large corporations; government interaction with business; business ideology and values; methodological approaches to measuring the social impact of business activities; corporations and political activities; and the influence of corporate management on the formulation of public policy.

The next circle is made up of books that deal with the impact of corporate activities in specific functional areas. The issues covered here include marketing and social conflict; accounting, accountability, and the public interest; corporate personnel policies and individual rights; and computers and invasion of privacy.

The outermost circle consists of books that are either interdisciplinary or cross-cultural in nature or both. Here we are concerned with the synergistic effect of various economic activities on the society as a whole. On one dimension we are concerned with issues such as how technology gets introduced into society; the economic effects of various types of social welfare programs; how various social activities like health, sanitation, mass transit, and public education are affected by the actions of business; and the social consequences of zero economic growth or population growth. On another level, studies will include comparison between corporate behavior in different social systems.

The concentric circles are not intended to be mutually exclusive, nor do they reflect a certain order of priority in the nature of problems or publication schedule. They are simply a convenient arrangement for thinking about the relationships among various problem areas.

In addition to their role as part of the training provided by collegiate schools of business and management and other social science disciplines, most of the volumes in this series are also of use and interest to managers and to the general public. The basic purpose of the series is to help provide a better understanding of the relationship between our economic institutions and the broader social system, and it is obvious that the need which the series hopes to satisfy is not confined to students of business and management or for that matter even to students. The ultimate goal, we suppose, is not just better corporate social policy but better public policy as well, in the formation of which all citizens participate Consequently, we have urged the authors of these volumes to keep in mind the broad, in addition to the narrow, targets and to couch their work in language, content, and style that meet both kinds of requirements.

S. Prakash Sethi
Dow Votaw

University of California
Berkeley, California

PREFACE

This book examines the values, ethics, and ideology of American business. Business values and peoples' expectations of business and work have a profound impact on such things as product quality, job design, new products, productivity, and government industrial policy. Thus values have an immense influence on the firm and on the manager. Business and work are so central to our society that they also have a great influence on our personal values, goals, and life styles.

Therefore, the purpose of this book is:

1. To examine the values and ideology upon which the free enterprise system of production and exchange is built,
2. To provide the reader with the language and tools to do ethical analysis, and some practice in dealing with ethical problems,
3. To aid readers in formulating and clarifying their own personal values and goals,
4. To aid business managers in designing products, work, and the work environment, taking into account values and ethics,
5. To help all citizens in clarifying their expectations of business and government.

Corporate planning and national economic policy are interdependent, and currently neither have a clear and consistent direction. To plan either with any hope of long-term success demands an understanding of our common values. To aid this understanding, both traditional business values and the challenges to these values will here be presented clearly and strongly. The reader will note how highly I regard the basic American free enterprise system. Nevertheless, entrepreneurship, a longer-term point of view, and creative, energetic and cooperative managers and workers are needed in order for American business to survive and continue to be productive. I do confess a bias, but it is one I share with most of you. It is that of the central importance of *each* individual person. Every business decision, action, and policy should be made with the best interests of *all* people in mind: customers, employees, neighbors, suppliers, and the larger community, along with the traditional concern for shareholders and management. Not to be forgotten are the most disenfranchised.

American Business Values retains the best elements of *American Business*

Values in Transition, yet adds many important new features. Chapter 5, "Ethics in Business," is entirely new and fills a serious need. As an ethically-based, yet practical, treatise on business ethics, it is useful to business managers and students alike. Chapters 6 and 7 are also almost totally new. Chapter 6 discusses contemporary business and its values. As a point of entry, one could begin reading here. Chapter 7 underscores the importance of values and ideology, examines trends, and projects future shifts in values. The first four chapters, which have been widely praised by readers, are left substantially as they were. Chapters 1 and 2 provide an historical overview of persons, problems, and events that have brought us to where we are today. Chapter 3 on the Marxist position, which remains the most telling indictment of free enterprise, is now included with the historical chapters. Chapter 4 examines actions, motivations, and stresses on the person in the organization through the eyes of the psychologist and sociologist. Each of these chapters has been updated with new materials. A number of figures and tables have also been added, along with discussion questions at the end of each chapter. A summary of content: chapters 1-3 are historical, chapter 4 is behavioral, chapter 5 treats business ethics, and chapters 6 and 7 cover business and society material.

This book is the result of two decades of stimulating and enriching dialogue with associates: fellow faculty, business people, students, and brother members of the Society of Jesus. It has benefited from the comments of many who have used the first edition. Otto Bremmer, Kirk Hanson, and Manuel Velasquez provided suggestions that greatly aided this new book. Arthur McGovern applied his professional expertise and wrote most of chapter 4. Margaret Betz, Garth Hallett, and Jennifer Coury read substantial portions and provided many helpful comments. The first edition benefited from the insights of Michael Lavelle, John Maurer, Margaret Betz, Prakash Sethi, Dow Votaw, Joseph Daoust, Theodore Purcell, and Henry Wirtenberger. Prentice-Hall's editors have helped shephard the manuscript through to completion; I am especially indebted to Kim Gueterman and Linda Albelli. Kathleen Daniels helped immensely by researching data, critiquing the manuscript, and doing the index. Virginia Carson typed substantial portions of the manuscript. For this and other support, I am grateful to the College of Business and Administration of the University of Detroit. Finally, mature graduate business students, who have for some years held management responsibilities, have provided important inputs, emphases and qualifications to the book. To them, too, I am grateful.

Gerald F. Cavanagh, S.J.

University of Detroit
Detroit, Michigan

AMERICAN
BUSINESS
VALUES

CHAPTER ONE
VALUES AND IDEOLOGY IN AMERICAN LIFE

Probe the earth and see where your main roots are.

—Henry David Thoreau

Values undergird, and sometimes determine, the important decisions that any individual makes. Whether these values are acknowledged or implicit, they are there; moreover, they have a profound influence on our lives and actions. To be aware of and to probe one's values allows a person to understand those values better and hence have greater control over her or his own life and actions.

A value system forms the foundation upon which decisions are made. This is equally true of business decisions as it is of other, more personal decisions. Values become so much a part of us that we are often unaware of their precise content and impact. An analogy might help: the way we operate an automobile. As we learn the process, it becomes more and more automatic. Gradually that procedure becomes so much a part of us that we only become explicitly aware of it when we take time to reflect on what we are doing. Yet without knowing that procedure, it would be impossible to drive. In the same way, without a value system or ideology, it is impossible to make consistent and reasonable decisions on important alternatives. To deny the importance of values is shortsighted and condemns one not to understand fully one's own and others' actions.

Americans have some values that are unique; others we possess in common with other peoples. Here we will examine briefly our traditional American values and ideals in historical and critical overview. Before plunging into history, let us try to clarify what we mean by values, ideology, and ideals.

Let us define *values* as the criteria upon which important choices are made.

1

These criteria are not merely objective but also influence our emotions. Values are not only in the head but are real and active enough in the person actually to affect decisions and actions. An *ideology* is a constellation of values that have been integrated into a coherent, comprehensive, and motivating statement of purpose.) As is true of values, an ideology is not merely a theoretical statement of purpose; it contains considerable motivating force. It is the rationale for life and action. An ideology provides answers to such questions as What are my most important activities and values? How do I explain those actions and values to people of other groups, nations, or generations? How do I defend my life and values when they are criticized either from within the group or from outside? An ideology also embodies accepted *ideals*, (the long-range goals an individual or a society holds for itself.) Hence, (ideals can significantly influence values) Ideals are sometimes distant, whereas values affect actions. Unless, and until, ideals are integrated into an ideology, they generally do not have much influence on actions and choices.

EARLY AMERICANS AND ENTERPRISE

The immigrants who came to the New World risked their lives and their fortunes in the hope of finding freedom and new opportunities. They came to a land that seemed to have limitless natural resources—timber, coal, much good farming land. Clearing the land was back-breaking, but it was good, fertile acreage that could be handed on to one's children. The changing climate encouraged work—it was brisk and invigorating—and the winters, when there would be no fruits or crops, demanded that settlers plan ahead and save something from the harvest. Two wide oceans provided natural defenses that until recently allowed the New World to focus on its own needs and development without much fear of foreign intrusions.

All these natural characteristics affected the values and ideology of the people. But when the settlers came, they also brought with them their own values and ideals that heavily influenced these attitudes. Most of the early American immigrants were religious people. In fact, many of those who came to the colonies did so largely because of religious persecution in their native countries; they sought a land where they could live and pray as conscience dictated. The men and women who settled along the coasts came from Europe, and so brought with them the religion that predominated there—Christianity. Of these groups, the Puritans, who came very early, probably had the most profound influence on early American values and ideology.

The Puritans fled Europe so that they might freely follow their antihierarchical religious faith and practices. To these men and women, who came well before the American Revolution, their work or their "calling" was an essential part of their total world view. To us today, the Puritan ideal is a delicate, even mysterious, paradox. It is succinctly described by the Puritan preacher John Cotton (1584-1652):

> There is another combination of virtues strangely mixed in every lively, holy Christian: and that is, diligence in worldly businesses, and yet deadness to the world. Such a mystery as none can read but they that know it.[1]

Puritans plunged into their work with a dedication that could come only because it was their "calling." In John Cotton's words, "First, faith draws the heart of a Christian to live in some warrantable calling . . . though it be of an hired servant."[2] Worship of God was not shown in hymn singing, colorful religious services, or sterile monasticism; worship was a simple, reverent prayer. Moreover, the Puritans' prayer was not separated from work, for work was their most effective means of giving glory to God. So work was disciplined and clear-eyed, because ". . . when he serves man, he serves the Lord; he doth the work set before him and he doth it sincerely and faithfully so as he may give account for it."[3] This early Puritan ideology strengthened the emerging social order by giving importance to every type of work. Again, in John Cotton's words, "[faith] encourageth a man in his calling to the most homeliest and difficultest and most dangerous things his calling can lead and expose himself to."[4] Self-discipline was also important, for Puritans were not to be caught up in their own success or failure. They were ascetics in the world; although in it, they were detached from it.

Two generations later, Cotton Mather (1663-1728) was born into the same family of erudition and clerical leadership. Like his grandfather, Mather held that "A Christian has two callings: 1) a general calling 'to serve the Lord Jesus Christ,' and 2) a particular calling which was his work or his business. Both of these callings are essential if the Christian is to achieve salvation. The Puritan divine says, 'Contemplation of the good means nothing without accomplishment of the good. A man must not only be pious; he must be useful.' "[5] The Puritan businessman fully integrated his work with his workshop. Often he would mention God in his invoices, thanking him for a profit, or accepting losses for his greater glory. Moreover, each individual determined his or her calling, and work was generally done individually. In the same fashion, people achieved salvation individually.

American Puritans did not invent this position; they took the theology of John Calvin and spelled out in some detail the implications for the businessman. The businessman in turn, eager for some justification of the efforts to which he devoted most of his waking hours, happily received the Puritan preacher's words.

[1]Perry Miller, *The American Puritans* (Garden City, N.Y.: Doubleday, 1956), p. 171.
[2]Ibid., p. 173.
[3]John Cotton in ibid., p. 176.
[4]Ibid., p. 177.
[5]A. Whitney Griswold, "Two Puritans on Prosperity," in *Benjamin Franklin and the American Character*, ed. Charles L. Sanford (Boston: D. C. Heath, 1955), p. 41.

So there began the mutual understanding and support between preacher and businessman that became a hallmark of New World society.

Benjamin Franklin's Way to Wealth

In the prerevolutionary period, Benjamin Franklin accepted the work values of the Puritans, shifted them from a religious to a secular foundation, and restated them for Americans. Franklin, especially in *Poor Richard's Almanack*, was prolific, mundane, incisive, and widely influential. Many of his homely bits of advice have become embedded in our language and now belong to us all. Looking back over twenty-five years of his *Almanack*, Franklin brought together his writings on the world of work and of business and published them in 1758 as the essay "The Way to Wealth."

> God helps them that help themselves. . . . Diligence is the mother of good luck, as Poor Richard says, and God gives all things to industry. Then plough deep, while sluggards sleep, and you shall have corn to sell and to keep, says Poor Dick. Work while it is called today, for you know not how much you may be hindered tomorrow. . . . Be ashamed to catch yourself idle. . . . When there is so much to be done for yourself, your family, your country, and your gracious king, be up at peep of day; . . . 'Tis true that much is to be done, and perhaps you are weak handed, but stick to it steadily, and you will see great effects, for constant dropping wears away stones . . . and little strokes fell great Oaks.[6]

In his own simple way, Franklin focuses on the importance of saving and the need for capital when he urges: "A man may, if he knows not how to save as he gets, keep his nose all his life to the grindstone. . . . If you would be wealthy, think of saving as well as of getting."[7] It must have been immensely satisfying to Franklin's early American contemporaries to see him supporting the same values and justification for their work as did their ministers. He provided a rationale for work and a purpose for life; at the same time, he buttressed the existing social order.

Franklin's writings were best sellers in his day and have exerted a tremendous influence up to the present. In his *Almanack*, his *Autobiography*, and his very life Franklin embodied the Puritan virtues. Here was a man who was eminently successful as an inventor, statesman, diplomat, and businessman and who espoused the same virtues as did the Puritan ministers. Although some aristocrats of his day, such as John Adams, resented Franklin's popular wisdom, he was popular with the people. Harvard-educated John Adams was a New England patrician: brilliant and courageous, but also haughty and stubborn. Adams conceded that Franklin was a genius, wit, politician, and humorist, but questioned

---

[6]Benjamin Franklin, *The Autobiography and Other Writings* (New York: New American Library, 1961), p. 190.

[7]Ibid., p. 192.

his greatness as a philosopher, moralist, or statesman.[8] In spite of Adams's petty quarrels with Franklin, history shows Franklin to have had greater influence on values. Thomas Jefferson agreed with the hard-working, individualistic ideals of Franklin, although Jefferson, who wrote the *Declaration of Independence*, was convinced that these virtues could best be fostered, and the new nation grow best, as an agricultural society.[9] Jefferson felt that as long as one had one's own land to till and crops to care for, the economy would thrive and people would be happier.

At this time more than 80 percent of the American work force were farmers, and if Jefferson had had his way, that is how it would have remained. Jefferson was opposed to the industrialization he had seen in England. He would rather import finished manufactured goods than undergo the undesirable changes manufacturing inevitably brings: urbanization, landless workers, banking. In an agricultural society, where work and initiative immediately pay off for the individual, and for the society as a whole, government intervention could be kept to an absolute minimum. It could only retard the natural forces of growth and encumber society with additional overhead, regulations, and bureaucracy. In Jefferson's own oft-quoted words, "That government is best which governs least." The ambivalent feelings toward and even fear of industry appeared early, for industry spawns cities. An agrarian society is simpler; duties and rewards are more easily seen and measured. Early Americans were therefore not always favorably disposed toward industry or the cities.

The American Frontier

The continuing westward expansion served to keep alive the simpler, measurable agrarian values. The effect of this westward movement and the frontier on the American character was spelled out by Fredrick Jackson Turner[10] just before the turn of the twentieth century. For successive waves of hunters, traders, ranchers, and finally farmers, there were always new lands to conquer. It seemed to be a world without limits. The Indians were nomadic, and there were few of them to offer resistance. For the brave and hearty immigrant, it was worth taking great risks, whether in moving or in building. Success meant wealth; failure, the chance to try again somewhere else.

The new territories demanded the strenuous labor of clearing the land. The first farmers faced the immense task of pulling out trees and building their homes and barns. Nevertheless, the rewards were also great: They would have homes and incomes and could pass on those farms to future generations. The rewards were clear, tangible, and permanent, and they gave settlers incentive and zest.

[8]For this essay, see John Adams, "An Exaggerated Reputation," in Sanford, *Benjamin Franklin*, pp. 22-26.

[9]Arthur M. Schlesinger, "Ideas and Economic Development," in *Paths of American Thought*, ed. Arthur M. Schlesinger, Jr., and Morton White (Boston: Houghton Mifflin, 1963), pp. 108-9.

[10]Frederick Jackson Turner, *The Frontier in American History* (New York: Holt, 1920).

The land is measurable and unambiguous. It is open to human effort; if one works harder, one will be able to produce more.

Turner himself sums up how the frontier has given the American intellect its striking characteristics:

> That coarseness and strength combined with acuteness and inquisitiveness; that practical, inventive turn of mind, quick to find expedients; that masterful grasp of material things, lacking in the artistic but powerful to effect great ends; that restless, nervous energy; that dominant individualism, working for good and for evil, and withal that buoyancy and exuberance which comes with freedom—these are traits of the frontier or traits called out elsewhere because of the existence of the frontier.[11]

Turner's thesis has been widely quoted and has had a great influence on thinkers and on men and women of affairs. President John F. Kennedy's "New Frontier," in the 1960s, was an attempt to tap that vision, along with the energy, initiative, and sense of accomplishment that come with it. Perhaps there was a new frontier in the 1960s; clearly, profound new challenges face Americans today. Although there are few new physical lands to conquer, the current challenges demand something of the same creativity, risk taking, energy, and sense of purpose.

Tocqueville's View of Americans

As anyone who has lived in another culture for any length of time knows, the peculiar characteristics of that culture stand out in bold relief to the foreigner. In that same process, of course, one is also far better able to recognize the unique qualities of one's own culture. A people's characteristic values and ideology can best be understood in comparison with another culture. Thus a perceptive foreign visitor often is able to describe the values and characteristics of the host people with penetrating insight. Because of this, Alexis de Tocqueville remains one of the best commentators on the American character.

A young French lawyer, Alexis de Tocqueville came to the United States in 1831 to observe and learn from the people. His reflections, *Democracy in America*, were written for the French, but they attained instant success not only in France, but in England and the United States as well. Published in English translation in 1838, the work was immediately praised for its insight and lack of bias, and it is still regarded, 150 years later, as one of the finest commentaries on American life. Tocqueville tried to understand Americans on their own terms. The well-known leader of English liberalism, John Stuart Mill, reviewed Tocqueville's work and was deeply impressed with it.[12]

On arriving, Tocqueville noted the physical expanse of the new country: "The inhabitants of the U.S. constitute a great civilized people, which fortune

---

[11]Ibid., p. 37.

[12]For the substance of the review, see the Introduction to *Democracy in America,* tr. Henry Reeve (New York: Knopf, 1946), pp. xxix-x1.

has placed in the midst of an uncivilized country."[13] It was this same combination, of course, which was to help give rise to the independence, resourcefulness, and frontier spirit of which Fredrick Jackson Turner was later to write. Tocqueville noticed that, preoccupied by the great task to be accomplished, Americans tend to value facts more than consistent ideals, that which works more than the beauty of a comprehensive ideological system. He characterized the American "philosophical method," the American method of reflection and learning, as "to evade the bondage of system and habit, of family maxims, class opinions, and, in some degree, of national prejudices." Americans accept tradition only as a starting point, the existing situation only "as a lesson to be used in doing otherwise and in doing better."[14] Each individual seeks to understand for himself or herself. All these characteristics Tocqueville summed up as an individualism of thought: ". . . each American appeals only to the individual effort of his own understanding." This mentality shows that what we today call the generation gap is no new thing: ". . . every man there readily loses all traces of the ideas of his forefathers or takes no care about them."[15] Looking back on recent history, we see that the exaggerated stability that characterized the 1950s and early 1960s was actually a temporary interlude, and by American standards it was precarious and unreal.

Tocqueville saw Americans as hardworking and individualistic. The only rationale they might have for their actions and attitudes is enlightened self-interest. They are not inclined to reverence for tradition, philosophy, or even much reflection. He focused on the same favorable attitude toward work that has been attributed to the Puritan, the immigrant, and the frontier settler. Americans see work "as the necessary, natural, and honest condition of human existence."[16] Labor is not only not dishonorable, it is held in honor among the people. Even the rich person feels the obligation to take up some sort of worthwhile work, whether this work be private or some sort of public business.

When Americans were asked *why* they work, act, and think as they do, Tocqueville reported that they gave a rather consistent response:

> The Americans . . . are fond of explaining almost all the actions of their lives by the principle of self-interest rightly understood; they show with complacency how an enlightened regard for themselves constantly prompts them to assist one another and inclines them willingly to sacrifice a portion of their time and property to the welfare of the state.[17]

Although not unique to America, by the time of Tocqueville's visit, enlightened self-interest had taken firm root here. In the generation following the publication

[13]Ibid., vol. I, p. 422.
[14]Ibid., vol. II, p. 3.
[15]Ibid., vol. II, p. 4.
[16]Ibid., vol. II, p. 152.
[17]Ibid., vol. II, p. 122.

of *Democracy in America,* social Darwinism was to make the self-interest doctrine even more popular, as we shall see later.

With remarkable insight, Tocqueville underscored both the strengths and
the weaknesses of this philosophy. The principle of self-interest is not a lofty goal,
but it is clear and certain. It does not demand much of a person, yet observing
it does produce results. It is not difficult to understand for all sorts and classes
of people. As a principle of human life, self-interest builds on peoples' infirmities:

> By its admirable conformity to human weaknesses it easily obtains great dominion;
> nor is that dominion precarious, since the principle checks one personal interest
> by another, and uses, to direct the passions, the very same instrument that excites
> them.[18]

The principle of enlightened self-interest produces no great acts of self-sacrifice,
but it encourages a daily discipline of self-denial. By itself self-interest cannot make
people good and virtuous and hence can hardly serve as a cornerstone of morality.
Nevertheless, said Tocqueville, "it disciplines large numbers of people in habits
of regularity, temperance, moderation, foresight, self-command."

Enlightened self-interest is closely related to individualism. Tocqueville's work
was the first to discuss individualism and, in fact, the first to bring the word into
the English language. It is characteristic of Americans that individualism was not
a common word among them, even though it so well described some of their
salient attitudes and values. People develop a vocabulary for those things of concern to them, those things they therefore want to discuss. Americans were not
then, nor are they now, a very reflective people. Tocqueville suggested that there
is probably no other civilized country in which less attention is paid to reflection
and philosophy than the United States.

Tocqueville described individualism as a mature and calm feeling, which
disposes each member of the community "to sever himself from the mass of his
fellows and to draw apart with his family and his friends." Each individual retreats
to his or her own familiar turf, and thus "leaves society at large to itself." The
Frenchman contrasted individualism and selfishness, and he found both seriously deficient:

> Selfishness originates in blind instinct; individualism proceeds from erroneous judg-
> ment more than from depraved feelings; it originates as much in deficiencies of the
> mind as in perversity of heart.
> Selfishness blights the germ of all virtue; individualism, at first, only saps the vir-
> tues of public life; but in the long run it attacks and destroys all others and is at
> length absorbed in downright selfishness.[19]

Tocqueville quite early pinpointed possibly the most serious weakness of
the American character. Enlightened self-interest and individualism narrow one's

[18]Ibid., vol. II, pp. 122-23.
[19]Ibid., vol. II, p. 98.

perspective. They encourage one to think less of public responsibilities, and they lead eventually, and almost inevitably, to selfishness. He almost sounded like a contemporary critic reflecting on the weaknesses of the corporate executive or the bureaucrat. Tocqueville's sensitive assessment of the American character—its impatience with tradition, reflection, and abstract ideals; its task-orientation and individualism; its self-interest leading to selfishness—still stands as one of the great social commentaries. Later observers often used Tocqueville as a starting point, but few have done a better overall appraisal than he.

Social Darwinism and Herbert Spencer

Adaptable survival depends on enteeval environment. Popular in U.S. turn of century. Not popular during depression - if rich are better why did depression happen!

Herbert Spencer (1820-1903) proposed a harsh "survival of the fittest" philosophy. Spencer's thesis was that the bright and able contribute most to society and so are to be encouraged and rewarded. The poor, the weak, and the handicapped demand more than they contribute and so should not be supported but rather be allowed to die a natural death. Contact with harsh and demanding reality is a maturing experience that should not be diluted by well-intentioned but in reality destructive charities and handouts. If "natural" principles were followed, evolution and the survival of the fittest in the competition of human life would be the result. Spencer did not set out to examine any particular society and its values; rather, his critique was proposed as "culture-free." According to Spencer, it applied to all people, for it was derived from basic, organic principles of growth and development. Spencer applied to society the same principles that Charles Darwin saw in biological life—hence the name social Darwinism. *incorrect application*

The events of the latter half of the nineteenth century had a profound impact on attitudes. The Industrial Revolution, the growth of cities, and the beginning of the concept of evolution shook the foundations of life and thought. Speaking of evolution, the contemporary American historian Richard Hofstadter has said: "Many scientific discoveries affect ways of living more profoundly than evolution did; but none have had a greater impact on ways of thinking and believing."[20]

Spencer, William Graham Sumner, and others who became prophets of the new evolutionary social ideology were impressed by the suffering of the poor, but they nevertheless felt that progress in an industrial society could come only through long hours of work, saving, self-discipline, and even the death of the less able. Rather than considering this a tragedy, they were convinced that through this process of natural selection, those of greater talent, intelligence, and ability would survive and be successful. The physically and mentally handicapped, unable to compete successfully, would be less apt to survive. It would obviously be a mistake for the government to provide assistance to these handicapped and deficient persons. That would allow them to stay alive, and worse, to reproduce, and so transmit their deficiencies to future generations.

Any attempt to minister to the needs of the poor or needy is misguided

Spencer - wealthy are superior. they are economically successful.

[20]Richard Hofstadter, *Social Darwinism in American Thought* (New York: Braziller, 1959), p. 3.

Poor inferior ∴ Helping poor hurts society. Poor will rise in social status (on own accord.) No need to help them. Natural.

Made sense to rich not to poor minorities

on several counts. It keeps alive those who are less able. It diverts the attention and abilities of able people who would be better off pursuing more profitable careers. And, finally, it insulates the less able from a sobering contact with harsh reality and poverty, an opportunity that might have jarred them from their complacency and encouraged them to work harder to better themselves. Although it might be painful to the weak in the short run, the overall good of society in the long run demands that these less fit individuals not be supported or encouraged. According to Spencer, society improves because of the survival of the fittest:

> The poverty of the incapable, the distresses that come upon the imprudent, the starvation of the idle, and those shoulderings aside of the weak by the strong, which leave so many "in shallows and in miseries," are the decrees of a large, farseeing benevolence. . . . Under the natural order of things society is constantly excreting its unhealthy, imbecile, slow, vacillating, faithless members.[21]

It is especially clear in primitive societies that the strongest and cleverest survive best. But this is a natural process, and so it occurs in civilized societies, too. People would be wise to prepare themselves and their children for this struggle.

Society as a whole will benefit from this struggle for survival. Since the most intellectually and physically fit survive, the race will improve. Given a difficult and demanding environment, over several generations the ideal man and woman will develop. There should therefore be little state interference in this natural selection process. The state must not regulate industry, impose tariffs, give subsidies, establish a church, regulate entry into the professions, operate schools, or run the mail service. Most especially, the government must not provide for the poor, improve sanitation, or look to the health needs of the less able.[22]

Herbert Spencer's philosophy was far more popular in the United States than in his native England. His praise of the strong, clever, and aggressive individual coincided with the spirit of the times. Further, his theory of inevitable progress was received enthusiastically in a country already marked with general optimism. Spencer's thinking provided both a rational foundation for already existing attitudes and a justification for many public and private practices. In the last third of the nineteenth century, Spencer was an influential leader of thought and a hero to many in the United States.

The personal attributes Spencer extolled are what many currently call "free enterprise." They focus on the hearty, adaptable individual in a hostile climate: careful planning ahead, hard work, loyalty and responsibility to family, and individual self-sufficiency. And as radical as they may have seemed to his contemporaries, Spencer's theories were actually quite conservative in overtone. Spencer saw great good in the way things were; paradoxically, there was no need to change or to plan ahead on a national or local level. Since natural processes will inevitably produce the best people and the best society, any sort of government or even

---

[21]Herbert Spencer, *Social Statics* (London: Appleton, 1850), pp. 323–26, 353.
[22]See Donald Fleming, "Social Darwinism," in Schlesinger and White, *Paths of American Thought,* pp. 124–25.

private intervention in the process will only hurt society in the long run. Citizens must repress their feelings of pity for the poor and allow natural processes to work themselves out. Although Spencer's theories challenged all the established theologies of the time and were thus opposed by most clergy, to others his position seemed a natural extension of the traditional Puritan ethic and especially its secularized counterpart, as expressed by Benjamin Franklin. It is thus no surprise that Spencer's theories were enthusiastically received by the business community of his day, but we will wait until the next chapter to examine their implications for business in greater detail.

Recent Foreign Views

A Frenchman, William Rappard, writing in the 1950s, attempted to probe the basic values of the American people. He found that he

> . . . admires unreservedly the Americans' courage, energy and generosity as individuals, the way they work together as a harmonious team, and the healthy social atmosphere which on the whole they have managed to create and maintain.[23]

He sees these characteristics as not only a cause of prosperity in this country but also an effect. He finds other tendencies much less attractive:

> . . . to subordinate the spiritual and artistic values to that of material success. Their impatience and restlessness, their cult of speed, and the breathless pace of their lives.[24]

These values, both the attractive and the unattractive, support the great economic prosperity of the United States. They underlie the passion for productivity and efficiency and the spirit of competition, which in turn contribute to the traditional measures of economic success.

Underscoring these same work-oriented yet approachable qualities of the American is the French Jesuit paleontologist Pierre Teilhard de Chardin, who spent many years in the United States. Teilhard had a sympathetic view of the American character in spite of his own penchant for reflection and asceticism. Writing from an expedition where he was working with Americans in the Gobi Desert, Teilhard said:

> People here are inclined to treat the Americans as a joke, but the more I see of them the more I admire their ability to work and get things done, and the kinder and more approachable I find them. . . . In my own branch of science it's the Americans who are showing us how we must set to work on the earth if we are to read its secret and make ourselves its masters.[25]

[23]William E. Rappard, *The Secret of American Prosperity*, tr. Kenneth A. J. Kickson (New York: Greenberg, 1955), p. 123.

[24]Ibid.

[25]Pierre Teilhard de Chardin, *Letters from a Traveller*, tr. Rene Hague, Violet Hammersley, Barbara Wall, and Noel Lindsay (New York: Harper & Row, 1962), p. 106.

Granting an American's ability to get a job done, that orientation to action is also the source of much criticism. Many foreigners see Americans as shallow and materialistic—more wedded to things than to goals, more inclined to do than to reflect. An Englishman gives his impression of American shallowness by pointing to "a general preoccupation with trivia—I mean Coke machines, launderettes . . . laxatives and baseball." He sees being caught up in superficialities as "the American attempt to exclude the bigger reality—reflection and looking to larger goals."[26]

On the other hand, Jacques Maritain, a shrewd interpreter of medieval European philosophy and contemporary humanism, defends Americans against the charge of being excessively materialistic. Maritain speaks of the people among whom he spent the last decades of his life:

> I would say that the accusation of materialism, technocratic inhumanity, etc., appears especially unfair. . . . Of course, here [in America] as elsewhere in the world, industrial civilization entails the temptation of materialist technocratism. But this country, which seems at first glance more threatened by such a temptation because it is more industrialized, has, in reality, a better chance of overcoming it, because from the very start the American effort is directed toward the good of man, the humble dignity of man in each one of us.[27]

Maritain articulately summarizes the national characteristic that foreign and domestic observers view as being basic to American survival and growth, not only as an economy, but as a people: their attitude toward every man and woman. It is the characteristic, a combination of humaneness and pragmatism, that may be the best foundation for the solution of future dilemmas.

Foreign social commentators, then, have felt the pulse of America and pointed to elements in our national character that make us simultaneously proud and humble. It is essential that we be aware of these characteristics if we are to make any intelligent assessment of our national character. It is even more important if we expect to have any influence on our own values and the values of our nation.

Social commentators and intellectual historians have thus provided us with considerable insight into our own origins and character. Examining their commentaries has enabled us better to grasp our own root values, those values that provide the foundation for our current business ideology. The physical environment, combined with the attitudes and values of the people who came to the New World, has given the United States a unique world position: rich and abundant farmland, protected east and west borders, and the frontier, coupled with the Puritan ethic. This ethic, more on the history of attitudes toward business, and the development of the contemporary American business creed will be discussed in the next chapter.

[26]Robert Robinson, quoted in *U.S.A.: The Permanent Revolution,* by the editors of *Fortune* (Englewood Cliffs, N.J.: Prentice-Hall, 1951), p. 220.

[27]Jacques Maritain, *Reflections on America* (New York: Scribner's, 1958), pp. 89-90.

THE FUNCTION
OF IDEOLOGY

[handwritten: Syntax internal set of decision making rules. People are inclined to disagree, ignore, or disbelieve conflicting information.]

An ideology is a coherent, systematic, and moving statement of basic values and purpose. It is a constellation of values generally held by a group, and members of the group tend to support one another in that ideology. An ideology seeks and provides some systematic answers to these questions: What are we about? Why are we doing this? How can I explain my life and my society to myself and to others? *[handwritten: ARISTOTLE]*

[handwritten: detailed explanation]

An ideology is an explication of values. It is a spelling out of attitudes, feelings, and goals. Without an explicit ideology, a nation or group is left without clearly stated purposes and hence without consensus or the drive that comes from purpose. When an ideology is spelled out, it can be examined, challenged, and altered as conditions change and new needs arise. It is then in the open for all to accept or reject as they see fit. When an ideology is not explicit, it is sometimes claimed that there is no ideology; but this is hardly true. The ideology is merely implicit, unspoken, and hence unexamined. This is a precarious position for any society, since questions which arise can thus cause confusion and chaos.

Ideologies possess certain common features. They are selective in the issues they treat and in the supporting evidence and argument they use. They are straightforward and uncomplicated, even when the actual material is quite complicated. Their content is limited to what is publicly acceptable. Finally, although ideologies are answers to questions and hence address the intellect, they nevertheless do so in a manner that also engages the emotions. They can inspire and motivate men and women to cooperate and even undergo great hardship for the sake of a compelling goal.

The positive effect of an ideology is that it gives a people direction, coherence, norms, criteria, and motivation. It can bring clarity and assurance to the mind and hence vigor and enthusiasm to life and work. These are great advantages, especially to a society troubled by doubts and by lessened confidence in institutions and inadequate leadership. A group possessing an ideology is thus given meaning, direction, and drive. Nations and peoples have left their mark on history, whether for good or ill, almost to the extent to which they have fashioned for themselves a comprehensive and compelling ideology—for example, ancient Rome, Victorian England, and Nazi Germany.

Almost everything that we do of any substance flows from an often implicit ideology, from raising children to going to work, from conducting foreign policy to meeting neighbors. Even a position that ideologies are unnecessary, or demeaning, or oppressive is in itself an ideology. Subgroups within a society, even the Rotary Club, possess some sort of constellation of values, however limited or narrow. Generally the more embracing a group, a movement, or a state, the more complete will be its ideology.

On the other hand, ideology has some disadvantages. It can rigidify. It tends to lock persons and systems into classes, roles, and expectations. A doctrinaire ideology can cause fanaticism, intransigence, and uncompromising attitudes. It can impede progress and cause anxieties for those in the group who find difficulties with the ideology, often those who are the most innovative and talented. The group as a whole then tends to expend a great deal of effort on defending its position instead of looking to the future.

"Ideology" was made a term of abuse by traditional Marxists. To them, it is the rationalization of privilege by the upper classes. These classes use ideology to justify the arrangements associated with their own positions and interests by claiming that they are essential for the good of the country and for humanity. Marx calls this "collective illusion," another tool of oppression of the ruling classes. He makes the excellent point that this sort of ideology mistakes the contingent and historical situation for a permanent and natural one.

Today many people are suggesting that we examine our current place in history and spell out our national values and the ideology in which they are embedded. There is a similar need for a rationale for our business activities, and that is the subject of this book. Demands for an exposition of our ideology come from a variety of sources:

1. Young, well-educated people are increasingly asking themselves, their peers, and their national leaders: What are we about? What are our goals? What is worth living for? Why?
2. Any successful effort to lessen government intervention demands that individuals and organizations have their own clear sense of goals, ethics, and self-discipline—all of which takes into account the public interest and the common good.
3. As population increases and we live closer together, we find that what one person does often infringes on others. For example, building new houses on farmlands, driving a fuel-inefficient and smog-producing automobile, or moving a plant to the water-scarce sun belt—all these actions place costs on other people. As managers, citizens, or government officials, we need criteria for making such decisions.
4. Disagreements over public policy—for example, social programs, pollution control, tax cuts, nuclear weapons and armaments—come back to the earlier questions as to what kind of society we want, what our collective priorities are, and the trade-offs we are willing to bear. Special interest groups plead their own cause, but do not address the common good. Americans often find it easier to agree on what they dislike than on the far more important question of what they like: their positive values, goals, and policies.

There is a need for answering these questions and clarifying personal and corporate values and goals. Each person is challenged to work out his or her own answers to basic value questions, to formulate his or her own constellation of values. Some consensus is necessary on these values and on public issues in order to have an effective and consistent national policy. Without an agreed-upon ideology, decisions are often made on crass, unexamined, and immediate criteria or by means of some current popular myth or shallow set of values. The agreed-upon values, especially those that touch on public life and issues, can be called an ideology. As such, they can provide direction and verve. And an awareness of the dangers in ideology—for example, that it may be a mask for privilege or that it may rigidify—should better enable us to avoid these pitfalls.

Origin and Impact of Ideology

A continuing dispute pits those who say that an ideology comes after the fact as a rationalization of reality against those who maintain that an already-existing ideology has a powerful influence on the world. These positions are reconciled by Berger and Luckman:

> It is correct to say that theories are concocted in order to legitimate already existing social institutions. But it also happens that social institutions are changed in order to bring them into conformity with already existing theories, that is, to make them more "legitimate."[28]

An ideology as a rationalization of the existing order obviously tends to defend the status quo. An ideology based on ideals that aim to change that status quo into something that is viewed as better is often called utopian. To Americans, "utopian" has an idealistic, pie-in-the-sky, pejorative connotation. Here we will use it as a descriptive term only.

Karl Mannheim, in his classic *Ideology and Utopia*,[29] says that a state of mind is utopian if it has some elements that transcend reality as it exists. In addition, when these elements pass over into conduct, they "tend to shatter, either partially or wholly, the order of things prevailing at the time." In other words, ideas and ideals that tend to change reality can be called utopian. According to Mannheim, ideologies become utopian when groups begin to act on them and to challenge the existing order.

Many utopias of today become the realities of tomorrow. Indeed, one definition of utopia is that it is merely premature truths. The principles of democracy and freedom were utopian in the minds of those who founded the United States. Their notions of representation and individual rights were ideals which, when they were written into documents and acted upon, challenged the status quo, shattered the existing order, and even caused a revolution. Looking back over this same period of rising aspirations, especially in the Western world, Mannheim calls the prevailing ideology of freedom a utopia:

> The utopia of the ascendant bourgeoisie was the idea of "freedom." It was in part a real utopia, i.e., it contained elements oriented towards the realization of a new social order and which were instrumental in disintegrating the previously existing social order and which, after their realization, did in part become translated into reality. Freedom in the sense of bursting asunder the bonds of the static, guild, and caste order, in the sense of freedom of thought and opinion, in the sense of political freedom and freedom of the unhampered development of the personality became . . . a realizable possibility.[30]

[28]Peter L. Berger and Thomas Luckman, *The Social Construction of Reality* (Garden City, N.Y.: Doubleday-Anchor, 1967), p. 128. For Berger's more current critique, see *Facing Up to Modernity* (New York: Basic Books, 1977).

[29]Karl Mannheim, *Ideology and Utopia,* tr. Louis Wirth and Edward Shils (New York: Harcourt, Brace & World, 1936), p. 192. Quoted with permission.

[30]Ibid., p. 203.

Generalizing, Mannheim points out that any nation or group which wants to translate its ideals into reality must formulate an ideology that builds on the existing values, needs, and aspirations of the people. This utopian ideology may then catch the imagination of the people and be the inspiration for change. For every utopian ideology that eventually becomes reality, there are dozens that never get beyond the stage of ideas. They may have caused some upset and discord in society, and their adherents are often considered fanatical.

There are a number of dangers inherent in any ideology in addition to those pointed out earlier. Those of being closed to facts and of fanaticism are highlighted by Mannheim: "Nothing is more removed from actual events than the closed rational system. Under certain circumstances, nothing contains more irrational drive than a fully self-contained intellectualistic world view." Those who feel they are well adjusted to the current state of affairs have little incentive to theorize, according to Mannheim.[32] These "conservatives" are happy with their situation, and so they defend the status quo. He points out that as long as people are content, they do little theorizing about situations in which they find themselves. They then tend to regard their current situation as part of the natural order of things; the way things are is the way they ought to be. For those whose position is unchallenged, there is little impetus to reflect on the situation. Rather, they tend to emphasize practical "how to do it" concerns—the means of coping within existing structures. It is only in the face of challenges to the status quo that conservatives do much reflecting. So the reflection and therefore the ideology of conservatives are generally not as profound or comprehensive as those of the challengers. It thus happens that the "most recent antagonist dictates the tempo and the form of the battle."[33]

Challenge Brings Understanding

A valuable by-product of this type of challenge and reformulation of goals and ideologies is that the society is compelled to examine itself. This sort of unmasking and examining of ideology can result in self-clarification for society as a whole. A society with a weak ideology, or one in which ideology is unimportant, can generally be characterized as stable, complacent, and content with its inherited laws, customs, and ideals. At the very end of his chapter on the utopian mentality, Mannheim paints a sad, even desperate, picture of a society or a people without a utopian ideology:

> The disappearance of utopia brings about a static state of affairs in which man himself becomes no more than a thing. We would be faced then with the greatest paradox imaginable, namely, that man, who has achieved the highest degree of rational mastery of existence, left without any ideals, becomes a mere creature of impulses. Thus, after a long, tortuous, but heroic development, just at the highest stage of

[31]Ibid., p. 219.
[32]Ibid., p. 229.
[33]Ibid., p. 231.

awareness, when history is ceasing to be blind fate, and is becoming more and more man's own creation, with the relinquishment of utopias, man would lose his will to shape history and therewith his ability to understand it.[34]

Mannheim presents an impersonal, alienating, and frightening prospect of a world without utopias—without ideals or engaging goals.

On the other hand, injustices can also be perpetrated in the name of an irrational but compelling ideology. Any strong, moving ideology risks being gross, oversimplified, and even unjust. Mannheim's own Germany a few years later was to undergo a tragic revolution in the name of "Aryan superiority" and the "master race." Nevertheless, without ideals worked into some sort of ideology, little new can be accomplished on any significant scale. People cease to question themselves and their society. They lose their direction and their enthusiasm for life. Hitler's ideology was a reaction to such a vacuum.

Suspicion of Ideology

Probably a majority of Americans share with Arthur Schlesinger, Jr., an abiding distrust of ideology. In an attempt to outline what has caused the rapid economic development of the United States, Schlesinger acknowledges the physical advantages of the continent. But he points out that the fertile lands and natural resources were there for the native Americans, too, but were never exploited.[35] Schlesinger maintains that the most important element in the success story of the United States was the spirit of the settlers. He contends that this spirit manifested itself in three important ways. The first was a faith in education; investment in people through education results in increases in productivity. A second factor encouraging development was the commitment to self-government and representative institutions. Democracy was important for releasing one's talents and energies.

The third uniquely favorable element in the American spirit, and probably the most important one according to Schlesinger, was a rejection of ideology: "America has had the good fortune not to be an ideological society."[36] Schlesinger defines ideology to be "a body of systematic and rigid dogma by which people seek to understand the world—and to preserve or transform it." Many Americans, with Schlesinger as a spokesman, feel that ideology constricts and distracts us from reality. They would not allow ideology to "falsify reality, imprison experience, or narrow the spectrum of choice."[37] This is part of an attitude that encourages innovation and experiment, part of the dominant empirical and pragmatic American approach.

The principal difficulty with an ideology is that it is a partial depiction of

[34]Ibid., pp. 262-63.
[35]See "Epilogue: The One Against the Many," in Schlesinger and White, *Paths of American Thought,* pp. 531-38.
[36]Ibid., p. 532.
[37]Ibid., p. 533.

reality. Certain elements are emphasized and others neglected. When decisions are made, they can thus be biased or even wrong. Communist states, for example, often do not tolerate positions that depart from the official ideology. The dominant American philosophy, pragmatism, is not heavily theoretical. It will be discussed in more detail in the next chapter, but suffice it for now to point out that pragmatism stays close to the facts; to simplify, it holds "that which works is true."

Schlesinger rightly rejects rigid dogma that would subjugate people and facts to an ideology. Americans have achieved much success in being flexible, open, and risk taking in a pluralistic society. He is, however, too quick and cavalier in his rejection of ideology. His definition of ideology as "a body of systematic and rigid dogma" better enables him to do this, since it embodies the undesirable properties he seeks to reject. Furthermore, he seems to miss the essential point that value judgments are being made constantly, and these value judgments, along with the world view in which they are embedded, are in fact an ideology. It only obscures understanding to deny this.

Schlesinger may not like ideology, but his own position is an ideology in its own right. It is an ideology that values freedom, laissez-faire, and selective nonintervention. Moreover, that freedom is especially for me and mine. It does not apply to the American Indians, who, in spite of the fact that they did not "exploit" their lands as Schlesinger would have liked, were pushed off those lands. The Indians did not have the freedom to decide how they would use their lands. This sort of double standard calls for government intervention to preserve *my* freedom and prerogatives; it calls for nonintervention when government regulations *restrict* my freedom, or the freedom of my organization. Schlesinger is consistent in using this same ideology in international relations. He supports the balance of power in the expectation that each nation will pursue its own self-interest; and he rejects any sort of moralism or altruism as a basis for policy between nations.

There is a typically American implied faith that, if each person or group uses its talents and intelligence to pursue its own long-term self-interest, it will work out most favorably for all. By any definition, this is an ideology. Its long-run effectiveness is questioned by minorities and others in the United States and around the world whose freedom and best interests have not automatically been served.

Values in American Life

Individualism and enlightened self-interest are still basic to the value systems of most Americans) Moreover, these values affect entire life styles, not merely work attitudes. Indeed, whenever predominant American values are listed, it is remarkable how many of them support work attitudes and are directly related to individualism and enlightened self-interest. The current serious challenge to some of these values will be discussed in later chapters. Here, let us make some attempt to indicate what these prevalent, traditional American values are.[38]

MeAsured in financial terms

1) Achievement and Success. American culture has been and still is characterized by a stress on individual achievement. Horatio Alger, who rose from rags to riches, has become a legend. The American myth says that anyone who works hard enough can succeed in what he or she sets out to do. Moreover, if we meet a successful person, we are much more impressed if he or she did not inherit wealth. (Someone who was born poor and then worked hard to obtain what he or she has is much more an idol for the young.) In fact, it is a bit embarrassing to us to be reminded that several of our recent presidents were born into wealthy families. This achievement and success ideal is, of course, best manifested in business. Achievement motivation is especially strong among executives and managers.[39]

(Success Symbol) Money and wealth are valued for the comforts they can bring, but even more because they are the symbols of having "made it." It is a measure to the person and to the world of one's own personal worth. Because these values developed in the westward expansion and the building of railroads and industry, there comes a correlative respect for size. (Large homes, automobiles, and businesses are respected; they are signals of success. *Material goods)*

time must be used to Advantage

2) Activity and Work. An extraordinary devotion to work on the part of both the unskilled worker and the executive has provided most of the wealth we now enjoy in the United States. Work is respected not only because it has resulted in immense wealth but also for its own sake—"The devil finds idle hands." In the United States a person's self-respect is severely undermined when he or she is without work. Americans have traditionally not valued leisure for its own sake; it is valued if afterward a person can work better. It is re-creation; and it, too, has a purpose. Task orientation has become a compulsion for which Americans are frequently criticized. *NON WORKERS/LAZY hAve NO SeIFRespect.*

Workers in a shop know that even though the job is well in hand, or ahead of the daily quota, they had best appear busy to their boss and especially to their boss's boss. Relaxing at the work station is rarely accepted. "Busyness" is a virtue in its own right. To call a person lazy is a serious criticism, especially because it is something over which that person seems to have control. Americans value the active virtues; they set out to shape and control their own lives and their world. They heed the biblical injunction "to subdue the world."

[38]For a basic work in this area, and one to which the author is indebted, see the chapter "Values in American Society," in Robin M. Williams, Jr., *American Society: A Sociological Interpretation*, 3rd ed. (New York: Knopf, 1970), pp. 438-504.

[39]There is, of course a great amount of literature on this, and the issue will be discussed in greater detail in Chapter 4. For now, see the insightful and synthetic work of Michael Maccoby, *The Gamesman: The New Corporate Leaders* (New York: Simon & Schuster, 1976).

3 Efficiency and Practicality.   Closely related to the foregoing cultural values are efficiency and practicality, which refer more to the method of working and acting. We have seen how Tocqueville was much impressed with American ingenuity and ability to "get the job done." Americans are often criticized for an overemphasis on technique, with little reference to goals.[40] These critics say that engineers and accountants run our society, and their values are at best instrumental and thus means. They may know how to accomplish a specific task, but rarely give any thought as to whether it is a good thing to do. A practical person, focusing on efficiency, assumes the basic worth of the task and of the social order itself. A practical orientation demands only short-range adjustments to immediate situations.

The American is known as one who can quickly and effectively search out the best way to accomplish the task. He or she is active in the search for solutions and is rarely contemplative. To call an American "impractical" would be a severe criticism. Characteristically, the best known American philosophers, such as Dewey, Peirce, and William James, are not idealists or absolutists, but rather relativists and pragmatists.

world view. It's all where you stand   PRACTical Application

4) Moral Orientation and Humanitarianism.   Although Americans are eminently practical, they still see the world in moral terms. Conduct of self and of others is constantly judged: honest, impractical, "a comer," lazy. Even our foreign policy is filled with righteous terms, such as "manifest destiny" and "to protect the world for freedom."

Basic honesty and frankness are also part of our moral and humanitarian value orientation. Foreign commentators are often surprised at how open and straightforward they find Americans to be. However, a highly moral person can quickly become quite cynical when his or her moral code is found to be superficial, inapplicable, or too idealistic. American charities, along with our social legislation since the 1930s, are examples of humanitarian attitudes. Increasing social security, minimum wage, and medical coverage are examples of the attempt to take care of the less fortunate. *Honest chARities, social Legislation*

5) Freedom.   As a prime value in American life, freedom is obvious to the most obtuse observer. In addition, it is probably the most spoken about of American values. The individual has freedom to operate in the social Darwinian world in which the fittest survive best, as we have seen earlier. He or she may freely move; change jobs; choose a home, friends, or a marriage partner. Freedom is the bedrock value not only of our laissez-faire, free enterprise economic system but for most of the rest of American life. Freedom has been touted alike by the Founding Fathers and the members of the local Rotary. American individualism, of course, is possible only when freedom is the foundation value.

The value of freedom has inspired the women's movement and other libera-

ConstitutioNAl Rights to do ✔ desire; speak, worship, Assemble etc.

[40]For a classic statement of this position, see Jacques Ellul, *The Technological Society* (New York: Knopf, 1964).

tion movements. Cultural norms that tie certain persons to predetermined roles and expectations can be oppressive. Freedom urges the elimination of these one-sided and unjust bonds. Defense of freedom is a foundation of American foreign policy, and freedom is the cornerstone of the U.S. Chamber of Commerce and the John Birch Society's defense of the American business system—*free* enterprise. As we have pointed out earlier, this freedom is primarily for me and mine, foreign policy protestations notwithstanding. Freedom as a value so permeates business ideology that it will come up frequently in subsequent chapters.

Every one Must be educated to make proper political decisions

6   Equality.   The American emphasis on equality goes back to early constitutional statements: *All men are created equal.* Citizens of the new world witnessed the elimination of indentured servitude, imprisonment for debt, primogeniture, slavery, and property requirements for voting and public office. New immigrants were able to acquire land and a free public education, and women and minorities have gained many important human rights. *Everyone is eligible to Learn.*

New arrivals and observers have often remarked on the unusual informality, frankness, and lack of status consciousness in our interpersonal relations. Such open and direct relations can endure over a long period only if they are supported by basic notions of the equality and importance of individual persons. But it became clear quite early that the value of freedom often ran counter to that of equality. When people pursued freedom in the rugged individualist climate in which the fittest survive, it resulted in some becoming rich and others remaining poor. An attempt at resolving this conflict is in the distinction that our ideals call for equality of opportunity, but not equality of result. Varying talents will also influence what a person can achieve.

Of all the government and corporate policies that have been developed to bring about better equality of opportunity in the workplace, none meets more opposition than "preferential treatment." In order to equalize past practices that were clearly discriminatory, many would contend that when equally qualified minority and white persons are presented for promotion, the minority should be chosen. Ironically, both the reason for the practice (to equalize past discrimination) and the major objections to it (reverse discrimination) stem from the American ideal of equality, especially equality of opportunity.[41]

Duty / loyalty to ones country &

7   Patriotism.   Every society has a sense of the greater value of its own people. Anthropologists tell us how in primitive societies the ordinary rules of respect for another's person and property do not apply to "outsiders." They apply only to the members of one's own tribe. On a contemporary national scale, this mentality emerges when during warfare we not only have less respect for lives of the "enemy," but sometimes rate our successes on the basis of how many of the enemy are killed. Racism, too, stems from these same parochial values.

the poorest Americans live better than 80% of world.

[41]See the detailed discussion of this complex question in Theodore V. Purcell and Gerald F. Cavanagh, *Blacks in the Industrial World: Issues for the Manager* (New York: Free Press, 1972), especially chap. 10, "Equal Versus Preferential Treatment," pp. 275–93.

In the United States our loyalties in the early days of the republic were with local cities (Boston, Philadelphia) and then with the states; finally, after several national efforts (especially the two world wars), our loyalties now lie primarily with the nation-state. Our attitudes toward Communist states and "un-American" activities find their roots largely in nationalism and loyalty to America.

A good leader to society's boundaries.

8   Material Comfort.   Americans generally place high value on the luxurious automobile, the ample home in the suburbs, and a good meal. The fact that these things are material comforts and that they are clearly highly valued does not in *Nothing better* itself indicate *why* they are valued. Underlying reasons may range from a simple symbol of achievement and success (moving to a larger home is a visible mark that I am moving up with the firm) to a hedonistic gratification in its own right.

The rise in popularity of spectator sports, packaged tours, the film, television, and alcohol indicates a greater passivity on the part of people. There seems to be less active participation and more watching and being entertained. The drug culture and chemically induced pleasure seem to take this tendency just one more step. Seeking pleasure coincides with a decline in the Puritan ethic values of self-denial and asceticism. *gold card speaks for you.   quality of life.*
Look to modest pleasures for more happiness.

9   External Conformity.   Probably the most common criticism Europeans have leveled at Americans is the one of a vast uniformity in speech, housing, dress, recreation, and general attitudes. Observers point to a certain flatness, to homogeneity, to lack of dissent and challenge. Although we went through a brief period in the late 1960s of racial and student dissent, to a large extent we now have returned to our more traditional attitudes of external conformity. Witness the new strength of fashions, television, and "dress for success."

To American rugged individualists, these criticisms may seem harsh and untrue. Yet, on closer examination, our individualism consists largely in the rejection of government interference and objecting to restrictions on personal and business activity. American society today lacks, and desperately needs, sufficient numbers of creative, risk-taking individuals and firms. *People are social animals - like to look alike - security. Looking your best helps.*

10   Rationality and Measurement.   This value is probably best exemplified in approaching a problem. A person is to be objective, gathering the facts first and not being unduly influenced by bias or emotions. The "scientific method," which embodies this approach, is the model for problem solving. If elements of the solution can be measured—whether length, time, or intelligence—that will make the solution more rational and objective. *Scientific method to winning a situation*

The value of science is demonstrated in its intelligent use in mastering the external environment. This value orientation is compatible with a culture that does not value emotion, tends to deny frustration, and looks on the world as open to effort and eventual control.

Optimism and the Inevitability
of Progress

The frontier, seemingly unlimited natural resources, and an immigrant people who were willing to work hard combined to provide an atmosphere of great optimism. Any job could be accomplished, if only one put one's mind to it. The result of this effort was growth: industrial, economic, urban. Growth has been so characteristic of the last two centuries that for most Americans it is inconceivable to think that growth and thus progress are not inevitable.

The optimistic euphoria that had enveloped the American people has only recently begun to dissipate. Only in the last decade has the possibility of continued growth been challenged and have we been asked to rethink what we mean by progress. We had defined progress largely in economic terms. As long as gross national product and sales were increasing, this spelled progress. The possibility of a more stable economy, the necessity of rethinking what "progress" is, and what impact these changes will have on business and business ideology will be discussed in greater detail in Chapters 6 and 7.

THE NECESSITY OF AN
IDEOLOGY FOR BUSINESS

An ideology, or some statement of goals and principles, is essential for any social system. It is especially necessary for business in our complex, contemporary society for several reasons:

1. For decades scholars and citizens have questioned the legitimacy of the corporation. Where resides the ultimate power and authority in the corporation, and the correlative responsibility that goes with it?
2. Managers are widely criticized for being too concerned with themselves and their own successful careers. They thus focus on short-term returns and neglect long-term planning and investment for the firm.
3. Some critics question whether the free enterprise system can survive in its present form because of its inequities and inefficiencies.

Without some rationale, it is impossible for businesspeople and others to evaluate these challenges, intelligently defend themselves against unfair attacks, and lay out new policies to rectify the abuses. In the future, as in the past, an ideology will undergird the acceptance of business and thus whatever stature and power it may possess. Without an ideology, the corporation risks losing its privileged position in the United States and perhaps even its legitimacy. As early as 1958, Adolph A. Berle put the issue strongly:

> Whenever there is a question of power there is a question of legitimacy. As things stand now, these instrumentalities of tremendous power have the slenderest claim

of legitimacy. This is probably a transitory period. They must find some claim of legitimacy, which also means finding a field of responsibility and a field of accountability. Legitimacy, responsibility and accountability are essential to any power system if it is to endure.[42]

The transitory period of which he spoke is still with us.

Notice how Berle links legitimacy, responsibility, and accountability. It is precisely in clarifying these basic issues that the corporation is on weak ground. Without rehearsing the entire classic position of Berle and Means,[43] suffice it to say that the corporation is responsible to no one. Management, often with little legitimacy and less ownership, unilaterally makes decisions. Stockholders have no real control over the corporation. The board of directors is elected from a slate that has been chosen by the board itself. The annual meeting of stockholders is a public relations gesture, with the stockholders exercising no real power. If a stockholder does not vote, the abstention is often counted as support for management.

The board of directors has no universal and clearly defined role. It is usually as active and effective as the chief executive wants it to be. And there are not many chief executives who want a strong board that might intervene. If they are "inside" directors, there will probably be conflicts of interest, and thus the directors lack objectivity. If they are "outside," they serve only part time. One principal difficulty is that they have very little time to devote to the affairs of the corporations of which they are directors; indeed, investment banker Gustave L. Levy was on the boards of twenty-three corporations.[44]

Eugene V. Rostow, then dean of Yale's Law School, even coined a word to describe this lack of responsibility in the corporation—endocratic: responsible to no one.[45] Management is also self-perpetuating; its members designate their own successors, and often even new board members. Corporate management controls the firm and thus is under no one else's control.

Probably the most able chairperson of the Security and Exchange Commission in a generation, ex corporate chief executive officer Harold Williams, charges management and the board with perpetuating a crisis:

The long-term health and dynamics of many American businesses and industries are being jeopardized by an undue emphasis on short-term considerations in their decision making. For more than a decade and a half, instead of formulating policies

[42]Adolph A. Berle, *Economic Power and the Free Society* (New York: Fund for the Republic, 1958), p. 16.

[43]Adolf A. Berle, Jr., and Gardiner C. Means, *The Modern Corporation and Private Property* (New York: Macmillan, 1932).

[44]"The Board: It's Obsolete Unless Overhauled," *Business Week*, May 22, 1971, p. 56. Quoted with permission.

[45]"To Whom and for What End Is Corporate Management Responsible?" in *The Corporation in Modern Society*, ed. Edward S. Mason (Cambridge, Mass.: Harvard University Press, 1959), p. 57.

that enhance the long-term strength of the American industrial system, we have tended to milk it for short-term benefit.[46]

Williams has long been an articulate advocate of an independent outside board of directors and of greater accountability of management. An outside board is less liable to be involved in conflict of interest, able to insulate the chief executive from the constant pressures from speculators and investment analysts for short-term return, so that he or she can attend to the long-term health and growth of the firm, and more apt to see to it that the corporation's goals are consistent with the goals of the larger society. Achieving these ends demands something more in the way of a corporate purpose than merely enlightened self-interest.

Furthermore, in recent decades some have severely criticized the corporation and questioned whether such "old-style capitalism" is consonant with modern democratic society. History shows the great evolution of American capitalism from that of the last century. Critics maintain that there will be similar changes in the coming decades, such that both capitalism and the corporation will be radically changed.[47] This question will come up in various forms throughout this book.

The last two generations of research on the power and legitimacy of the corporation, plus the more recent social demands on the firm, raise basic and serious questions about the role, purpose, and responsibilities of the corporation. Any response to these new needs demands some clearer notions on the even more basic issue of the ideology of the corporation—its goals, rationale, and responsibilities, its very reason for existence.

Without a basic ideology that is clear, consistent, and effective, these gnawing questions will continue to arise, and we will be incapable of answering them. In any social system, this sort of situation is not stable. Indeed, it is probably true that much of the current loss of respect for business, the corporation, and the businessperson stems from an inability to respond in more than a defensive or perfunctory fashion to these very questions. Without an ideology and consequent accountability, business risks losing its accepted position in American society and possibly even its legitimacy.

SUMMARY AND
CONCLUSIONS

This first chapter has set the general scene and defined terms. It has examined major values and ideals in American life and some of the elements of physical

---

[46]Harold Williams, "The Corporation as a Continuing Enterprise," address to the Securities Regulation Institute, January 22, 1981, Washington, D.C., 1981, p. 1.

[47]See the excellent papers in William R. Dill, ed., *Running the American Corporation* (Englewood Cliffs: Prentice-Hall, 1978), especially Dill's "Private Power and Public Responsibility"; also John L. Paluszek, *Will the Corporation Survive?* (Reston, Va.: Reston Publishing, 1977). For a minority view that the corporation has a natural right to exist and operate and does not require the permission of the state, see Robert Hessen, *In Defense of the Corporation* (Stanford, Calif.: Hoover Institution, 1979).

environment and personal character that have contributed to the development of those values. The vast expanse of virgin land was a challenge to the righteous, task-oriented Puritans. Their theology supported their work ethic: self-denial, hard work, thrift, early rising. Furthermore, the favorable results of these efforts indicated that the individual was saved. Benjamin Franklin, not a Puritan, found this work ethic attractive, and he presented a secularized version to his contemporaries.

Educated Europeans who have visited us over the last century and a half have noted an honesty, frankness, and directness in Americans. They have found us to be pragmatic and practical and to have little time for unproductive theorizing. Freedom is a value that has been institutionalized in our Constitution and laws and that remains predominant.

With this information as background, we then reflected on what an ideology is, what its function is, and some of its effects. An attempt was then made to spell out the main values in American life. This more general examination of American values and ideology has been necessary in order to mark out the turf where we will find business values. Business values exist in a larger context; and in this case, we already see how remarkably well the larger society's ideals support business ideology. Nevertheless, the very legitimacy of the corporation and business itself is being questioned. Moreover, it is increasingly clear that there can be no adequate response without some attempt at working out a purpose and an ideology for the business firm that coincides better with what the larger society expects of its business institutions.

The values of the American Puritan—hard work, saving, regular habits, diligence, self-control and sobriety—perhaps best characterize the American work ethic. These values have since come to be known as the Protestant ethic. It, and the conditions that led to these values, will be discussed in the next chapter.

DISCUSSION QUESTIONS

1. Distinguish among values, ideals, and ideology. How do values relate to an ideology?
2. According to the Puritans, what constituted a person's calling? How did Benjamin Franklin alter these values? *desecularized – work took religion out of it, savings*
3. Compare and contrast Benjamin Franklin's attitudes toward work and efficiency with those of Thomas Jefferson. *– against industrialization, spread economic power*
4. Outline Alexis de Tocqueville's appraisal of enlightened self-interest. According to Tocqueville, what are the strengths and weaknesses of enlightened self-interest as a basic motive for Americans? To what extent are his assessments still valid today?
5. What is social Darwinism? Why does Herbert Spencer maintain that evolution and the "survival of the fittest" are not to be thwarted?

*civilized
east* — *uncivilized
west*

6. Describe the effect of the <u>frontier</u> on American values. Compare the effect of the frontier with the effect of social Darwinism on American values. *p23*

7. What is an ideology? What does it do for a society? What are the advantages and disadvantages to a society of having a well-articulated ideology? What happens to a society without a utopian vision? *p 15-17*

8. Are the American values, as outlined in this chapter, predominant for the average American? In your environment? For you? *p 22*

9. Does business today possess a consistent ideology? What are the disadvantages of not having a business ideology?

Kant does not like self-interest at all

CHAPTER TWO
HISTORICAL ROOTS
OF THE BUSINESS SYSTEM

In the past the man has been first; in the future the system must be first.

—Frederick Winslow Taylor

We are a product of our past. No matter how rapidly society changes, current attitudes have their roots in history. History encompasses such diverse elements as the physical spread of our cities and the energetic, entrepreneurial attitudes of earlier generations of Americans. The past is indeed prologue. Where we go and what we do in the future are very much influenced by past values and attitudes. Whether we view the present as part of an organic development from what has gone before or as a rejection of it, that past has an immense influence. An inherited pragmatic faith in technology undergirds the conviction of many that we can readily overcome current productivity and energy problems. On the other hand, a recent concern for the quality of work life and a clean environment stems partly from a disenchantment with the attitudes of earlier generations that were excessively autocratic and wasteful. It is impossible to understand current values and what the future will bring without some knowledge of the path we have taken to get where we are.

QUESTIONING THE PAST

Members of industrialized societies are generally more questioning of their everyday behavior than those of more traditional societies. They feel a more acute need to understand underlying values and attitudes for several reasons, the most basic

[handwritten annotations:] why question work? today there Are more business And career opportunities of which is that change has taken place so rapidly in societies like those of the United States, Europe, and Japan that new explanations are needed for current activities and behavior. The traditional values and ideology that were sufficient in relatively unchanging societies are no longer applicable in these transitional, dynamic nations. The second reason is that a higher level of formal education encourages people to be more questioning and reflective. Third, and more immediate, the many more choices that people face in industrialized societies— choosing a career, a style of life, whether or not to marry and have children— encourage them to examine the criteria on which they base these decisions.

The fourth and last reason why greater understanding of basic values and goals is necessary is the fact that in industrialized societies, actions and rights are more often in conflict. The desire for increased productivity and the right to work collide in the person of the unemployed. The desire to produce at lowest cost conflicts with the air and water pollution that result. The resolution of these conflicts requires clarification of goals, principles, and criteria. Moreover, this inquiry is no mere academic venture; it is the foundation from which will rise public policy and legislation and eventually a type of society and style of life.

People are beginning to ask the most basic question of all: Why work? What is the value of work? Further, what is the value of business? Granted, if I want a car or a refrigerator, it must be produced and I must have some legitimate means of obtaining it for my own uses. But if I can obtain it in some lawful fashion without working, why not? Or, to pose the question in another way, is it acceptable to work only enough to stay alive? If I have a spouse and two children, why not obtain just enough to keep ourselves happy? Why should I try to accumulate more wealth than I actually need? Such basic questions are complex and difficult, yet people are asking them with increasing frequency. All over the world, people are inquiring into the value of work for themselves and are questioning the goals of the entire business system. Some satisfying responses are essential for a happy people and a successful society.

Of course these questions are not new, but now they are being asked by more people and with greater urgency. In earlier and more traditional societies, they were largely academic or philosophical questions, asked by the wealthy and leisured, not by the ordinary citizen. The ordinary worker's life was largely determined at birth. If that person's father was a shoemaker or a baker, he would become one too, and use the tools, workshop, and home that had belonged to the family for generations. Rarely was there any question of whether the person *would* work, or at what occupation. There was little choice. There was also little regret or frustration because there was no alternative. Heredity, custom, and geography determined one's life: "To ask men in such economically undeveloped traditional societies why they work is similar to asking them why they try to stay alive."[1] Furthermore, for the average person, there was little leisure in which to question the value of work.

---

[1] Sigmund Nosow and William H. Form, *Man, Work and Society* (New York: Basic Books, 1962), p. 9.

The business system, and especially its rapid growth, is almost wholly dependent on people's attitudes toward work. Earlier generations did not much question it. Indeed, as we have seen and will examine in further detail, the American Puritan ethic supported tireless work and thus economic growth. Now the business system itself and attitudes toward it are even more dependent on people's assessment of the place and importance of work in their lives. Let us first look to our roots.

LISTENING TO OUR FOREBEARS

Change has taken place very rapidly in the United States almost from its beginning as a nation. Almost all its people are immigrants from other lands, mostly from Europe. All the Founding Fathers were heavily influenced by European thinkers, such as John Locke, Rousseau, and Adam Smith, on such issues as the value of work, business, and private property. Although there were and are alternate strains of thought in the East, these values had little impact on the West. Hence we will limit ourselves largely to Western attitudes and philosophies on these practical issues.

Throughout most of recorded history, work has been an integrating force for the individual. It was a basic binding strand for the fabric of the social system, the family, and the city. It gave stability and meaning to people and their relations. A clear change, however, emerged with industrialization. Changes in work such as division of labor, mass production, and "scientific management" were introduced. And the individual worker had increasing choice as to the type and location of the work he or she might do. It is ironic that just when individuals began to be able to choose work and so look for greater satisfaction from their jobs, that work became more fragmented, repetitive, and less able to provide pride of accomplishment and workmanship.

The Ancient Greek Attitude Toward Business and Work

[handwritten: work was dirty /degrading — Aristotle — bad for health & character]

The ancient Greeks thought of work and commerce as demeaning to a citizen. At best, it was a burdensome task required if one was to survive. The meager legitimacy and value accorded to work came not because it had any value in itself but because it was a necessary evil. There are two limitations to our knowledge of ancient attitudes toward work. First, most of our information comes from written sources whose authors were generally not from the working class; they were citizens and hence persons of leisure. Second, most of the work was done by slaves under grueling, dirty, and very difficult conditions. These slaves were uneducated and often prisoners of war from other cultures.

Plato speaks of work as if it were a temptation to be avoided because it hinders a person's ability to live and to contemplate. In his *Laws*, Plato speaks for himself and his fellow citizens when he urges, "If a native stray from the pursuit of goodness into some trade or craft, they shall correct him by reproach and degradation until he be brought back again into the straight course."[2] Citizens of ancient Athens thought of work as something not worthy of a citizen. Plato, however, reveals the extent to which his contemporaries' attitudes are based on the accidental conditions under which work was done as he cuts to the heart of their disenchantment and even revulsion with work:

> . . . suppose the very best of men could be compelled—the fancy will sound ludicrous, I know, but I must give it utterance—suppose they could be compelled to take for a time to inn-keeping, or retail trade or some such calling; or suppose, for that matter, that some unavoidable destiny were to drive the best women into such professions: then we should discover that all are humane and beneficent occupations; if they were only conducted on the principles of strict integrity, we should respect them as we do the vocation of mother and nurse.[3]

Even under conditions of general disapproval, Plato recognizes that most of the objections to work are not basic to work itself. In fact, these occupations are in themselves "humane and beneficent."

Plato's pupil Aristotle is more severe in his condemnation of the life of the worker or tradesperson. To him, such a life is irksome and beneath the dignity of a citizen:

> . . . the citizens must not lead the life of mechanics or tradesmen, for such a life is ignoble, and inimical to virtue. Neither must they be husbandmen, since leisure is necessary both for the development of virtue and the performance of political duties.[4]

From his observations Aristotle found crafts, trade, and business detrimental to health and character. Much of the work was done in cramped and unhealthy surroundings, and it was necessary to have daily dealings with the rude, the unprincipled, and the unethical. So industrial and commercial life was thought to begin by robbing the body of its health and to end by degrading the character. Moreover, whether those who followed a trade or craft should even be admitted to citizenship was a problem for Aristotle. This sort of work was generally done by slaves, and many contemporary states did not admit the laborer and the skilled worker to citizenship. "Even in states which admitted the industrial and commercial classes to power, popular sentiment held trade and industry cheap."[5]

Aristotle speaks of two types of business and trade activity, and his distinction goes to the root of a difficulty that perplexes many to the present day: the

²Plato, *The Laws of Plato*, tr. A. E. Taylor (London: Dent, 1934), 847B, p. 235.

³Ibid., 918B-E, p. 311.

⁴Aristotle, "Politics," in *Basic Works of Aristotle*, ed. Richard McKeon (New York: Random House, 1941), p. 1141.

⁵W. L. Newman, *Politics of Aristotle*, vol. I (Oxford: Clarendon Press, 1887), p. 98.

difference between careful management of goods and what often seems to be merely selfish profit orientation. He approves of the first, but disapproves of the second. _Oeconomia,_ from which our word _economics_ derives, is literally "household management." It includes careful and intelligent use not only of the household but of all one's property and resources. On the other hand, _chrematistike_ is the use of skill and goods to achieve a profit. This term described the city traders, who were few in number compared with the farmers and skilled workers. The trader often resorted to deceptive practices, and it seemed to Aristotle, and scores of generations that followed him, that this sort of person really contributed little or nothing to society. Aristotle's objections are not unlike those of Marx: The trader adds no value to a good; his service as a middleman does not enhance the good in question. Not surprisingly, then, Aristotle approved of _oeconomia,_ but disapproved of _chrematistike._[6]

Plato and Aristotle generally agree in their objections to the pursuit of a career in trade or a craft, although Aristotle raises these objections more strongly: (1) The practice of business or a craft deprives a person of the leisure necessary to contemplate the good, the true, and the beautiful. (2) It hinders proper physical, intellectual, and moral development. (3) It is "illiberal" because it is done for pay. (4) It is less perfect because its end is outside of itself.

Work in the Bible

Unlike the Greeks, who had slaves, the ancient Hebrews could not remain aloof from work; it was an integral part of their lives. They saw work as necessary, but also as a hardship. Even the painful aspect of work had its self-inflicted cause in original sin. This gave reason, integrity, and even verve to what for most other cultures was only something to be endured. On the positive side, the Hebrews pointed to the commands of God in Genesis that men and women were to cultivate the world and subdue it (Genesis 2:15). Work was still drudgery for the Hebrews, but it was better integrated into their lives and had greater meaning for them. The God of the Hebrews is close to his people. He is often pictured as one who labors: a vine dresser (Ezekiel 15:6), a pottery maker (Genesis 2:7), a soldier (Isaiah 27:1).

Christianity built on the Hebraic tradition with regard to work, trade, and commerce. The new religion itself had working class origins. Jesus was a carpenter (Mark 6:3) and Paul, a tentmaker (Acts 18:2). The Apostles, all working men, were mostly fishermen. They were not from the priestly class. The Gospels caution against an excessive and exclusive concern with work and the things of this world (Matthew 6:24–34), but they also make clear that work is a serious responsibility for the Christian (Luke 12:41–49). Furthermore, in the often-quoted parable of the talents (Matthew 25:14–30), the servant who has intelligently and profitably invested his money and his efforts is the one who is given additional rewards.

---

[6]Robert L. Heilbroner makes this same distinction in _The Making of Economic Society_ (Englewood Cliffs, N.J.: Prentice-Hall, 1972), p. 39.

[handwritten: work to share wealth with others.]

But the unique contribution of Christianity to the value of work is that it is done also out of love and concern for one's brothers and sisters. Work is necessary "not only to earn one's living, asking alms of no man, but above all so that the goods of fortune may be shared with one's needy brothers."[7] In investigating the foundations of industrial civilization, John U. Nef points to this new concept of love preached by Jesus Christ and presented in the New Testament. He finds it "a peculiarly generous concept of charity, of the opportunity we have to give ourselves to others here and now, insofar as we love our neighbors for God."[8] Through the ages and in our own time Christians most often fall short of these ideals. Nevertheless, Nef is convinced that as a foundation for work and business values, especially in its emphasis on love of neighbor, Christianity was an important step forward. *[handwritten:)God portrayed as a craftsman]*

In the early centuries of the Christian era, the most important commentator was Augustine. He approved of handicraft, farming, and commerce on a small scale. But in any selling, no more than a "just price" can be asked; asking interest on the use of money is immoral. Those who have wealth should prize it as a trust from God. After their own modest needs are met, they should give the rest to the poor.[9] As early as the fifth century, Augustine held that work was obligatory for monks. During later centuries in the monasteries, especially among the Benedictines, a new work ethic developed.

Monastic Business   *[handwritten: techniques in work efficiency]*

Benedictine monasteries have been credited as being *[handwritten: Benedictine]* "perhaps the original founders of capitalism."[10] The Benedictine Rule, as embodied in tens of thousands of monasteries throughout Europe, brought a much more positive attitude toward production and work. For the monks, work was not merely a curse, and manual work not merely degradation. These men looked on work as an opportunity to build, to grow and develop individually and as a community. They chose to work together, and they were among the first to cooperate voluntarily in all tasks. Since the monks often worked in groups and varied their occupations, they found it helpful to work by the clock. They would begin and end their work together. They standardized tasks, so that any one could handle the work.

Living and working as a cooperative community helped to stimulate the use of various labor-saving devices. When, in 1115, Bernard of Clairvaux led a band of monks to found a new monastery, one of his prime requisites for a new site was that it have a rapidly moving stream that could be harnessed by the monks to help them do their work. Bernard himself provides us with a descrip-

[handwritten: work saving ideas to do more/get more done]

---

[7]Adriano Tilgher, "Work Through the Ages," in Nosow and Form, *Man, Work and Society*, p. 13.

[8]John U. Nef, *Cultural Foundations of Industrial Civilization* (Cambridge: Cambridge University Press, 1958), p. 89.

[9]Tilgher, "Work Through the Ages," pp. 14-15.

[10]Lewis Mumford, *Techniques and Civilizations* (New York: Harcourt, Brace, 1934), p. 14.

* woman's role

tion of his famous abbey at Clairvaux, and he provides considerable detail on the mechanical devices that are geared to waterwheels to make the work of the brothers easier.[11]

The monastery is built at the base of a mountain and literally over a fast-moving stream to make best use of the waterpower. The river is guided by "works laboriously constructed" by the monks so that the water may be of the greatest help to their efforts. The water thus "passes and repasses the many workshops of the abbey." In one instance, the water is channeled so that it "passes on at once to drive the wheels of a mill." In moving these wheels, "it grinds the meal under the weight of the mill-stones, and separates the fine from the coarse by a sieve." The river's waters are also harnessed to raise and drop hammers for the traditional fulling of cloth and to help the shoemaker in his chores. The waters are then split into smaller streams where they help "to cook the food, sift the grain, to drive the wheels and hammers, to damp, wash, soak and so to soften, objects; everywhere it stands ready to offer its help." The monks also constructed an elaborate irrigation apparatus to water the fields. Recall that all this happened in the 1100s, six centuries before the Industrial Revolution.

1st catholic to endorce work as relecance to All

A century later the great Christian theologian of the Middle Ages, Thomas Aquinas, provided a rationale for work. He spelled out clearly and in some detail the reasons why it seemed to him that manual labor was necessary for all: to obtain food, to remove idleness, to curb concupiscence, *idle Desires* and to provide for alms-giving.[12] Although Aquinas saw clearly that work was not only necessary but also of considerable value, there was still an element here of work being a burden, something to endure for the sake of some leisure. *Provided for Alms giving* *Charity*

Work, however, was not a burden for the monks; it was a vehicle of love and service. When setting up a new monastery, the monks would deliberately choose a site far from existing towns. They did this both because it would be a better locale for prayer and because they deliberately set out to communicate their new view of the value of work as it is rooted in charity. Benedict and Bernard expected their monks to work in the fields and the shops, whether they were sons of aristocrats or of serfs. According to Lynn White, Jr., historian of technology and industry, this provision

> . . . marks a revolutionary reversal of the traditional attitude toward labor; it is a high peak along the watershed separating the modern from the ancient world. The Benedictine monks regarded manual labor not as a mere regrettable necessity of their corporate life but rather as an integral and spiritually valuable part of their discipline. During the Middle Ages the general reverence for the laboring monks did much to increase the prestige of labor and the self-respect of the laborer. Moreover, since the days of St. Benedict every major form of Western asceticism has

---

[11]Bernard of Clairvaux, *Patrologiae Latinae*, ed. Migne (Paris: Garnier, 1879), vol. CLXXXV, pp. 570–74. A translation of much of this is in *Life and Works of St. Bernard*, by Samuel J. Eales (London: Burns & Oakes, n.d.), vol. II, pp. 460–67. The quoted words that follow are those of Bernard himself.

[12]Thomas Aquinas, *Summa Theologica*, II-II, qu. 87, art. 3.

held that "to labor is to pray," until in its final development under the Puritans, work in one's "calling" became not only the prime moral necessity but also the chief means of serving and praising God.[13]

The monks lived together and lived thriftily, and that enabled them to invest in productive machinery like that described above to aid them in their work. This is why some call the monks the first capitalists. Their resources and inventiveness combined and resulted in division of labor, interchangeable work, a clock-regulated workday, and ingenious labor-saving equipment—all of which added up to considerably greater productivity. They used the additional time that was then available for their common life and prayer. A few hundred years later, this same love-centered ethic was brought to the cities and marketplaces of seventeenth-century France by an eminent group of saints, artists, poets, and theologians. John Nef maintains that it was this unique emphasis on the centrality of love for one's brothers and sisters, especially as embodied in women, that made industrial society and its requirement of cooperation and hard work possible.[14] More specifically, he shows that the law of love and its vision as carried out by women were two of the greatest impetuses to the sort of civilization that makes industrialized society possible.

By 1700, Christianity, with its central love ethic, had helped to provide many of the elements necessary for the development of business and commerce. Work began to be looked on as something of value; it provided self-discipline and an integrating force in a person's life. Christianity helped the individual to focus on the value of the product of work; if the same thing could be produced more easily, this was good—especially when it enabled one to help one's family and neighbors. The importance of quantity and a new consciousness of time developed first in the monastery and then spread to the larger society. Furthermore, the Catholic church urged all to attend mass side by side: worker and artisan, rich and poor, along with the peasant, scholar, and duke—a practice that fostered communication and cooperation.

In its otherworldly theology, however, Catholicism thwarted the coming of capitalism. Material goods, wealth, and success were not the measures of holiness. According to this theology, the purpose of life on earth was not merely to build up material goods. This attitude led to suspicion of those who would lend money to others and charge them for the use of it. Even as late as the sixteenth century, theologians condemned the opening of state banks.[15] Lending money at interest in the Christian tradition was the sin of usury. **××**

In Christian society, work and industry were much more respected than

Todays "usury laws" prohibit very high interest rates.

[13]Lynn White, Jr., "Dynamo and Virgin Reconsidered," *American Scholar,* 27 (Spring 1958), 188. Quoted with permission.

[14]See Nef, *Cultural Foundations,* and also his briefer *Civilization, Industrial Society and Love* (Santa Barbara, Calif.: Fund for the Republic, 1961).

[15]Lewis Mumford, *The Myth of the Machine* (New York: Harcourt, Brace & World, 1966), p. 279.

they had been in aristocratic Greece or Rome. The average citizen had many reasons to do tasks well, and there were no slaves to do them for him. In addition, a person's trade or craft gave meaning and integrity to life. But it was the Protestant Reformation that provided the impetus for the development of attitudes that would propel Western society toward rapid economic growth.

From Luther and Calvin to the Protestant Ethic

MARTIN Luther exposed church as bad. Working class is best more honest

It was Protestantism that eventually established hard work as central to a Christian life. Ironically, Martin Luther (1483–1546), the initiator of this new movement, intensely disliked the commerce and economic individualism of his day. Luther was appalled at the regal high living of the popes and the local merchants and princes. The sharp contrast between the ideals of Christianity and what he actually found around him motivated Luther to push for reform. He called for a return to a simple, hardworking peasant life; this would bring sufficient prosperity for all. A person should earn a living and not make an excessive profit.

Luther saw a number of Christian institutions as actually encouraging idleness: the mendicant friars glorifying begging, the many religious holidays, and the monasteries' support of some who did not work. Idleness is unnatural, according to Luther; charity should be given only to those who cannot work. His original contribution was in emphasizing the importance of one's profession. The best way to serve God was to do the work of one's profession as well as one can. Thus Luther healed what had been a breach between worship and work. As long as work was done in obedience to God and in service to one's brothers and sisters, every type of work had equal value in God's eyes.

Luther held that a person's salvation is achieved solely through faith in God; good works do not affect salvation. Moreover, all legitimate human activities are acts of worship, no one more than another. Since formal prayer and worship, and especially the monastic life of prayer, are no more valuable than tilling the fields, Protestantism released all human energies for the world of work. The farmer, the smith, and the baker all do work that is quite as honorable as that of the priest. Although the life of the simple worker is better, Luther concedes that

> Trade is permissible, provided that it is confined to the exchange of necessaries, and that the seller demands no more than will compensate him for his labor and risk. The unforgivable sins are idleness and covetousness, for they destroy the unity of the body of which Christians are members.[16]

A charismatic speaker excommunicated for suggesting work

Luther was vehement in preaching against lending at interest, yet paradoxically his denial of all religious authority eventually set economic life free from strictures on usury. This denial left business and commerce to develop their own life and laws independent of existing moral authority. Capitalism thus set up its own

Started on church — eventually Lutherns

[16]R. H. Tawney, *Religion and the Rise of Capitalism* (New York: Mentor, 1947), p. 83.

Disliked freyers — encouraged idleness/begging
idleness is unnatural : ungodly. Limit charity to those unable to work.

Historical Roots of the Business System   37

norms of right and wrong; it became a life set apart from and beyond the influence of the church.

Luther's insistence on investing everyday life with the same value as worship and on breaking the system of canon law and religious authority eventually resulted in profound changes in economic and social life. The elaborate prescribed relationships with neighbor, family, and church were swept away. Although they were encumbering and limiting, they also provided roots, personal relationships, and a meaning for life. Secular interests, work, and business now formed another world, one rather unconnected with the religious and moral values that had until this time governed all aspects of life.

The most important influence on what we now call the Protestant ethic was that of John Calvin (1509–1564), who followed Luther as a reformer of Christianity. Calvin and his followers did not idealize the peasant as did Luther, but accepted urban life as they found it. As R. H. Tawney puts it, "Like early Christianity and modern socialism, Calvinism was largely an urban movement."[17] Calvin's central theological notion, which distinguishes his position from that of Luther and of Catholicism, is predestination. God is infinite, absolute, and supreme; he is totally above and beyond human beings. There is no way of grasping or understanding God and his ways. In his infinite power and wisdom, God has determined that it is fitting for his glory if only a small number of men and women be saved. Moreover, there is absolutely nothing a person can do to influence his or her own salvation; from all eternity God has freely predetermined it. A person lives to glorify God, and the major way a person glorifies God is in his or her very life. If a person bends every talent and energy in work, and achieves success, this may be an indication that he or she is one of the saved. Although these individual efforts cannot directly affect or ensure salvation, if successful they do glorify God and may thus be a sign that the person is numbered among the elect. Probably even more motivating was the conviction that if a person was idle, disliked work, or was not successful, these were most likely signs that that individual was not among the saved.

Calvin taught that all must work and must never cease working. Profits earned must not be hoarded, but must be invested in new works. Investment and resulting profit and wealth are thus encouraged: "With the new creed comes a new man, strong-willed, active, austere, hard-working from religious conviction. Idleness, luxury, prodigality, everything which softens the soul, is shunned as a deadly sin."[18] Calvin proposed a unique paradox: Deny the world; live as an ascetic in the world, because it cannot guarantee your salvation. Yet remember that your one duty is to glorify God, and the best way of doing that is by being a success at your chosen work, your calling. It is a precarious balance, difficult to achieve and even more difficult to maintain.

The Protestant ethic, therefore, stems directly from Calvin's teachings. He

---

[17]Ibid., p. 92.
[18]Tilgher, "Work Through the Ages," p. 19.

stressed the importance of hard work and the necessity to reinvest one's earnings in new works. Moreover, Calvin did not continue to condemn interest and urban trade as did Luther and Catholic leaders. Calvin not only urged working hard at one's occupation but also held that successful trade and commerce was but another way of glorifying God.

Weber and the Protestant Ethic

Before leaving the influence of the Reformation on business ideology, let us look at the summary of that influence drawn up some two hundred years later by the sociologist Max Weber in _The Protestant Ethic and the Spirit of Capitalism_. It is ironic that Max Weber, a German, cites no other person more often as an example of the Protestant ethic than Benjamin Franklin, an American (we have examined Franklin's attitudes in Chapter 1).

Weber begins his analysis by noting that "business leaders and owners of Capital, as well as the higher grades of skilled labor, and even more the higher technically and commercially trained personnel of modern enterprises, are overwhelmingly Protestant." He goes on to compare the Catholic and the Protestant: "The Catholic is quieter, having less of the acquisitive impulse; he prefers a life of the greatest possible security, even with a smaller income, to a life of risk and excitement, even though it may bring the chance of gaining honor and riches."[19] In trying to determine the reason why Protestants seem to be more successful, Weber examines the roots of the theology of Luther and Calvin, as we have done above. He notes that Reformation theology encouraged individuals to look on their work more seriously. Life demanded sobriety, self-discipline, diligence, and above all, planning ahead and saving. A person's attention to the life of this world was serious in the extreme. In addition to having its own rewards, success was a reflection of God's glory, and hence a hint as to whether that person was saved or not. It was therefore incumbent on all to be successful. Moreover, they had the means to achieve that success: "In practice this means that God helps those who help themselves. Thus the Calvinist . . . himself creates his own salvation, or, as would be more correct, the conviction of it."[20]

An asceticism adequate to achieve the goal flowed from the Calvinistic ethic: "Waste of time is thus the first and in principle the deadliest of sins." On the same theme, the Calvinist asceticism "turned with all its force against one thing: the spontaneous enjoyment of life and all it had to offer." On the positive side, in the Calvinist and Puritan churches Weber finds "the continually repeated, often almost passionate preaching of hard, continuous bodily or mental labor."[21] But Weber observes that even in his day, "The people filled with the spirit of capitalism today tend to be indifferent, if not hostile, to the Church." Then it most often

---

[19]Max Weber, _The Protestant Ethic and the Spirit of Capitalism_, tr. Talcott Parsons (New York: Scribner's, 1958), pp. 35–41. Quoted with permission.

[20]Ibid., p. 145.

[21]Ibid., pp. 157–66.

happens that the pursuit of business and a career takes on the vehemence and all-embracing aspects of active religion; "business with its necessary work becomes a necessary part of their lives." But this is what is "so irrational about this sort of life, where a man exists for the sake of his business, instead of the reverse." The Protestant ethic changed history. Contrary to the ethical convictions of centuries, "money-making became an end in itself to which people were bound, as a calling."[22]

In his last chapter Weber quotes both John Wesley and John Calvin when they point out a paradox. It is religion that makes people careful, hardworking, frugal; and this, in turn, enables them to build up wealth. "But as riches increase, so will pride, anger, and love of the world," in Wesley's words. Speaking of those on the lower end of that same economic ladder, Weber quotes Calvin: "only when the people, i.e., the mass of laborers and craftsmen, were poor did they remain obedient to God."[23] Therein lies a paradox, and the men who themselves are most responsible for the Protestant ethic foresee it. Their religion demands hard work and saving, and this provides wealth. But wealth brings pride, luxury, and lack of will. It is therefore a highly unstable ethic, in part because its religious foundations tend to dissolve. But as we have seen in Benjamin Franklin and many others, the ethic can take on a secular life of its own. It can perhaps continue with other, changed though not less vital, sources of vision and motivation. It remains for us to ascertain precisely what this new secular vision and new motivation will be.

TABLE 2-1	The Protestant Ethic

THE PROTESTANT ETHIC URGES
Hard work
Self-control and sobriety (that is, humorlessness)
Self-reliance
Perseverance
Saving and planning ahead
Honesty and observing the "rules of the game"

The Protestant ethic urges planning ahead, sobriety, diligence, and self-control for the individual. It promises a material reward; and in its religious strand, a good chance of salvation. Moreover, the Protestant ethic serves an additional,

---

[22]Ibid., pp. 70-73.

[23]Ibid., pp. 175-77. Some reject the attempt to link economic success with religious faith. They maintain that there are more plausible explanations for commercial success, such as "special education, family relationships and alien status." See Kurt Samuelson, *Religion and Economic Action*, tr. E. G. French (New York: Basic Books, 1961), p. 154. Nevertheless, the fact that Weber's theses are so widely accepted makes it a theory to be reckoned with. Whatever the causal relationships, religious values and economic development are there to be observed, and they have had a marked influence on one another.

and psychologically perhaps more important, purpose. It assures the successful and wealthy that their wealth is deserved. They have property because they have worked for it, and so have a right to it. As Weber himself has observed, the wealthy man is not satisfied in knowing that he is fortunate:

> Beyond this, he needs to know that he has a *right* to his good fortune. He wants to be convinced that he "deserves" it, and above all, that he deserves it in comparison with others. He wishes to be allowed the belief that the less fortunate also merely experience their due.[24]

Thus the Protestant ethic not only provides a set of directions on how to succeed and a motivation for doing so, but also attempts to legitimate the wealth that is acquired. The successful person says, "Anyone who was willing to work as hard as I did could have done as well, so it is clear that I deserve the wealth I have."

John Locke and the Right to Private Property   *defended Rights of individual ownership*

John Locke (1632-1704) had a considerable influence on the Founding Fathers and through them on the American Constitution. He and Jean Jacques Rousseau also influenced the French Revolution and most of the subsequent efforts to move toward more democratic governments. The Oxford-educated Locke was both a philosopher and a politician. He was a practical man, having served various government figures of his day, and his philosophy showed a great concern for political and social questions.

Locke was concerned with various natural rights, but the right to which he devoted most of his energy was the right to private property.[25] Locke held that an individual has a right to self-preservation, and so has a right to those things that are required for this purpose. Individuals require property so that they may feed and clothe their families and themselves. A person's labor is what confers primary title to property. If individuals settle on land and work it, they therefore deserve title to it. Locke's ideal was America, where there was unlimited property available for anyone who was willing to clear and work it.

Locke has been criticized for overemphasizing the rights of private property and thus catering to the interests of his landowning patrons, and this may be true. But he did not allow for a person's amassing wealth without limit. Whatever is beyond what the individual can use is not by right his or hers; it belongs to others, and should be shared with them. *helps people defend themselves from others - grow own food etc.*

[24]Max Weber, "The Social Psychology of World Religions," in *Max Weber: Essays in Sociology,* ed. H. H. Gerth and C. Wright Mills (New York: Oxford University Press, 1946), p. 271.

[25]John Locke, *An Essay Concerning the True Original Extent and End of Civil Government,* especially chap. V, "Of Property," and chap. IX, "Of the Ends of Political Society and Government." See also the summary in Frederick Copleston, *A History of Philosophy,* vol. V (London: Burns and Oates, 1964), pp. 129-31.

Rousseau's Social Contract Agrees w/ Locke

Jean Jacques Rousseau (1712-1778) shared with other members of the French Enlightenment a distrust of contemporary society and its institutions. He saw that society, and even Enlightenment ideals such as reason, culture, and progress, as having created unhealthy competition, self-interest, pseudosophistication, and a destruction of the "simple society" he valued. He saw that society as unjust, effete, and dominated by the rich and by civil and church authorities. According to Rousseau, "Man was born free and everywhere he is in chains." Man's original state in nature is free; and although some form of society is necessary, freedom, reverence, family life, and the ordinary person must be central to it.

The *Social Contract* is an attempt to achieve the necessary activities, associations, and governments required in a civilized society without losing basic individual rights. A citizen's duty of obedience cannot be founded simply on the possession of power by those in authority. To be legitimate, it must rest on some sort of freely given consensus.[26] (Rousseau's distrust of society's institutions also included private property) According to him, when private property is introduced into a society, equality disappears. Private property marks a departure from primitive simplicity and leads to numerous injustices and evils such as selfishness, domination, and servitude. In the state he proposes, Rousseau supports a sharply increased tax on the property that is not necessary for a man to modestly support himself and his family. Beneath this level, there should be no tax at all. With regard to the illegitimacy of excessive wealth, Rousseau agrees with Locke.

Divided Labor — Competition is a driving force
1st economist

Adam Smith's Capitalist Manifesto

influenced by Hobbes men are greedy - self seeking, wealth is power

The Scot Adam Smith (1723-1790) is the grandfather of capitalism and of free enterprise economics. As a political economist and moral philosopher, he was among the first to emphasize free exchange and to present economics *1st* as an independent branch of knowledge. His classic work, *Wealth of Nations*, *economic* was published in 1776, and so provided independence for economics and business *textbook* in the same year that the American colonies declared their political independence from England. *Professor of moral philosophy - Oxford*

In explaining economics Smith says, "Nobody ever saw a dog make a fair and deliberate exchange of one bone for another with another dog." A bit later he spells out the implications of this inability to exchange by showing that each animal is obliged "to support and defend itself, separately and independently, and derives no sort of advantage from that variety of talents with which nature

wealth of a nation/country is its industrial resources
larger the market — lower prices

[26]Jean Jacques Rousseau, *The Social Contract and Discourse on the Origin and Foundation of Inequality Among Mankind* (New York: Washington Square Press, 1967). See also the summary of Rousseau in Copleston, *History of Philosophy*, vol. VI, especially pp. 68-69 and 80-100.

Remove everything that resist commerce

divide Labor for efficiency more produce.

has distinguished its fellows." Human beings, says Smith, are quite different in that they can take advantage of one another's unique genius. What a man is good at he does in abundance, sells to others, and thus "may purchase whatever part of the produce of other men's talents he has occasion for."[27] Smith's first and most familiar example is of the division of labor of the pinmaker. One man, working alone and forming the entire pin, could perhaps "make one pin in a day, and certainly not make twenty." But when the operation is divided up into a number of separate operations so that "one man draws out the wire, another straights it, a third cuts it, a fourth points it, a fifth grinds it at the top for receiving the head," and so on, Smith says he has observed a man is able to make a batch which, divided by the number of workers in the group, comes to 4,800 pins.[28]

In addition to the value of exchange and the division of labor, Smith also examines the value of the free market, competition, and profit maximization. Smith was among the first to make a clear and plausible case that when individuals follow their own self-interest, it automatically works to the benefit of society as a whole. As individual competitors pursue their own maximum profit, they are all thus forced to be more efficient. This results in cheaper goods in the long run. Free competition in all markets and with all goods and services is thus to be encouraged; government intervention serves only to make operations less efficient and is thus to be avoided. The same principles apply to international trade. There should be a minimum of government interference in the way of duties, quotas, and tariffs. Smith's is the classical argument in support of free trade.

Smith takes some of his basic inspiration from the English philosopher Thomas Hobbes (1588–1679). Hobbes had maintained that individuals act simply to gain that which gives them pleasure, or to avoid that which causes displeasure. Since this may differ in each individual, there is no objective good or value in reality itself. Hobbes's view of human motivation is that of "egoistic hedonism." Since human nature is largely self-seeking, and further since there is no objective morality, it is not surprising that Hobbes held that might makes right. It is important to have power to protect one's person and goods. Whatever a person has the power to take belongs to that person. Hobbes acknowledges that this leads to conditions of insecurity and even war but maintains that they are an inescapable part of the human condition. On the theme of trade and economic activity, Smith quotes Hobbes that "wealth is power." It enables its possessor to purchase what he or she wants, and this in itself gives that person considerable control over others. So it is to the benefit of individuals to increase their wealth.

To explain profit maximization, Smith uses the example of rent. Even though the owner of the land contributes nothing to production beyond the fact of ownership, nevertheless the owner will strive for a contract that will give the highest rent the tenant can possibly afford to pay. The landlord will strive to leave the tenant as little as possible of what he or she earns. Smith contends that this is

---

[27]Adam Smith, *Wealth of Nations*, ed. J. C. Bullock (New York: Collier, 1909), pp. 19–23.
[28]Ibid., pp. 9–10.

Profit maximization – charge as much as you can

as it should be. On some occasions the landlord may leave the tenant a bit more for himself, but this is and should be exceptional; it is due to "the liberality, more frequently the ignorance, of the landlord."[29]

As the grandfather of modern economics, Smith spells out clearly and graphically most of the current major principles operating in economic and business theory. He illustrates the great advantages of the division of labor, the free competitive market, and profit maximization and how they contribute to more efficient production. In pursuing these self-interested goals, Smith's famous "invisible hand" guides economic and business activities so that they are more productive and cheaper and thus benefit society as a whole. Industry and commerce in the two centuries following Adam Smith have been extraordinarily successful. Moreover, these activities have closely followed the model Smith described. The free market encouraged rapid economic growth. Economic motivation for most people up to Smith's time had been based more on obligations to a lord, proprietor, or one's family and on threats, fears, and sanctions. The free market and potentially unlimited monetary rewards shifted the entire basis of economic activity.

The free market and the possibility of unlimited profits are at the heart of the system's greatest strength: It taps positive motivation and rewards. It draws a man or woman into greater activity and creativity and quickly rewards those efforts. Furthermore, the rewards are tangible and measurable; by these standards there is little doubt as to who is a success. On the other hand, this new model for economic activity also includes the system's greatest weakness. It insulates a person from the older and clearly perceived obligations to friends, family, fellow citizens, and the larger community, and replaces them with an easily broken contract whose purpose is to obtain individual profit. Hence, individuals can much more readily come to feel that they are alone, that they are isolated, and that they are easily replaceable. Current literature on the attitudes of managers and blue-collar workers alike shows this feeling of isolation and alienation.[30]

Put in another way, Adam Smith, and the Industrial Revolution that followed, shifted people's view of themselves and others from what could be compared to an organism to a machine. In earlier society men and women knew they were part of something larger than themselves. Families worked together, and they cared for their neighbors. They were dependent upon one another— like an organism. They had a stake in their community and they belonged. This was replaced by a situation in which one's own work was sold. One no longer belonged, and one's very self became just another commodity in the market system. Every individual can and will be replaced when he or she becomes obsolete, old, and inefficient, just as is the case with parts of a machine.[31]

---

[29]Ibid., pp. 153-71. See also Harold L. Johnson, "Adam Smith and Business Education," *AACSB Bulletin* (October 1976), 1-4.

[30]See, for example, evidence of this dissatisfaction in Theodore V. Purcell and Gerald F. Cavanagh, *Blacks in the Industrial World: Issues for the Manager* (New York: Free Press, 1972), especially pp. 72-75, 236-38.

[31]For this and many other insights in this second edition, the author thanks Otto Bremmer, University of California, Berkeley.

Adam Smith provided a remarkably accurate and integrated picture of developing business activities. He clearly detailed the advantages of free exchange and the free market. As such, he was to people of the nineteenth century a father of "liberal economics." Smith is still widely quoted and, although challenged and criticized, remains to this day a principal spokesperson for capitalism and free enterprise.

communication & info.

THE PROTESTANT ETHIC
AND THE GROWTH
OF A NATION

Agriculture — Industry — Service

The year 1776, when a new nation was born on an unspoiled continent, is an appropriate time to shift our attention back to the United States. In Chapter 1 we surveyed the early values that developed in the American colonies, with an examination of the Puritans and the work of Benjamin Franklin. After independence, those values and attitudes had an unprecedented opportunity to be realized. The nation provided an ideal testing ground for enterprising farmers, traders, prospectors, entrepreneurs, and theorists. Business and commerce grew at an extraordinary pace. It is important to examine that growth briefly and, more to our purpose, the attitudes that undergirded it.

The early days of the new republic were dominated by the farmer. The colonial merchant provided the trading link between the early Americans, responding to needs and transporting food and goods. From 1800 to 1850, wholesalers took the place of merchants. They "were responsible for directing the flow of cotton, wheat and lumber from the West to the East and to Europe."[32] The rapid growth of the American industrial system that was to make the United States the most productive nation in the world had begun by the middle of the nineteenth century. "In 1849 the United States had only 6,000 miles of railroad and even fewer miles of canals, but by 1884 its railroad corporations operated 202,000 miles of track, or 43 percent of the total mileage in the world."[33] The number of those working in factories also grew very rapidly during this period. In terms of manufactured goods, "By 1894 the value of the output of American industry equalled that of the combined output of the United Kingdom, France and Germany."[34] Growth continued to accelerate, until within twenty years the United States was producing more than a third of the industrial goods of the world.

The mining city of the West was the site of new activities that called for strong, resourceful people. Tales of silver, gold, and other minerals in the mountains thrilled imaginations across the continent. Hundreds of thousands took the challenge, risking their fortunes, their lives, and often their families to try to get

---

[32]Alfred D. Chandler, "The Role of Business in the United States: A Historical Survey," *Daedelus,* 98, 1 (Winter 1969), 26.

[33]Ibid., p. 27.

[34]Ibid.

at the newly found ore. Vast amounts of capital and superhuman energies were spent. The "get rich quick" spirit of these prospectors was a prelude to that of the entrepreneurs who came later. Virginia City, Nevada, was built over the famed Comstock Lode. What was bare desert and mountains in 1860 became within five years one of the most rapidly growing and thriving cities of the new West. The energies and genius of thousands sank dozens of shafts into the rock, supported them with timbers, built flumes—and an entire city. Between 1859 and 1880 more than $306 million worth of silver was taken from the mountains.[35] The magnitude of the effort and the accomplishment can be gathered from this description:

> In the winter or 1866 the towns and mills along the Comstock Lode were using two hundred thousand cords of wood for fuel, while the time soon came when eighty million feet of lumber a year went down into the chambers and drifts. Since the mountains were naked rock, flumes had to be built from the forested slopes of the Sierras, and by 1880, there were ten of them with an aggregate length of eighty miles.[36]

Adolph Sutro owned a quartz mill on the other side of the mountains on the Carlson River, and he thought he saw an easier way to get the ore out of the mountains. He envisioned a three-mile-long tunnel through the mountains from the river valley that would intersect the Comstock mines 1,600 feet below the surface. The tunnel would drain the series of mines to that level, and would also enable the ore to be taken out through the tunnel for processing where fuel and water were plentiful. By 1866, Sutro had obtained contracts from twenty-three of the largest mining companies to use the tunnel when it was completed.

> . . . after incessant effort, in which any man of less marvelous pluck and energy would have failed, he raised sufficient capital to begin the project. In 1869 he broke ground for the tunnel and set a corps of drillers upon the task that was to occupy them for eight weary years. It was the labor of a giant.[37]

Sutro finished his tunnel and put it in use in 1877. But within three years, the boom collapsed. The value of the silver mining stock sank from a high of $393 million in 1875 to less than $7 million in 1880. People slowly began to leave Virginia City, and today it is literally a ghost town, with only remnants of roads, homes, and a few of the more substantial large buildings left to remind us of what it once was.

Virginia City illustrates how the great talents and wealth of a society can be quickly channeled to accomplish tremendous feats; it also shows how that ac-

---

[35]Allan Nevins, *The Emergence of Modern America,* vol. 8 (New York: Macmillan, 1927), p. 137. For a discussion of these and other issues raised in this chapter, see Daniel T. Rodgers, *The Work Ethic in Industrial America, 1850-1920* (Chicago: University of Chicago Press, 1978).

[36]Nevins, *Emergence of Modern America,* p. 136.

[37]Ibid., p. 137.

complishment can be and often is short-lived, and not designed to encourage stability. This sort of activity appeals to the energetic and fast-moving entrepreneur; it does not appeal to family people, who look to their own and their children's future. Virginia City illustrates both the strengths and the weaknesses of the American entrepreneurial spirit. The same sort of gold rush a decade earlier in California left a more permanent mark, since the new inhabitants did not leave when the gold ran out. The prospectors, miners, and fortune seekers converged from all parts of the country, disrupting communities and families. Before their coming, California had had a unique style. "To these California imperatives of simple, gracious, and abundant living, Americans had come in disrespect and violence."[38] Exploitation of the land kept people moving, and California chronicler Kevin Starr focuses on some of the problems they left in their wake:

> Leaving the mountains of the Mother Lode gashed and scarred like a deserted battlefield, Californians sought easy strikes elsewhere. Most noticeably in the areas of hydraulic mining, logging, the destruction of wildlife, and the depletion of the soil Americans continued to rifle California all through the nineteenth century.
>
> The state remained, after all, a land of adventuring strangers, a land characterized by an essential selfishness and an underlying instability, a fixation upon the quick acquisition of wealth, an impatience with the more subtle premises of human happiness. These were American traits, to be sure, but the Gold Rush intensified and consolidated them as part of a regional experience.[39]

Throughout these years of rapid economic change, the role of the entrepreneurs was central. Their brains, ingenuity, and willingness to risk gave us most of our economic success and growth. At the same time, their myopic desire for short-term gain caused many failures and much personal anguish. With this as background, let us return to the leaders of thought who have had such a profound influence on American business values.

American Individualism, Ralph Waldo Emerson Style

Rehtorical proponet to being ones own self.

To this day, the American businessperson is characterized as an individualist. One articulate, persuasive, and most influential champion of freedom and the importance of the individual was Ralph Waldo Emerson (1803-1882). Following on the French Enlightenment and Rousseau, Emerson is the best known American proponent of individualism. He sees human nature as having natural resources within itself. Societal structures and supports tend only to limit the immense potential of the individual. Given freedom, individuals can act, grow, and benefit themselves and others. But they require an absence of restraints imposed by people, cultures, and governments. Emerson's friend Henry David Thoreau acted on this ideology and built himself a hut at Walden Pond, outside Boston,

---

[38]Kevin Starr, *Americans and the California Dream* (New York: Oxford University Press, 1973), p. 33.

[39]Ibid., pp. 65-66.

where he reflected and wrote alone in the unimpeded, open atmosphere of trees, grass, and water.

In his book of essays *The Conduct of Life,* Emerson has one entitled "Wealth."[40] Here he applies his philosophy of individualism to economics and the marketplace. A person should contribute and not just receive. If an individual follows his or her own nature, he or she will not only become a producer but will also become wealthy in the process. Individuals contribute little if they only pay their debts and do not add to the wealth available. Meeting only one's own needs is expensive; it is better to be rich, and thus be able to meet one's needs and add to wealth as well. And doing both coincides with a person's own natural inclinations. Emerson insists that getting rich is something anyone with a little ingenuity can achieve. It depends on factors a person has totally under one's own control:

> Wealth is in applications of mind to nature, and the art of getting rich consists not in industry, much less in saving, but in a better order, in timeliness, in being at the right spot. One man has stronger arms, or longer legs; another sees by the course of streams, and growth of markets, where land will be wanted, makes a clearing to the river, goes to sleep, and wakes up rich.[41]

Emerson's heroes are the independent Anglo-Saxons. They are a strong race who, by means of their personal independence, have become the merchants of the world. They do not look to government "for bread and games." They do not look to clans, relatives, friends, or aristocracy to take care of them or to help them get ahead; they rely on their own initiative and abilities.

Struggle for Survival

The businessperson, and especially the entrepreneur, has always found the world to be nothing less than a struggle for survival. One may want to be humane and conscientious, but one cannot afford it. Herbert Spencer's theories of the survival of the fittest and what has come to be known as social Darwinism were discussed in Chapter 1. Spencer's philosophy had an immense influence on the America of the late nineteenth century. In fact, it described the American experience. *Rich are best of race*

William Graham Sumner (1840–1910) was a social science professor at Yale and a disciple of Spencerism. Sumner's father was an immigrant English workingman who gave his children the Puritan virtues of thrift, self-reliance, hard work, and discipline.[42] His son was convinced that egalitarianism, made fashionable by the French Revolution and the freeing of the slaves, would undermine

---

[40]Ralph W. Emerson, *The Conduct of Life and Other Essays* (London: Dent, 1908), pp. 190–213.

[41]Ibid., p. 192.

[42]Donald Fleming, "Social Darwinism," in *Paths of American Thought,* ed. Arthur M. Schlesinger, Jr., and Morton White (Boston: Houghton Mifflin, 1963), p. 128.

the initiative and independent spirit that encourage the best people to develop their talents fully. According to Sumner, the less able and adept are jealous of the successes of the more talented, and through the political process they will require the latter to support them. This perversion undermines the creativity and motivation of the better and more talented people. Sumner applauded the era in which people would work and live, not because of inherited position and status, but because they themselves chose to do so through the new democratic device of contract. He clashed with Yale President Noah Porter when the latter objected to Sumner's assigning Herbert Spencer's book to students but won the long-term battle with one of the first clear statements of academic freedom.

Sumner and Spencer urged a tight-fisted, unemotional aloofness. Both one's self and one's wealth must be saved and not spent without chance of a good return on investment. Free emotions and spontaneity were suspect; a person could lose all in a lighthearted or thoughtless moment. In the same vein, Sumner urged that government should not intervene in social and economic affairs. The environment should be kept clear of restrictions, taxes, restraints, and other needless and even harmful laws and regulations.

The opposition was led by Lester F. Ward (1841–1913). Ward's indictment in his *Dynamic Sociology* is that people should control their environment, not allow it to control them. Evolution and natural selection as outlined by Darwin led to change without direction and without goals. According to Ward, the great value of evolution and natural selection was that they had brought people to the position in which they found themselves now. Moreover, it was precisely in Ward's era that individuals became able to take over and control their own future, and not leave it to blind, natural chance. For him, it would have been the supreme paradox for men and women, now that they had discovered these natural laws and forces, to retreat and allow themselves to become victims of them. Ward labeled Spencerism a do-nothing philosophy.

Establishment Churches and Business

Churches have a double and often conflicting role to play in society: to help people to worship God and to sensitize the consciences of their members. As a church becomes a large, recognized, and respectable institution in society, it can easily be deterred from its role as a prophet and prodder of consciences. A church ministers to its members, yet it can be so influenced by its "respectable" membership that it becomes part of the Establishment and preaches against change, "rabble rousers," and social justice. The church and its members risk losing too much by change. A lesson for today can be learned by examining the actions of the larger and more respected churches in the United States in the last century.

The dominant American churches in the nineteenth century, while preaching charity and concern for the poor, nevertheless vehemently defended the economic system that had grown up with the Protestant ethic. In this period, churches and schools had considerable influence over American life and morals. The prestigious

private colleges of the eastern Establishment taught the values of private property, free trade, and individualism. These religiously oriented schools (both Harvard and Yale were still Congregationalist at this time) generally taught conservative economic and business values along with their moral philosophy.

To many of the clergy, since God had clearly established economic laws,
it would be dangerous to tamper with them. Francis Wayland, president of Brown
University and author of the most popular economics text then used, intertwines
economics and theology in stating his basic position: "God has made labor
necessary to our well being." We must work both because idleness brings punishment, and because work brings great riches; these are two essential, powerful,
and immutable motives for work.[43] Wayland concluded from this simple principle that all property should be private and held by individuals. Charity should
not be given except to those who absolutely cannot work, and the government
should not impose tariffs or quotas or otherwise interfere.

Approaching economic and social life from a different perspective, some
religiously inspired groups did set up experimental communal and socialist communities. But the important church leaders and the major religious denominations vigorously defended the status quo against these new sectarian challenges.
However, in the last twenty-five years of the century, these churches went through
an agonizing reexamination. Up to this time, the major Protestant churches had
bought Adam Smith's economics and canonized it as part of the "Divine Plan."
They defended private property, business, the need to work, and even wealth.
Then three severe, bloody labor disturbances in these decades forced the churches
to reconsider their traditional survival-of-the-fittest theories.

The first of these conflicts followed a severe economic depression in 1877.
Wages of train workers were cut by 10 percent, and they protested. They picketed
and halted trains. Army troops were called to defend railroad property, and they
fought with desperate mobs of workers. In the confusion, scores of workers were
shot. The churches generally sided with the Establishment and self-righteously
preached to the workers on the Divine wisdom of the American economy. Hear
the *Christian Union:*

> If the trainmen knew a little more of political economy they would not fall so easy
> a prey to men who never earn a dollar of wages by good solid work. . . . What
> a sorry set of ignoramuses they must be who imagine that they are fighting for the
> rights of labor in combining together to prevent other men from working for low
> wages because, forsooth, they are discontented with them.[44]

The religious press, reflecting the attitudes of its patrons, took a hard line against
what it saw as anarchy, riots, and support of weak and lazy men.

A decade later another serious confrontation occurred. On the occasion

---

[43]Henry F. May, *Protestant Churches and Industrial America* (New York: Harper & Row, 1949),
p. 15.
[44]Ibid., p. 93.

of a labor meeting at the Haymarket in Chicago, the police shot several of a group of strikers. A few days later, a bomb was thrown at the police. As is often the case in such situations, facts and circumstances were forgotten as near hysteria swept the religious press. The Protestant *Independent* was typical: (A mob should be crushed by knocking down or shooting down the men engaged in it; and the more promptly this is done the better)"[45] Only when these strikingly un-Christian outbursts had ended did the clergy have the opportunity to reflect on what had happened and how they themselves had reacted. (It then became clear how bi-ased, inflexible, and violent had been their stance—hardly what one would ex-pect of churches.) During this period the clergy were anxious to accommodate their churches' position to the new industrial movements. They changed no creeds or confessions, but "progressively identified [themselves] with competitive in-dividualism at the expense of community."[46] From the rubble of these mistakes and later recognized biases came the impetus toward a new social consciousness, specifically in the form of the Social Gospel. *protestant movement in US (help the poor)*

Acres of Diamonds

Defense of free enterprise was not limited to the Establishment Congrega-tional and Presbyterian churches. The Baptist preacher Russell Conwell traveled the country giving his famous speech, "Acres of Diamonds." He delivered it more than five thousand times around the turn of the century to enraptured audiences eager to hear that to gather wealth was God's will.

Conwell's speech tells of a man who goes out to seek wealth, and his suc-cessor on the farm finds diamonds in the yard he had left behind. His message: Any man has it within his grasp to make himself wealthy, if he is willing to work at it:

> I say that you ought to get rich, and it is your duty to get rich. How many of my pious brethren say to me, "Do you, a Christian minister, spend your time going up and down the country advising young people to get rich, to get money?" "Yes of course I do." They say, "Isn't that awful. Why don't you preach the gospel in-stead of preaching about man's making money?" "Because to make money honestly is to preach the gospel." That is the reason. The men who get rich may be the most honest men you will find in the community.[47]

Conwell demonstrates what to him was the happy confluence of deeply felt religious convictions and the life of the marketplace. Because of the more tradi-tional religious values of poverty and humility, riches often brought qualms of conscience to contemporary believers. Conwell represents the tradition that tries to wed faith and fortune: There can be no better demonstration of faith in God

[45]Ibid., p. 101.

[46]Martin Marty, *Righteous Empire: The Protestant Experience in America* (New York: Dial, 1970), p. 110.

[47]Russell Conwell, *Acres of Diamonds* (New York: Harper, 1915), p. 18.

than to use one's abilities to their fullest, to be a success and to accumulate the goods of the earth (to be used responsibly, of course). Conwell himself made a fortune from his lectures and, following his own advice on investment, used the money to found Temple University.

Carnegie's Gospel of Wealth

A handful of industrialists called the robber barons had an immense, enduring influence on America and American industry around the turn of the century. The immigrant Scot Andrew Carnegie was one who enjoyed his role as industrial and moral leader. With the help of the financier J. P. Morgan, Carnegie had put together United States Steel in 1901; he accumulated immense wealth in the process and loved to tell all who would listen why he deserved it. Furthermore, with millions at his disposal, Carnegie set out to establish libraries in every city and town in the United States, each proudly bearing the Carnegie name.

Carnegie had amassed a huge personal fortune, even though he was well aware that many of his own steelworkers were not well paid. He maintained that God gave him his wealth. Carnegie made no apology for the inequality, and in fact defended it as the survival of the fittest. The millionaire's money would do no good if it were paid to the workers:

> Much of this sum, if distributed in small quantities among the people, would have been wasted in the indulgence of appetite, some of it in excess, and it may be doubted whether even the part put to the best use, that of adding to the comforts of the home, would have yielded results for the race at all comparable.[48]

According to Carnegie, it is only the wealthy who can endow libraries and universities and who can best look to the long run good of society as a whole. The money is much better spent when the wealthy accumulate it in large amounts so that with it they can accomplish great things.

For this reason, Carnegie felt that the wealthy person should "set an example of modest, unostentatious living, shunning display or extravagance." He should hold his money in trust for society and be "strictly bound as a matter of duty to administer in the manner which, in his judgement, is best calculated to produce the most beneficial results for the community."[49] Inequality and the accumulation of great fortunes are good for society, along with "the concentration of business, industrial and commercial, in the hands of a few." This concentration of wealth enables the most able to use the funds for the best interest of society.

Carnegie defended his fortune, his right to have it and dispose of it as he saw fit. He was not totally objective in his examination of the socioeconomic

[48]Andrew Carnegie, "Wealth," in *Democracy and the Gospel of Wealth*, ed. Gail Kennedy (Boston: D. C. Heath, 1949), p. 6.

[49]Ibid., p. 7. David M. Potter, in *People of Plenty: Economic Abundance and the American Character* (Chicago: University of Chicago Press, 1954), maintains that in an even more fundamental sense, a democratic system depends on economic surplus (pp. 111f).

system; he was profiting too much from it. Thus, not surprisingly, he was able to overlook the injustices he and his company supported.

Manufacturing and
Scientific Management

The growth of manufacturing did, in fact, provide a new and much faster means of attaining wealth and economic growth. With increases in productivity, higher wages could be paid and greater profits obtained for the owner at the same time. This was a considerable departure from past eras, when fortunes had been made by trade, transport, or lending (and, of course, wars and plunder). As a result, wealth had been considered more of a fixed quantity: What one person gained, another lost. The advent of manufacturing demonstrated clearly that the economy was not a zero-sum game—it was *possible* for each party in the exchange to benefit financially. It depended largely on productivity.

Frederick W. Taylor, founder of scientific management, focused on better methods in manufacturing as a way to increase productivity. Productivity is, of course, the amount of a product that is produced, given an hour of labor. Clearly, mechanization and careful planning would enable workers to produce more than they might without planning. This was Taylor's insight: Worker and management experience plus intuitive judgment are not enough. For the sake of greater production, which would benefit all concerned, the work setting and even the motions of the job itself ought to be carefully studied to discover the most efficient tools and techniques.

As factory work became more complex, Taylor had greater support for his argument. No single person, worker or supervisor, could be aware of all the mechanical, psychological, and technological factors involved in planning even one job. Efficiency required careful planning by a team with varying competences. Intuition, experience, and seat-of-the-pants judgments would no longer do. Scientific management unwittingly undermined Spencer's notions of survival of the fittest. Taylor pointed out that allowing the "best person" to surface naturally was inefficient. In the contemporary complex world, few single persons had the ability to achieve maximum productivity. Greater efficiency and productivity demanded the intervention of planners.[50]

Taylor was in favor of higher wages and shorter hours for workers, but he saw no need for the union. If scientific management is implemented, and the best and most efficient means of production achieved, there will be no grounds for petty quarrels and grievances. Policies and procedures will be set by scientific inquiry into what objectively is most efficient. And that which is most efficient will benefit worker and management alike, since both will share in the results of this greater productivity: greater profits. In Taylor's scheme, the personal exer-

---

[50]See Daniel Nelson, *Frederick W. Taylor and the Rise of Scientific Management* (Madison, WI: University of Wisconsin Press, 1980); and Reinhard Bendix, *Work and Authority in Industry* (New York: Wiley, 1956), pp. 275-79.

cise of authority would be eliminated. Managers would be subject to the same policies, rules, and methodology as the workers themselves.

Although he agreed with the traditional managerial ideology that workers pursue their own self-interest and try to maximize their own return, Taylor challenged the notion that each person worked out this struggle in isolation, apart from and even in competition with other human beings. In an industrial organization greater productivity can be achieved only when each worker, along with management, cooperates to achieve the best means of production. Taylor pointed out how the returns to all were diminished if a single worker is not working at his or her most efficient job and pace. Prior to this, a person caught not working was fired. Now Taylor set out to help both worker and management achieve maximum efficiency, which could be done only in cooperation. Up to this time a lazy man or woman had been penalized; now Taylor proposed to reward workers by enabling them to work to their greatest capacity and receive greater financial return.

Scientific management was not greeted happily by either workers or management, because it tended to deprive each of a measure of freedom and judgment. Nevertheless, in the long run Taylor's methodology, and perhaps even more his ideology, have had an immense impact on industrial life. In a sharp break from earlier American individualism, Taylor demonstrated that productivity and the system, in this case manufacturing, were more important than the lone individual. The emerging corporation itself bore additional testimony to the new importance of planning, expertise, and cooperation. In subsequent decades the corporation was to provide even more individual needs: vacations, retirement, and medical care. It was no longer the individual standing alone, but rather the person working and cooperating with a larger group to achieve greater productivity that characterized American business.

Schumpeter's Prediction of Decay

The dynamism and intensity of the single-minded effort directed toward economic growth in America throughout this period seemed boundless. The very best minds and talent were drawn into business and industry. Moreover, the effort was rewarded as the economy grew more and more rapidly. As long as people's goals are to increase financial return and the amount of material goods available, seeking greater efficiency in production, and hence higher productivity, is paramount. Once these goals become less pressing, the talent, concern, and effort that go into industrial activity may decline. The possible result, decay of the economic system, was foreseen by the economist Joseph Schumpeter in the early 1940s.

In his *Capitalism, Socialism and Democracy*, Schumpeter provides a brilliant and detailed description of the undermining and decay of capitalism. He points out that the very success of the capitalist economic mechanism in providing goods and income paradoxically lessens dependence on and concern for the system. As free enterprise is successful, human needs are satisfied and investment opportunities tend to vanish. That same success undermines the need for, and so the position and prestige of, the entrepreneur, who is no longer a dominant or even a highly respected person in society.[51]

Contributing to the growing hostility to capitalism are the intellectuals. Academics and intellectuals are quick to see inequities and evils in any system. The problems are there for any perceptive eye to see, and it is the vocation of the intellectual to be a cultural critic. Moreover, Schumpeter would say that most intellectuals have had no experience in trying to manage an organization; at best they serve as staff persons or consultants. The ultimate responsibility for making an organization work has never been theirs, so they do not possess the wisdom and practicality of those who have gotten their hands dirty. In addition, they have a captive audience in the universities, and thus have a ready-made forum for their critical views. Schumpeter was convinced that the intellectuals had undermined capitalism.[52]

He was also convinced that these criticisms generated increasing government regulation to constrain the free movement of people and capital. Schumpeter is at pains to point out that he is not opposed to this change, but it is no longer capitalism. Moreover, the professional manager does not have the same long-term will and vision as the owner she or he replaces.[53] A manager need not stay and fight for the integrity of a firm or system; he or she can move on to another job that offers greater financial return. Schumpeter's indictment is a broad-gauged one; he even goes into some detail as to how capitalism and its attendant attitudes tend to undermine family life and child rearing. In his view, capitalism faces imminent death.

Schumpeter picks out another increasingly obvious weakness of capitalism: It has no compelling, motivating, all-embracing ideology and set of values. It is a pragmatic system, designed and pursued for a rather narrowly conceived end— economic growth. He then contrasts capitalism with Marxism. Marxism has a vision of the world and a systematic ideology; it calls on its followers to sacrifice for the sake of the poor and the oppressed and for a more equal distribution of goods. Its vision is sufficient to inspire people and to initiate revolutions. According to Schumpeter, Marxism has all the marks of a religion: vision, doctrine, rules, and a call for self-sacrifice. In contrast, capitalism promises only a higher standard of living and in itself cares nothing for the poor and disadvantaged. It is effective in production, but crass and parochial in its view of people and their world.

Three decades later, the economist Paul Samuelson updated and paraphrased Schumpeter's penetrating assessment: "I told you so. The successes and rationalism of bourgeois capitalism will breed a swarm of discontented intellectuals—to fan the flames of hostility toward an efficient but unlovable system with no mystique to protect it."[54] Schumpeter's critique was widely quoted in his

[51]Joseph A. Schumpeter, *Capitalism, Socialism and Democracy* (London: Allen & Unwin, 1943), pp. 131–39.

[52]Ibid., pp. 143f.

[53]Ibid., p. 156.

[54]Paul A. Samuelson, *Newsweek*, April 13, 1970, p. 75.

own day, but it is clearly even more relevant now. His insights remain valid and painfully obvious.

Measures of Success

Americans implicitly and often without much reflection look on rising gross national product and the level of median family income as yardsticks of a successful civilization. Since it is true that we have been eminently successful in the production and consumption of material goods, it is probably not so surprising that we would like to make that the measure of success for all cultures. Frederick Winslow Taylor, the founder of scientific management, put it succinctly when he said, "In my judgment the best possible measure of the height in the scale of civilization to which any people has arisen is its productivity."[55]

Another point of view was presented a generation before Taylor when England was at its height as an industrial and trading power. Matthew Arnold raised the same question, alluding to those who said that England's greatness was based on its railroads and its coal:

> If England were swallowed up by the sea tomorrow, which . . ., a hundred years hence, would most excite the love, interest, and admiration of mankind—and which would most, therefore, show the evidences of having possessed greatness?

Would it be the England of the preceding two decades, a period of industrial triumph, or would it be an earlier period when culture was more valued? Arnold answers for his contemporaries:

> Never did people believe anything more firmly than nine Englishmen out of ten at the present day believe that our greatness and welfare are proved by our being so very rich.

And then he goes on to give his own response:

> . . . the use of culture is that it helps us, by means of its spiritual standard of perfection, to regard wealth as but machinery, and not only to say as a matter of words that we regard wealth as but machinery, but really to perceive and feel that it is so.[56]

This same question faces Americans in the 1980s. How are we to judge the success of our civilization? What is our goal, and therefore what are our criteria for judging whether or not we are successful? Frederick Taylor says it is productivity; Matthew Arnold says productivity and wealth are merely tools to achieve something more. In this perennial discussion, on which side do we stand? Or

---

[55]Frederick W. Taylor, *Hearings Before the Special Committee of the House of Representatives to Investigate the Taylor and Other Systems of Shop Management,* vol. III (Washington, D.C.: Government Printing Office, 1912), p. 1471.

[56]Matthew Arnold, *Victorian Prose,* ed. Frederick William Roe (New York: Ronald Press, 1947), p. 399.

must we fashion some middle ground? If so, what elements will go into it? The point of this book is to provide some basis for resolving the dilemma.

THE AMERICAN BUSINESS CREED

The first empirical study of the principal values and the ideology of the American business system took place in the mid-1950s.[57] This inquiry focused on public and official statements of businesspeople and organizations such as the U.S. Chamber of Commerce, the Committee on Economic Development, and the National Association of Manufacturers. Using material from the decade prior to 1955, they produced a comprehensive, heavily documented, and carefully constructed analysis of the American business creed.

According to the authors, the American business creed is not monolithic. Members of the business community disagree on many issues, sometimes publicly. There is no official text of the creed. But there is enough consistency in what is said and done that it is not inaccurate to call the business ideology a creed.

"Praise for the achievements of American capitalism is one of the dominant themes in the literature of the Business Creed."[58] Production and higher standards of living are listed first. In a secondary and quite subordinate position are nonmaterial achievements such as freedom. Even more important is the firm link that is forged between the accomplishments and the system: Without American capitalism, we would not have this prosperity. The achievements are a result of the system and thus validate it. Most businesspeople would add American democracy and the free political system to free enterprise to form a highly interdependent system. To their minds, tampering with any one element will destroy the whole. Americans should defend the free market as strongly as they defend their right to vote.

The authors also found two discernible positions in the creed: (1) the classical strand of business ideology and (2) the managerial strand. The classical strand emphasizes the traditional notions and values; it has continued with little substantial change since the days of the Puritans and Benjamin Franklin. In the authors' opinion, Jeremy Bentham's description of economics as "the dogmatics of egoism" could easily be applied to the classical position. The managerial strand held many of the same positions, but broke sharply with the traditionalists on such issues as social consciousness and concern for the public image of the corporation and its members. It is more characteristic of the larger corporations and their managers. The Committee for Economic Development, a nationally respected group of business executives which publishes policy papers, generally represents the managerial strand of business ideology.

[57]Francis X. Sutton and others, *The American Business Creed* (Cambridge, Mass.: Harvard University Press, 1956). Quoted with permission.

[58]Ibid., p. 19.

(The creed itself maintains that the American business system has several important attributes.) It is *unique;* there is nothing like it anywhere else in the world. The system is also *natural;* it flows from the natural, free needs and desires of people and so could operate in other cultures. Since it is natural, it is easy to see that it is also *stable.* Unless attacked from the outside, it will remain and continue. As a result, challenges to the system result, not from its own deficiencies, but solely from outside, foreign interests. But the system, though natural and stable, must still be *chosen* by each individual. It cannot work well if large numbers of people do not understand it, or refuse to cooperate and contribute. This is a moral choice, and those who refuse to cooperate are considered "enemies."[59] Although these attributes obviously reflect the post-World War II atmosphere, they remain strong elements of the creed today.

When Francis Sutton and his colleagues investigated business-government relationships in terms of the creed, they found business generally critical of government. Government power should be restricted; government should stay out of economic life as much as possible. On this point, both the classical and the managerial strands of the business ideology agree. Some regulation may be necessary, but restraints in general are evil because they are limitations on individual liberty.[60] Individuals are responsible for their own material well-being, according to the ideology. Whether executives or laborers, they are responsible for their own future. "Virtue pays; hard work, thrift, initiative, imagination, and venturesomeness are rewarded not only in the next world but in this. Failure, like success, is deserved."[61] The values found to be inherent in the business ideology are these:

- Individualism—moral responsibility and freedom
- Materialism and productivity
- Practical realism
- Activism based on realism
- The continuing goal of progress
- The need for optimism and the spirit of adventure
- Competition
- Democracy and equal opportunity
- Service and social responsibility (in the managerial strand)[62]

The ideology's most glaring weakness is its uncritical adulation of material prosperity. More material goods and a higher standard of living seem to be worthwhile for their own sake:

[59]Ibid., pp. 36-44.

[60]Ibid., pp. 184-86. See also Friedrick A. von Hayek, *The Constitution of Liberty* (Chicago: University of Chicago Press, 1959).

[61]Ibid., p. 208.

[62]Ibid., pp. 251-63.

> Much of [the business creed's] apparent materialism arises from a tendency to value material riches without special regard to their ultimate uses. It does this above all in stressing the active pursuit of *productivity*. Business ideologists are not ashamed to stand with John Bright against Matthew Arnold and measure the greatness of a society in terms of its size and industrial equipment.[63]

Although the ideology does not necessarily encourage hedonism in the use of material comforts, it has never realistically faced the question: Productivity for what?

Every ideology grows out of a total cultural tradition, and the business ideology is no exception:

> The stamp of Western tradition is clearly set upon the general character of the business ideology. It is overwhelmingly secular in character; its values are temporal—almost embarrassingly so. Despite its use of religious symbols, the creed does not proclaim the workings of God's ways to men.[64]

The business creed, following Franklin more than the Puritans, is secular. Its few references to God are ritualized; when examined, they have little content. To have a "calling" means to have an occupation; it has moved from being a religious duty to being an expectation of the larger society. When individuals understand their "calling" and the "dignity of work," they need make no apologies for the often narrow, specialized concern with production and sales that takes up the major portion of their lives.

When a large group of managers were asked about their own value systems, 70 percent favored an individualistic, free enterprise ideology. Fewer, however—60 percent—thought that such an ideology would be the most effective in solving the problems of the future. When the study was reported in 1975, only 25 percent of these executives felt that a free enterprise ideology would dominate the United States ten years later; 73 percent of these managers thought that a more community-oriented value system would prevail.[65]

In summary, the American business creed, although oversimplified and selective, has been and remains the basis for giving business a legitimate position within the larger society. Furthermore, it has given vision, provided motivation, and lessened anxieties for generations of businesspeople. The creed proudly extols the material and practical achievements of the system and holds these to be justifications in themselves for American capitalism. There are few claims of cultural or esthetic gain from the system, and spiritual and moral achievements are limited largely to those connected with freedom.

[63]Ibid., p. 255.

[64]Ibid., p, 274

[65]William F. Martin and George Cabot Lodge, "Our Society in 1985—Business May Not Like It," *Harvard Business Review* 53 (November-December 1975), 143-52. See also George Cabot Lodge, *The New American Ideology* (New York: Knopf, 1975).

Free Men and Friedman

The central importance of free enterprise and its supporting values still remains perhaps the tenet most widely held by business leaders. That set of values, first outlined by Adam Smith and developed through two centuries of hard experience, is still vital and compelling for businesspeople. The most respected and articulate contemporary spokesperson for this free market ideology is the economist Milton Friedman. He considers freedom the most important value in any economic or political system, and he sees economic freedom as absolutely essential to political freedom.

Friedman's position in defense of the free market and in opposition to government intervention goes all the way back to Adam Smith. His is the now familiar conviction that allowing every person the opportunity to buy and sell openly and without restriction will ensure that people will obtain the goods and services they need at the lowest possible price. Free competition in the marketplace will bring about the greatest efficiency in producing the goods society is willing to pay for. The corporation, as the currently predominant economic institution, is a focus of Friedman's concern. He sees that institution as solely an economic one, responsible primarily to its stockholders. The corporation, or more properly corporate management, has no right to dispose of stockholders' profits in any manner that does not directly benefit the corporation. Management has no right to contribute to universities, to install pollution-control equipment, or to spend to make the workplace safer, unless in some way these actions benefit the corporation itself, at least in the long-term.

Friedman is convinced that government has no role in central economic planning. He speaks disparagingly of the government exercising control over the market in the "public interest."[66] Moreover, on the whole he finds that public interest groups have a negative influence:

> . . . whatever the announced objectives, all of the movements in the past two decades—the consumer movement, the ecology movement . . . the protect-the-wilderness movement, the zero-population-growth movement, the "small is beautiful" movement, the antinuclear movement—have had one thing in common. All have been antigrowth. They have been opposed to new developments, to industrial innovation, to the increased use of natural resources.[67]

Although the details of Friedman's indictment are not entirely accurate, it is clear that he finds that these public interest movements have hurt rather than helped the operation of the market.

There are only a limited number of strategies available to address such prob-

---

[66]Milton and Rose Friedman, *Free to Choose: A Personal Statement* (New York: Harcourt Brace Jovanovich, 1980), pp. 54-56, 95.

[67]Ibid., p. 191.

lems as product reliability, worker safety, and industrial pollution. If government legislation and regulation are to be kept to a minimum, and if public interest groups do more harm than good, then the only alternative for solving such problems is management initiative. Yet here, too, Friedman is convinced that management has no right to take the initiative on these issues out of a recognition of the common good. Friedman vehemently denies that corporations do have, or even *can* have, social responsibilities: ". . . the only entities who can have responsibilities are individuals; a business cannot have responsibilities."[68] To presume that a corporation can have social responsibilities

> . . . shows a fundamental misconception of the character and nature of a free economy. In such an economy, there is one and only one social responsibility of business—to use its resources and engage in activities designed to increase its profits so long as it stays within the rules of the game, which is to say, engages in open and free competition, without deception or fraud.[69]

He is convinced that the growing sense of corporate social responsibility undermines basic freedoms:

> Few trends could so thoroughly undermine the very foundations of our free society as the acceptance by corporate officials of a social responsibility other than to make as much money for their stockholders as possible. This is a fundamentally subversive doctrine. If businessmen do have a social responsibility other than making maximum profits for stockholders, how are they to know what it is?[70]

He then goes on to point out the difficulty in making such a decision, citing the fact that some German businesspeople contributed to the Nazi party in the early 1930s. Managers thus wrongly presumed an authority and a wisdom they did not possess.

Friedman argues for the abolition of all corporate taxes and for ensuring that corporate profits are returned to the stockholders, who can then as individuals decide how they will spend their money. It is *their* money, so it should be their decision whether or not to use it for community purposes. His position is simple, straightforward, and consistent: The interests of stockholders, consumers, and citizens as a whole are best served if the corporation sticks to its traditional role of producing goods and services and does that as efficiently and inexpensively as possible. This is the best long-run service that the business firm can provide for society. He does, however, recognize the problem of unemployment and disability, and he was one of the first to propose a guaranteed minimum income (or "negative income tax," as he calls it) for all those of wage-earning age in the

---

[68]Milton Friedman, "Milton Friedman Responds," *Business and Society Review*, 1 (Spring 1972), 6.

[69]Milton Friedman, *Capitalism and Freedom* (Chicago: University of Chicago Press, 1962), p. 133.

[70]Ibid.

economy. He would substitute a minimum income for the variety of welfare, disability, and unemployment programs that have proliferated, all of which now require separate, expensive, and inefficient administrative apparatuses.

The same principles apply to such diverse areas as schooling and medical care. Friedman does not think the government should be in the business of education, for public education then becomes a monopoly insulated from the challenges to excellence and efficiency that come from *free* competition. Rather, the government should provide redeemable tuition certificates for parents and children to use at the school of their choice. As in producing goods and services, he is convinced that better and more effective education will result when there is free competition.[71] His position on the medical profession and the monopoly that certification gives to the American Medical Association is the same. Better, more efficient, and cheaper medical service would result if there were no monopoly. If anyone with some medical knowledge could hang out a shingle, the public would eventually find out who was giving better service and who should not be patronized. Friedman criticizes the guru status we have bestowed on the medical profession and claims that this does not produce the most effective and efficient treatment.

Milton Friedman acknowledges that his views on the corporation and the socioeconomic system do not possess the depth, insight, or balance of his Nobel Prize-winning work in economics. Especially in his later work, he fails to grapple with the basic criticisms of free enterprise: It encourages selfishness and results in costs to third parties and in serious inequities. Furthermore, Friedman has little patience for any of the major alternative solutions: government regulation, public interest group pressures, or voluntary actions by management.

The Ideology of Chief Executive Officers

For a decade, beginning in the late 1950s, the chief executives of some of the largest corporations in the United States (General Electric, Sears Roebuck, du Pont, U.S. Steel, American Telephone and Telegraph, and International Business Machines) delivered an annual lecture at Columbia University's Graduate School of Business Administration. The aim of the series, known as the McKinsey lectures, was to explore larger issues of value and ideology. The executives attempted to present their views of the business system and their conceptions of how that system relates to the larger society. In "The View from the Top," Robert Heilbroner analyzed these lectures for their approach, content, and basic ideology.[72] His definition of ideology is "the various ways in which privileges and disprivileges of any society are justified to those who enjoy or suffer them." It

---

[71]Friedman, *Free to Choose*, pp. 150-88.
[72]Robert Heilbroner, "The View from the Top," in *The Business Establishment*, ed. Earl F. Cheit (New York: Wiley, 1964), pp. 1-36.

is a pragmatic and self-serving conception, but we must probably concede that it accurately describes how ideologies are usually formed.

In making his analysis, Heilbroner looked for common threads. He found that these executives tended to dwell on several main themes. They emphasized a clear break between "old-fashioned" exploitative capitalism and modern capitalism. Modern capitalism is more responsible and more socially aware. Indeed, one of the main elements in this new capitalism is its professional responsibility. Like the proponents of what earlier was identified as the managerial strand of the business creed,[73] these executives too found a sharp break with the old brand of capitalism. Although very much in favor of the free market and free competition, they nevertheless argued the need for large-scale organizations. Not surprisingly, since each headed a giant firm, they did not see the need to revive federal antitrust activities. These executives acknowledged the need to be sensitive to the basic human needs of the men and women who work for them, whether managers or blue-collar workers.

Heilbroner is somewhat severe, and probably rightly so, in his criticisms of these lectures. He found that much of what these executives said was not borne out by their everyday actions. It was not that they deliberately set out to deceive; they seemed to take seriously what they said but never to have examined the inconsistencies:

> . . . one searches the McKinsey lectures in vain for a recognition of truly great issues. A few token gestures, a respectful doffing of the cap before the "challenges of our time," only serve to give greater inanity to the declarations of economic patriotism that follow. It is not moral leadership that the McKinsey lectures finally offer us; it is a pep talk.[74]

Heilbroner goes on to ask what it is in these lectures that deprives the business ideology of the quality of inspiration it seeks. He says that it is, in part,

> . . . the more or less transparent defense of privilege masquerading as philosophy, the search for sanction cloaked as a search for truth, the little evasions and whitewashings that cheapen what purports to be a fearless confrontation of great issues.[75]

But there is something even more basic lacking in the business creed: "What it lacks is a grandiose image of society, a projection of human possibilities cast in a larger mold than is offered by today's institutions."

In his *The 20th Century Capitalist Revolution*, the perceptive Adolph Berle located the "conscience of the corporation" in the person of the manager. Berle wrote during the same period and at the same university at which the McKinsey lectures were held; indeed, the lectures may well have been prompted by a desire to investigate his theories, which compare the power of the manager with that

---

[73]Sutton and others, *American Business Creed*, pp. 33-36

[74]Ibid., p. 35.

[75]Ibid.

of the kings of earlier centuries and argue the necessity for restraint and responsibility. From the time of William the Conqueror, power has been accompanied by responsibility. This is especially true of absolute power; and in the corporation, "within a wide range, management power is absolute."[76] Berle sees the necessity for such corporate and managerial power, but he also sees clear dangers.

In medieval times, there was a higher law; "the Cross could frequently stop the king."[77] Some higher law would provide a more balanced exercise of power in contemporary society, but there is none. Hence, corporations need an active conscience: "This conscience must be built into institutions so that it can be invoked as a right by the individual and interests subject to corporate power." Berle argues so strongly for management conscience that he adds this to the qualifications necessary for the corporate executive:

> for the fact seems to be that the really great corporation managements have reached a position for the first time in their history in which they must consciously take account of philosophical questions. They must consider the kind of community in which they have faith, and which they will serve, and which they will help to construct and maintain.[78]

This sort of vision is essential for the executive, for it is easy to forget that "Capitalism is not a way of life, but a method of achieving economic and social results." Yet the decisions of the management of Exxon or Sears Roebuck & Company in the aggregate "do form life and community."[79]

Berle's thesis is well argued and substantiated with considerable evidence; furthermore, though it was presented thirty years ago, the question of how accurate he is remains unanswered. Concerning whether the free market has within itself the ability to handle current difficulties, or whether the increasing power of corporations must be balanced by a corporate conscience, Berle clearly comes down on the side of the latter. Laws and regulations must be developed, but Berle argues for the necessity of greater vision and moral sensitivity on the part of corporate executives. For although it is clear that corporate decisions in the aggregate help to create the type of society we have, the free enterprise economic system in itself as yet has no categories for the more subtle considerations of human happiness, interpersonal relations, and the quality of life.

During the 1960s and 1970s, it became clear that the public did not have great trust in or high regard for business. Hence businesspeople felt misunderstood and embattled[80] and set out to change this popular perception. They orga-

---

[76]Adolph A. Berle, Jr., *The 20th Century Capitalist Revolution* (New York: Harcourt, Brace & World, 1954), p. 64.

[77]Ibid., p. 69.

[78]Ibid., p. 166.

[79]Ibid., pp. 181–83.

[80]See, for example, Ernest van den Haag, ed., *Capitalism: Sources of Hostility* (Washington, D.C.: Heritage Foundation, 1980); Robert Hessen, *In Defense of the Corporation* (Stanford, Calif.: Hoover Institution, 1979); and M. Bruce Johnson, eds., *The Attack on Corporate America* (New York: McGraw-Hill, 1978).

nized and developed strategies and have been rather successful in getting their message to the public and in obtaining more political clout. Moreover, during this period some executives developed corporate policies that show greater concern for customers, employees, suppliers, and other groups of the larger community. These efforts of the last decade will be discussed further in Chapter 6.

From these activities it is clear that the classical and the managerial strands of the American business creed continue to the present day. Most of President Ronald Reagan's advisers adhere to the classical strand: The first and almost exclusive duty of the firm and its management is to produce effectively quality products and services at a profit to the firm, the stockholders, and themselves.[81] On the other hand, many corporate executives hold to the managerial strand of the American business ideology. These managers agree on the importance of efficiently producing quality products at a profit, but they also maintain that this is not sufficient. Their corporate policies demonstrate a larger sense of social responsibility to the various constituencies that are touched by the firm.

Masculine Management

The world and the ideals we have been discussing in this chapter are those of the businessman. For centuries, business, commerce, and trade have all been largely "for men only." Women did not even obtain the right to vote until the twentieth century. Fully half of the potential technical and managerial talent has been lost. Also, a glance at any firm's equal employment opportunity figures, especially at the "officials and managers" category, immediately spotlights the results of centuries of racial prejudice. Moreover, it has been only within the past generation or so that the religious prejudice in the executive suites of the largest corporations has broken down (the WASP (white Anglo-Saxon Protestant) clique is cracking. Blacks, Jews, Catholics, and women are only now climbing up the managerial ladder into the executive suites.)

SUMMARY AND CONCLUSIONS

From ancient times to the Middle Ages, Western attitudes toward work lost their negative cast and became progressively more positive. Biblical injunctions and monastic practices helped to integrate work, labor-saving devices, and a planned day into the average person's life. Then, in the sixteenth century, the Protestant Reformation made the successful performance of an individual's "calling" or occupation one of the primary duties of life. Although a rather joyless vision, it encouraged a focusing of energies that made rapid economic growth possible. The

---

[81]For this position, see George Gilder, *Wealth and Poverty* (New York: Basic Books, 1980); and Michael Novak, *The American Vision: An Essay on the Future of Democratic Capitalism* (Washington, D.C.: American Enterprise Institute, 1978).

central importance given to private property and the freedom of the individual further supported this growth.

The American business ideology as described in this chapter was ideal for a period of expansion, rapid growth, and exploitation of land and resources. It gave the poor immigrant an opportunity; and it gave a new nation its railroads, mines, industries, and cities.

It was an ideology that advocated such personal qualities as hard work, competition, self-reliance and self-discipline, individualism, and saving and planning ahead. The vision that called forth these qualities, preached in church, school, and town meeting alike, was one of growth, superiority, and making the world a better place for the next generation. Quality of life.

Several elements converged to fashion this new and unique vision called the American business ideology:

1. The *frontier* opened up for the immigrants who had come to the New World looking for a challenging new life in farming, mining, or manufacturing where potential rewards were immense.
2. The *Protestant ethic*, which underscored the value of hard work in a person's occupation, was carried to the New World by the Puritans and translated into a secular vision by people like Benjamin Franklin.
3. *Faith in free enterprise* gave the individual security, confidence, and vigor. The system obviously worked well in encouraging economic growth and, moreover, was shown to be intellectually sound by the classical economists.
4. *Competition* became more explicit and central with the advent of the theory of evolution and the recognition of the principles of natural selection and the survival of the fittest. Natural forces, if allowed to operate without constraint, would provide the best specimen of human being and, in a parallel fashion, the most efficient firm.
5. *The role of government* was to apply as few constraints as possible to business activity; its central purpose was to protect the private property of its citizens. On this, Thomas Jefferson is often quoted: "That government is best which governs least."

survival
of the
most
adaptable.

It is an irony of history that emphasis on the rugged individualist peaked during the latter half of the nineteenth century, just at the time the business scene was dominated by oligopoly and trusts. A few firms in an industry virtually controlled production, prices, and even wages. It was difficult for an individual, no matter how rugged, to raise the capital necessary to compete. At that time and since then, it has become apparent that this American business ideology, although it may provide a motivation and a vision for the enterprising individual, does not really give an accurate description of the marketplace. For the market is not totally free.

The goal of the traditional American business ideology is expansion and growth; its focus is on material reward for the individual. But the assumption that an individual always wants more in the way of material goods leads to further questions. Is the goal of more material goods sufficient to motivate the individual to give most of his or her physical and psychic energy to the business enterprise? When accumulating material goods is the major reason for working, and if an

individual is satisfied with less, why should he or she work harder, work overtime, or take work home? Is the goal of more material goods the most basic motivation? Are there other, more subtle values of the individual in an affluent society
that must be tapped if we are to continue to be economically healthy? From another perspective, to what extent will one's "calling" continue to be central in one's
life? On a question that will have profound impact on national policy: Is a goal
of material growth necessary for a business creed for the future? If so, what sort
of growth? These and other, similar questions will be addressed in the following
chapters.

Sect = religious group who cut themselves off from group

DISCUSSION QUESTIONS

4th century BC

1. What was the attitude of Plato and Aristotle toward work? What influence did Jesus and the Gospels have on the value of work?

2. What attitudes toward work did the early Benedictine monasteries contribute? What meaning might these attitudes have for work today?

3. Describe how John Locke's attitude toward private property influenced
   the Protestant ethic and early American attitudes? How does this influence current business values?

4. Was Martin Luther favorable toward business and commerce? Was
   John Calvin? Why did Calvin think that the Protestant ethic would
   decay?

5. Why is Adam Smith called the grandfather of economics? Compare his
   attitudes on work and efficiency with those of Benjamin Franklin.

6. Using historic events and attitudes, indicate what characteristic American values were illustrated during the silver-mining days at Virginia
   City, Nevada. Compare these values with those of the Establishment
   churches during roughly the same period (that is, about 1860–1890).

7. What are the similarities and dissimilarities between the Protestant ethic
   and American individualism? Outline how the Protestant ethic aided
   in the economic development of the New World.

8. What was Andrew Carnegie's position on wages, wealth, and the responsibilities of the rich? Compare his attitudes on work with those
   of Fredrick W. Taylor (scientific management). What do they have in
   common? How do they differ?

9. Why did Joseph Schumpeter say that capitalism would decay? Compare his views on this subject with those of John Calvin.

10. How does one measure the success or failure of a culture? By its gross
    national product? Average per capita income? By its literature or art?
    By its care for the poor and disadvantaged? What other criteria?

CHAPTER THREE
MARX'S CHALLENGE
TO FREE ENTERPRISE

[handwritten annotations: inevitable struggle btwn. 2 classes. workers win. Is it a 'pecking order' leader/wchange - mid. - very poor. Abused INNATE?]

> The communist ideological and social system alone is full of youth and vitality, sweeping the world with the momentum of an avalanche and the force of a thunderbolt. . . . (communism) is the most complete, progressive, revolutionary and rational system in human history.

[handwritten: MARX'S]

[handwritten annotations: eg. now Jew moved to England mid industrial - Fred Ingalls Rich friend. Revolution - BAD time. Dad: only looked At world then. Never Saw 3 classes like us. Rich - in btwn - poor.]

—Mao Tse-tung*

No critique of free enterprise has proved as perceptive, trenchant, or appealing historically as that of Karl Marx. Marxism raises serious questions about the social and moral consequences of the economic system we have adopted. It also presents an alternative economic system and a supporting ideology. For Marxism has given us not only critics of the free enterprise system, but also a block of Communist nations whose people now outnumber those of the capitalist nations of the world.

Marxism and the Marxist nations of the world are a separate chapter of world history; they deserve their own chapter here also. Their ideology is so unique, its presuppositions so different, that it stands in marked contrast to the ideology of Western nations. Moreover, nations which embrace Marxism have chosen to separate themselves physically from their neighbors in order to develop and retain the purity of their value system. Marxist leaders regard Western self-oriented materialism as a corrupting influence; it is best to keep at a distance that value system that emphasizes self interest.

Free enterprise, or capitalism as it is called by its critics, is the socioeconomic

---

*Mao Tse-tung, *Quotations from Chairman Mao Tse-Tung.* (New York: Bantam Books, 1967). Quoted with permission.

The principal author of this chapter is Arthur F. McGovern, S.J., professor of philosophy, University of Detroit. He is the author of the now classic *Marxism: An American Christian Perspective* (New York: Orbis, 1981).

land owners   o. workforce
Aristocracy o. WC.

England System had distinctive classes — even dialect

system of most of the developed, industrialized countries. North America, Western Europe, and Japan form the powerful core of these wealthy "first world" countries. Russia, China, Cuba, and Eastern Europe operate with a Marxist socioeconomic system; they are called the "second world." The nations of Asia, Africa, and South America, which are very poor and do not clearly belong to either ideological camp, are thus called "third world" countries.

Although Marxism has been a remarkably successful system for organizing an economy, it is by no means the first social system to be built on cooperative ideals. Monastic living, discussed in Chapter 2, is an enduring model of living and working together and sharing goods in common. But such a community, which depends on closely shared values and a lifelong commitment at least on the part of some, was never intended for all people. Medieval European communities were more cooperative than their contemporary counterparts. Guilds, stable populations, and extended families all living within walking distance gave these early communities cohesion. On the other hand, they also had a rigid hierarchical social system. If the father was a butcher, so was the son.

Criticisms of capitalism and advocacy of socialism did not originate with Marx. As the Industrial Revolution took hold of Europe in the nineteenth century, a plethora of critics and socialist theories emerged. Saint-Simon, Fourier, Cabet, Moses Hess, Blanqui, Robert Owen, and countless others attacked the capitalist system and proposed various ways of achieving socialism: state ownership, national workshops, voluntary communes, revolutionary overthrow by elitist conspiracy groups, revolutionary overthrow by the masses. The communes advocated by Cabet, who first coined the term "communism" in the 1830s, and by Fourier inspired some of the ventures in communal ownership attempted in the United States. One such was Brook Farm, which was located in West Roxbury, within the city limits of present-day Boston.

Before going on to examine various cooperative socioeconomic systems, it might be wise to step back for a moment to examine some of *our own* beliefs and presuppositions. Each of the following questions can be asked also of any of the major leaders of thought discussed in this book. But in order to obtain additional clarity on our own goals, beliefs, and value system, let us ponder some questions. What do I believe regarding the following most fundamental issues:

1. Is humanity on an inevitable, long-term road to progress and the better life? Or, on the contrary, is humanity headed for a collapse of civilization and catastrophe?
2. If neither progress nor collapse is inevitable, do men and women have it in their power to affect future society (e.g., society one hundred years hence)? In what way?
3. Is anything always wrong or always right (e.g., murder)? Is lying or stealing always, or generally, wrong? Or is it all relative? a matter of social expectations and the law?
4. Does life end at death? Is there an afterlife? How does this influence my work, my life, and my attitudes?
5. Is human nature essentially good, needing only support and encouragement to develop it, or is human nature essentially self-seeking, so that an economic system ought best build on this selfishness and make the best of it?

(margin notes, left side: monarchy — capitalism — communism (social state))

(bottom notes:)
Eng. not Agri. economy   *All Revolutions come that in Agrarian Economy*
Hasn't happened yet in industrial countries.

(note above question 3:) *education*

the Roy of history   Economic Structure gives rise to class differences

3 Forces shape history   social, economic, political

6. Is competition the most effective motivation for me? Is cooperation more effective? Or do I respond to some combination?

7. Have I ever thought about the above questions? Or do I put them aside, either because I do not understand their relevance or because they are too difficult?

Adam Smith — profit MAXIMIzation — charge All ucan.

Our answers to these questions expose a framework upon which both our daily and long-term decisions are built. Whether we answer yes or no has a profound influence on our goals, values, and attitudes. On the other hand, it is also possible that we have not thought much about these questions. We may have answered them in some implicit fashion, or it may be that we have never faced these issues at all. Perhaps our values and attitudes have been merely absorbed from television, other people, and our surroundings. In this case we are making daily decisions with far-reaching implications without having examined the presuppositions which mightily affect those decisions. Problems which stem from this posture, and how we cope or fail to cope, will be discussed in the next chapter. *Acquinas*

It would be instructive to raise these questions with regard to what we know of Benedictine Bernard of Clairvaux, John Calvin, Benjamin Franklin, Adam Smith, and now Karl Marx. But let us first return to an examination of cooperative socioeconomic systems in the United States.

USA No permanant working class Am. dream
W/ same 'some have more #

ALTERNATIVES TO CAPITALISM: THE EARLY AMERICAN EXPERIENCE

The New World was attractive, not only to the individualist and those who were enraptured with the frontier mentality, but also to those with cooperative ideals. In the nineteenth century, as Europe was swept with the Industrial Revolution, many came to the New World to begin living and working again in a more cooperative fashion. Hundreds of cooperative, "communist" communities were formed in the United States during the nineteenth and early twentieth centuries.[1] These were not merely a few people or a single house like most of our contemporary communes; they were, rather, communities that counted their members in the hundreds and sometimes thousands. These communities shared work and income equally. They were opposed to the competition encouraged by capitalism and felt that only through cooperation could a human society develop. The clearly alternate life style they constructed was available to Americans through the early part of this century.

The Shakers were a religious group that at one time had nineteen separate

[1]Rosabeth Moss Kanter, *Commitment and Community* (Cambridge, Mass.: Harvard University Press, 1972); see also Norman J. Whitney, *Experiments in Community* (Wallingford, Pa.: Pendle Hill, 1966), and the earlier account by William A. Hinds, *American Communities* (Chicago: Charles Kerr, 1902).

communities scattered throughout New England and the Midwest; their land hold-ings included nearly 100,000 acres.[2] The suburb of Cleveland called Shaker Heights takes its name from the Shaker community there. Its beautiful Shaker Lakes were built as millponds by the Shakers. The men lived communally, as did the women; there was little contact between men and women at work or social-ly. There was no marriage; new members had to be converted. In the early days there were converts, and the number of Shakers eventually reached 6,000. They called themselves the Millennial Church; it was outsiders who observed the long, loud, and active shaking movements in their prayer services and dubbed them Shakers.

Most of the members of these communities farmed, like everyone else, but some later moved into manufacturing. Notable among the latter is Oneida Com-munity in New York State, which was founded by the minister John Humphrey Noyes in 1848. Although it is no longer a commune, it has paradoxically de-veloped into a multimillion-dollar international business. It is now the nation's largest maker of stainless steel tableware.[3] Probably the best known of the com-munal experiments was that of Robert Owen at New Harmony, Indiana. Owen was a weathly Scot factory owner who was the first in England to limit the work-day to ten hours. He both advocated and initiated other work and social reforms among his employees. But Owen's dream was a community in which all work, life, and leisure would be shared. Unlike most other early commune organizers, Owen's vision was not religious in origin.

In 1825, Owen purchased an established community built by a religious group called the Rappites and renamed it New Harmony. He advertised for members and accepted almost all comers; more than 900 came, among them some well-known professional people. But because of his other obligations, Owen himself found little time to be at New Harmony in the early days. Farming and other basic skills were scarce among the community members, and lack of com-mon vision and subsequent discord brought the community to an end in 1827. It was a highly publicized, expensive, and noble experiment, but was shorter lived than most cooperative communities.

All these early cooperative communities began with strong leadership, and most were religious in origin. For a commune to survive, it must continue to at-tract the vigorous and talented, and not merely the weak and those who are look-ing for a refuge from the problems of the outside world. Self-discipline and exter-nal order are necessary to solve the multitude of differences that arise in a com-munity, yet these values are impossible to sustain without a shared vision. Most of the communes failed after the original leader was gone and the early goals and inspiration for the community began to fade. It is thus clear that the com-

[2]Hinds, *American Communities*, p. 27. See also Marguerite F. Melcher, *The Shaker Adven-ture* (Princeton, N.J.: Princeton University Press, 1941), p. 302.

[3]Hinds, *American Communities*, pp. 173-214. On recent successes, see "It Started Out as a Commune in 1848, and Today Oneida Is a Thriving Business," *Wall Street Journal*, April 4, 1973, p. 8.

munes we find in the United States today are not a new social phenomenon.[4] Moreover, in the light of history, it can hardly be said that communes and cooperative living are "un-American."

[handwritten: Social State = gov't owns goods & services producing co.'s All productive capacity]

THE MARXIST CRITIQUE

[handwritten: Should share wealth]

Although French and English Utopian Socialists anticipated the idea of public or communal ownership as an alternative to capitalism, it was Karl Marx (1818-1883) who first forged a theory of communism as we know it today. Marx's criticisms of the capitalist system were incisive and based on careful empirical studies. His language is intentionally polemic. Marx and Marxists speak of "exploitation," "imperialism," and "alienation." Such language generally jars Americans and often provokes defensiveness and anger. The criticisms come from a viewpoint that is designedly quite foreign to that of the American business community. Marxist critics make little effort to be balanced or conciliatory. In addition, their criticisms recall the rhetoric of radical activists, and some may feel that we have already heard too much of it. But despite differences in language, values, and attitudes, the Marxist critique can provoke us to examine our own national priorities and the values that govern our economic, political, and social policies. If we are here attempting an objective examination of the goals and values of free enterprise, we must not neglect its harshest critics.

[handwritten margin: Argument, Refutation]

[handwritten margin: disprove beliefs]

A man of real genius, Marx combined analytic and critical power with an ability to weld his ideas into an overall theory of history. According to his theory, economic forces are the primary determinant of history. Economic structures give rise to class differences; class conflicts provoke social and political struggles. The capitalist class conflict between workers and owners would inevitably erupt in revolution and would usher in a new socialist system of production. Our concern here, however, is, not with the Marxist theory of history, but with its criticisms of our economic system. Not every person cited in this section is a strict Marxist (many would certainly not advocate social revolution), but all are severe critics of our current system. One critic acknowledged as a Marxist economist is Paul Sweezy. Sweezy contends that the essence of Marx's criticism can be found in the very method he used to analyze the economy.[5] Until Marx's time, according to Sweezy, economic theory viewed economic factors (capital, labor, prices) as things. But Marx insisted that economics does not deal simply with things; it deals with *social relations*. Every commodity produced and sold, every wage paid, in-

[handwritten: entropy]

---

[4]For a sociological analysis of historical and contemporary American communes, see Benjamin Zablocki, *Alienation and Charism: A Study of American Communes* (New York: Free Press, 1979). A well-written, carefully researched firsthand account of scores of modern communes in the United States is Robert Houriet, *Getting Back Together* (New York: Coward, McCann & Geoghegan, 1971).

[5]Paul Sweezy, *The Theory of Capitalist Development* (New York: Oxford University Press, 1942), pp. 1-5, chap. II passim.

volves very definite relationships between human beings. In failing to recognize these social relations, (capitalism and capitalist theory consequently ignore the real effects of the system on human society.)

This basic critique can be divided into several accusations made by Marxists and other critics of the capitalist system. For some readers, these accusations may seem exaggerated, one-sided, and wearisome. But they are presented with the conviction that criticism can also lead to constructive change and a healthy reappraisal of views.

(dehumanization Exploitation) of the Worker leads to Revolt
#1 for efficiency concern #2 for worker

The free enterprise system operates on the theory that when people work for their own self-interest, they will simultaneously contribute to the welfare of all. Everyone profits from economic growth, and presumably each person receives in proportion to effort and skill. Marxists challenge these assumptions. That economic growth has occurred since the beginning of the modern industrial age is evident. That all have profited from this growth in any degree proportionate to their work is quite dubious. For Marx, who knew the Industrial Revolution in its grimmest stage, it was difficult to see how the working class benefited at all from their labors. The masses of factory workers lived in hovels, worked exhausting ten- and fourteen-hour days, and died prematurely. Marx's classic, *Capital*, chronicles in page after page the price paid in human suffering for industrial growth: workers suffering from pulmonary diseases caused by the dust and heat of factories, small children working fifteen-hour days, a young girl dying of exhaustion after twenty-six consecutive hours of work.[6] Workers were forced to live on bare subsistence wages, while owners gained fortunes and lived in luxury.

Today the extremes between impoverished workers and wealthy owners described by Marx no longer prevail, in the United States at least. Labor unions and government legislation forced better wages and working conditions, which have significantly raised the standard of living of most workers. But if one looks to the *distribution* of wealth and income in the United States, great disparities remain. Five percent of family units have upward of 40 percent of all personal wealth, and the bottom *half* of wealth-holders account for only 3 percent of the net worth of all Americans. The top 20 percent of family units have three times the net worth of the bottom 80 percent.[7] U.S. Census statistics show that wealthy families in the United States, with $60,000 or more in gross assets, hold $629 billion in corporate stocks. The wealthiest 1 percent accounted for one-fourth the value of all gross personal assets, worth one trillion dollars. They hold 56 percent of all corporate stock, 60 percent of the bonds, and nearly 90 percent of trusts.[8]

---

[6]Karl Marx, "The Working Day," *Capital*, vol. I (New York: International Publishers, 1967), pp. 244-54.

[7]Maurice Zeitlin, ed., *American Society, Inc., Studies of the Social Structure and Political Economy of the United States*, 2nd ed. (Chicago: Rand-McNally, 1977), p. 63.

[8]*Statistical Abstracts of the United States* (Washington, D.C.: U.S. Bureau of the Census, 1981), p. 453.

Capitalist - get paid for Not working - own lAnd - control workforce
- industrial Rent -

low wages

Rich can Afford biggest/Best mAchines/tools .

For a Marxist, the reason for this disparity is clear. At best, workers can only bargain for higher wages. But the capitalist class, the owners and executives, determine the whole productive process—what is produced, how it is produced, the selling prices of products—and payment for respective contributions—how much to wages, to executive salaries, and to stockholders. Through power of ownership the capitalists control the system, and the great disparities which develop are a consequence of their control. Workers are not paid the real value of their work contribution, according to Marx. The difference, the surplus value, between what they should receive and the actual wages they do receive is the real explanation of the owner's profit.

A Belgian Marxist explains this notion of surplus value and the exploitation it involves quite graphically.[9] As long as the productivity of labor remains at a level where one person produces only enough for his or her own subsistence, no social division of owner and worker occurs. But once a surplus is available, the possibility of exploitation develops. Exploitation was blatantly clear in the slave plantations of the Roman Empire. On six days of the week the slave worked on the plantation and received nothing. Most often slaves had to produce their own food by working a tiny plot of land on Sundays. The great domains of the Middle Ages furnish another illustration. Serfs worked three days on land whose yield belonged to them; the other three days they worked on the lord's land without remuneration. The revenue of the capitalist class, according to Ernest Mandel, is simply a more subtle form of the same exploitation. It is the uncompensated labor the wage worker gives to the capitalist without receiving any value in exchange. Or, in Marx's own words: "Suppose the working day consists of 6 hours of necessary labor and 6 hours of surplus labor. Then the free laborer gives the capitalist every week 6 times 6 or 36 hours of surplus value. It is the same as *ultimate goal in business* if he worked 3 days in the week for himself and 3 days gratis for the capitalist."

It is not sufficient to respond that executives also work and merit their salary, or that costs of raw materials and maintenance must also be computed. Marx argues that profit is precisely the surplus over and above all costs and salaries. The Marxist recognizes the need for capital investment for expansion and new industry; his quarrel is with its private possession and control. If workers are the prime source of production, then they, and not private owners, should be the prime beneficiaries and should also have a significant voice in the whole process of production. The fact that labor unions have reduced the inequities between wages and profits does not alter the basic fact of exploitation for a Marxist. The capitalist still seeks to pay as little as possible for workers' services. The resulting profits or "surplus" are not the rewards of the capitalist's hard work or enterprising spirit, but due simply to ownership of property and control over the work of others.

The contemporary Marxist challenges the contention that wealth in the United States has really been the product of "free" enterprise. Can American busi-

[9]Ernest Mandel, *An Introduction to Marxist Economic Theory* (New York: Pathfinder Press, 1970), pp. 7-9.

[10]Marx, *Capital*, vol. I, p. 236.

Assembly line most efficient — everyone share work, if done differently Not all benefit. together

ness be said to have "earned" its total income in the past without reference to the takeover of native American territories, to slavery, or to the minimal wages paid immigrant workers? Or in the present, do even the relatively well-paid blue-collar workers receive a share proportionate to their work when executives of the same company earn ten times or more their salary. Inequality shows itself first in the difference between worker and executive salaries. Leo Huberman provided a graphic, if now dated, example:

> In 1946, the union of shipyard workers in the Bethlehem Steel Company fought for and won an increase of 15 percent which raised the minimum shipyard rate to $1.04 an hour. That's $41.60 a week or $2,163.20 a year. In 1946, the executives in Bethlehem were given a 46 percent salary boost. Mr. J. M. Larkin, vice-president of Bethlehem, who insisted that the incentive rates for workers had to be cut, was given a bonus of $38,764 to his salary of $138,416. That's $177,180 a year, $3,407.30 a week, $85.18 an hour.[11]

But top executives are not just salaried managers; they are often owners as well. Richard Barnet notes that chief executive officers in major corporations averaged about $380,000 in after-tax incomes in 1972. Fifty-three percent of that income came from stockholdings valued at more than $5 million each. The top five executives in each company drew 42 percent of their income from stockholdings.[12]

"Let your money work for you," the advertisement reads. That is precisely the problem, say radical critics of the free enterprise system. Great wealth, C. Wright Mills argued, has never resulted from work and salary alone. Great wealth derives from investment or ownership, not work. Mills illustrated this quite graphically in *The Power Elite*. If you had bought $9,900 worth of General Motors stock in 1913 and had gone into a coma for forty years, you would have awakened in 1953 worth $7 million.[13] A study of people who reported million-dollar incomes in 1961 showed that of their total income less than $30 million came from salaries or partnership profits. Nearly $700 million was derived from dividends and capital gains.[14] Graduated income taxes are supposedly designed to redistribute wealth. In fact they do not. The proportion of income held by the top 5 percent of the population drops less than 2 percent after taxes.[15]

Alienation of the Worker

poor working conditions

In his earliest writings, Marx used the term "alienation" to describe the effects the capitalist method of ownership and production had upon the working

Capitalism leads to imperialism   Britain has Colonies (empire) worldwide

[11]Leo Huberman and Paul M. Sweezy, *The Introduction to Socialism* (New York: Monthly Review, 1968), p. 47.

[12]Richard J. Barnet and Ronald E. Muller, *Global Reach: The Power of the Multinational Corporations* (New York: Simon & Schuster, 1974), p. 292, and note, p. 458.

[13]C. Wright Mills, *The Power Elite*, reprint (New York: Oxford University Press, 1969), p. 111.

[14]Ferdinand Lundberg, *The Rich and the Super-Rich* (New York: Bantam Books, 1968), pp. 43, 935–36.

[15]Richard C. Edwards, Michael Reich, and Thomas E. Weisskopf, eds., *The Capitalist System* (Englewood Cliffs, N.J.: Prentice-Hall, 1972), p. 210.

imiserates workers

class. Capitalism alienates the workers first of all because it takes from them the product and profit they produced. Their life energy is poured into their work, yet they have little to show for it. "The more the worker exerts himself, the more powerful the alien objective world he fashions against himself; the poorer he and his inner world become, the less there is that belongs to him."[16]

But Marx's concern was not just distribution of wealth and fair return for work done. He felt an almost greater concern for the way people work. Under capitalism, he charged, work is forced and dehumanizing. The work is forced because the average worker, though theoretically free to accept a job or not, has little choice but to take a job or go unemployed. Nor do workers have much freedom in the way they carry out the work. They do the work assigned, at the pace designated. The work is thus dehumanizing because it does nothing to develop the human potential of the workers (for example, to be inventive, to make decisions, to develop different skills). The worker is simply an appendage to a machine. He "does not affirm himself in his work but denies himself, feels miserable and unhappy, develops no free physical and mental energy but mortifies his flesh and ruins his mind."[17] The capitalist works him as he would "a horse that he has hired for a day."[18]

Many critics, Marxist and otherwise, believe that capitalism still sacrifices humanizing work to efficiency and profit maximization. Kenneth Keniston describes the impact of alienated work in terms that echo Marx's analysis a century before. In most traditional societies, he observes, one's work was one's life. Work, play, and social life flowed into each other. Work meant simply tasks to be done, without any division of life into work and nonwork. For most Americans, in contrast, work has unpleasant connotations. The reason for this lies in the characteristics of most jobs. With increasing specialization, each worker finds herself or himself assigned to a smaller and smaller portion of a task. The product is finished far down the line: out of sight and out of mind. There is little sense of satisfaction from work. Moreover, too few jobs challenge one's abilities, imagination, or spirit; most call simply for a capacity to follow exact routines in an orderly way. As a result, most Americans speak of "working for a living" and rarely of "living for their work." Many have stopped even expecting work to be meaningful.[19]

Harry Braverman's *Labor and Monopoly Capital* is an important Marxist study of "the degradation of work in the 20th century." He begins by noting rising discontent in the labor movement today stemming from job dissatisfaction. Expressive of this discontent was the Lordstown, Ohio, strike in 1972, directed against the increased pace of work demanded in a General Motors plant.[20] What

---

[16]Loyd D. Easton and Kurt H. Guddat, tr. and ed., *Writings of the Young Marx* (Garden City, N.Y.: Anchor, 1967), p. 289.

[17]Ibid., p. 292.

[18]Marx, *Capital*, vol. I, p. 185.

[19]Kenneth Keniston, "The Alienating Consequences of Capitalist Technology," in Edwards, Reich, and Weisskopf, *The Capitalist System*, pp. 269-73. See also Herbert Gintis's essay on alienation, ibid., which follows Keniston's.

[20]Harry Braverman, *Labor and Monopoly Capital, The Degradation of Work in the Twentieth Century* (New York: Monthly Review, 1974), pp. 31-39.

distinguishes *human* work from animal instincts, Braverman argues, is the power of conceptual thought. True human labor unites mental and material action. The degradation of labor in capitalist society results from their separation.

The "scientific management" which Frederick Taylor proposed in the late nineteenth century, and which greatly influenced the U.S. system of production, very deliberately divorced mental and material labor. Taylor wrote:

> The managers assume . . . the burden of gathering together all of the traditional knowledge which in the past has been possessed by the workmen and then of classifying, tabulating, and reducing this knowledge to rules, laws, and formula. . . . All possible brain work should be removed from the shop and centered in the planning or laying-out department.[21]

The introduction of assembly lines carried this concept of mechanized labor to its fullest expression. Henry Ford's decision in 1914 to raise workers' pay to $5 a day was hailed as an enlightened, progressive move to enable workers to become more affluent customers. This view overlooks the fact, says Braverman, that Ford faced an angry revolt by workers against his new assembly lines. The turnover rate in 1913 had forced the Ford Motor Company to hire 963 workers in order to sustain the 100 needed.[22]

If the separation of mental from manual work has been most obvious in factory work, it has increasingly influenced clerical work as well. The drive for speed and efficiency has reduced more and more work to simplified, routinized, and measured tasks.

If work has been dehumanized, unemployment proves far more degrading still. To speak of *only* 7 percent unemployment—a figure once thought intolerable—does little to describe the powerlessness, frustration, and alienation of millions of unemployed people. Welfare may permit an income on which to live, but it can only be dehumanizing. From a Marxist perspective, worker exploitation and alienation are among the most serious failures of the free enterprise system.

Imperialism: Exploitation of Other Countries.

In recent years, much of Marxist criticism of free enterprise has been directed against the influence of capitalism in poor countries. When Americans praise the achievements of free enterprise, they point to the overall affluence of the United States and the political democracy which accompanies it. But in Latin America and other parts of the third world, free enterprise means desperate poverty, oppressive right-wing military rule, and exploitation by foreign companies. Thus, in El Salvador free enterprise has for decades meant 2 percent of the population owning 60 percent of the land, and 8 percent taking half the entire income, with

[21]Cited in ibid., pp. 112–18.

[22]Ibid., p. 149.

Some exploited by leaders

German lost everything After WWII

the remaining 92 percent living in poverty and three-fourths of the children suffering from malnutrition. Yet efforts at reform and change have been crushed
by right-wing death squads.

Marxists argue that capitalist countries want to maintain the status quo in
countries of the third world in order to exploit them. Profit always has exploitation as its source, according to Marxist critics. Underdeveloped countries of the
world provide natural resources and cheap labor which make investment
tremendously profitable, if the political regimes remain favorable. Some Marxists
contend that without foreign markets, in which to sell goods and reinvest profits,
the capitalist system would face economic crisis. They quote Franklin D. Roosevelt, who acknowledged: "Foreign markets must be regained if America's producers are to rebuild a full and enduring domestic economy for our people. There
is no other way if we would avoid painful economic dislocations, social readjust-
ments, and unemployment."[23]

The very beginnings of capitalism in Europe, Paul Sweezy contends, were
made possible by the plunder and exploitation of foreign countries.[24] At first, European countries simply plundered the gold, silver, and minerals of countries in
the southern hemisphere. Then colonial rule put complete control of resources
in the hands of the colonizing countries. Specialized economies were developed
by foreign investors. Today we associate certain products with certain countries—coffee in Brazil, tin in Bolivia, copper in Chile, sugar in Cuba. But the development of such economies did not come from initiatives within those countries. Production of these raw materials was developed by European and U.S.
companies to meet needs in the "developed world." The concentration on one
or two products often upset a natural balance of production and created "one-
crop" economies very dependent on the fluctuating prices in the world market
for that one crop. Brazil's northeast was once that country's richest area; now
it is its poorest. Portugal granted lands to Brazil's first big landlords. Sugar production flourished for a time, but left washed-out soil and eroded lands.[25] Barbados,
in the West Indies, suffered the same fate. It once produced a variety of crops
and livestock on small holdings: cotton and tobacco, oranges, cows and pigs.
Canefields devoured all this; the soil was exhausted, unable to feed its population. The story is similar in Africa. Gambia once grew its own rice on land now
used to grow peanuts. Northern Ghana grew yams and other foodstuffs on land
now devoted to cocoa. Liberia was turned into a virtual rubber plantation. Seizures
of land, taxation, the undercutting of domestic prices, and forced migrations were
all employed by colonizers to gain control of the land.[26]

[23]Quoted in Carl Oglesby, *Containment and Change* (New York: Collier-Macmillan, 1967),
p. 67.

[24]Paul Sweezy, *Modern Capitalism and Other Essays* (New York: Monthly Review, 1972),
pp. 18ff.

[25]Eduardo Galeano, *Open Veins of Latin America, Five Centuries of the Pillage of a Continent*, tr. Cedric Belfrage (New York: Monthly Review, 1973), pp. 72-75.

[26]Frances Moore Lappé and Joseph Collins, *Food First, Beyond the Myth of Scarcity* (Boston:
Houghton Mifflin, 1977), pp. 78ff.

Thus the economies of most countries in the third world now depend on the one or two crops which foreign investors cultivated. Bananas accounted for 23 percent of Panama's export earning and 25 percent of Honduras's in the late 1970s. Coffee brought in 65 percent of Colombia's foreign exchange and 44 percent of Haiti's. Moreover, their export earnings on foodstuffs declined as the price of manufactured goods soared. In 1960, three tons of bananas could buy a tractor; in 1970, the same tractor cost the equivalent of eleven tons.[27]

What can be said of foreign enterprises, of the fruit companies, sugar companies, mining corporations, manufacturers, and banks that invest in the third world? Doesn't their presence ensure needed capital, technology, and know-how to help poor countries develop? Paul Sweezy noted that in the heyday of British imperialism (1870–1913) the flow of income *to* Britain exceeded the flow of capital *from* Britain by 70 percent. Foreign investments by U.S. corporations (1950–1963) showed an almost identical percentage of profit: net flow of capital *from* the United States, $17.4 billion; flow of income *to* the United States, $29.4 billion.[28] In a study some years ago John Gerassi noted that in Venezuela during the decade of the 1950s barely 10 percent of oil profits—$600 million of $5 billion—remained within the country.[29] If a box of bananas retails at $5.93 in the United States, producers in Honduras gross roughly 66 cents. Chain supermarkets in the United States gross $1.90 on the same box.[30]

"Let the market decide" and "consumer sovereignty" are bywords justifying the free enterprise system. But the consumer who decides is the consumer who has money, and profits are determined by this. The poor and hungry cannot buy food enough to match the profits that can be made on exports. Therefore Central America sends its vegetables to the United States, where 65 percent are dumped or used as animal feed because their quality is not good enough or markets are oversupplied. Mexico grows strawberries, cantaloupes, and asparagus for Del Monte and other U.S. corporations to sell in the United States. Colombian private owners grow flowers for export because one hectare of flowers brings nine times the profit that wheat or corn could.[31]

When poor nations attempt to change internally, the United States has often intervened—sending Marines into Guatemala in 1954, supporting the military overthrow of Goulart in Brazil in 1964, and using the CIA to subvert the Allende government in Chile in 1973. For Marxists, the reasons for such interventions are clear: protection of U.S. business investments. In Cuba, before Castro's revolution, U.S. companies controlled 80 percent of Cuba's utilities, 90 percent of its

[27]Ibid., p. 182. See also *Economic Survey of Latin America, 1977* (Santiago, Chile: United Nations, 1978), pp. 136, 278, 292, 373; and Harry Magdoff, *The Age of Imperialism: The Economics of U.S. Foreign Policy* (New York: Monthly Review, 1969), pp. 99–100.

[28]Sweezy, *Modern Capitalism*, pp. 22–23.

[29]John Gerassi, *The Great Fear in Latin America*, rev. ed. (New York: Collier-Macmillan, 1968), p. 370.

[30]Lappé and Collins, *Food First*, pp. 194–98.

[31]Ibid., pp. 255–56.

mines, and almost 100 percent of its oil refineries. U.S. firms received 40 percent of the profits on sugar, a crop that represented 89 percent of all Cuban exports.[32] Before the war in Vietnam, *U.S. News & World Report* ran an article entitled "Why U.S. Risks War for Indochina: It's the Key to Control of All Asia":

> One of the world's richest areas is open to the winner of Indo-China. That's behind the growing U.S. concern . . . tin, rubber, rice, key strategic raw materials are what the war is really about. The U.S. sees it as a place to hold—at any cost.[33]

Years later, presidential adviser Walt W. Rostow reaffirmed this same point: "The location, natural resources, and populations of the underdeveloped areas are such that, should they become effectively attached to the Communist bloc, the United States would become the second power in the world."[34]

Finally, if wars protect overseas markets, the massive defense industry is seen as essential to free enterprise. Defense contracts ensure new markets, new jobs, and new uses for capital. Without the artificial stimulus of defense spending, say Marxist critics, the United States would face crises of unemployment and severe recession.[35] Exploitation of other countries, war, and a giant defense industry—these alone, say Marxists, provide the outlets without which the free enterprise system would collapse.

At least Capitalist Domination of the State *give the Appearance of freedom*

Americans take pride in their democratic system: "Whatever its faults, it's the best in the world." Every citizen has a voice in the government. All can vote; all can aspire to political office. The two-party system offers alternatives in the choice of policies and candidates. The division of executive, legislature, and judiciary creates a balance of power. Opposition to Marxist communism most often expresses itself as a defense of democracy.

Marxists challenge this "pluralist" view of the state and its faith in U.S. democracy. Their quarrel is not with the principles and values of democracy as such, but with claims that they have been realized in the United States and in other capitalist nations. Marx had argued, in his early writings, that political freedoms created only an "illusion" of true human freedom. People's lives are determined far more by the conditions in which they live in society than by abstract political rights. Political power, moreover, reflects economic power. When John Locke, the seventeenth-century English philosopher, stated that the great and

---

[32]Felix Greene, *The Enemy: What Every American Should Know About Imperialism* (New York: Vintage, 1971), p. 139.

[33]Quoted in ibid., p. 108, from an article in *U.S. News & World Report*, April 4, 1954.

[34]Cited in Magdoff, *The Age of Imperialism*, p. 54.

[35]See Clemens Dutt, ed., *Fundamentals of Marxism-Leninism* (Moscow: Foreign Language Publishing House, 1961), p. 330.

chief end of persons uniting to form a government was "the preservation of property," he reflected all too clearly the goals of his social class. The democratic state in capitalist society claims to represent the common good of all its citizens, and indeed it must pass legislation needed to legitimize that claim. But it serves primarily to maintain the power and interests of the dominant class. Or, as Marx expressed it in *The Communist Manifesto*: "The executive of the modern State is but a committee for managing the common affairs of the whole bourgeoisie."[36] Marxists may be exaggerating and using heavy rhetoric when they speak of "capitalist domination of the state," but it is important to consider the arguments for the Marxist position.   *US. most are Lawyers then businessmen*

The first and most obvious evidence for the Marxist position is the disproportionate representation of the rich in high office. In theory anyone can be president of the United States. But in fact millionaires and multimillionaires, though they represent a miniscule fraction of the population, have been dominant over the last fifty years—Franklin D. Roosevelt, John F. Kennedy, Lyndon Johnson, Richard Nixon, Jimmy Carter, Ronald Reagan. Cabinet posts reflect the same "wealthy elite" representation. G. William Domhoff, in *Who Rules America?*, noted that five of eight secretaries of state and eight of thirteen secretaries of defense, over the thirty-six-year period he studied, were listed in the elite Social Register.[37]

Congress has a broader composition, but the power of wealth is quite evident there also. Congressperson Torbert H. MacDonald, a Democrat of Massachusetts, noted that: "In the nation's seven largest states in 1970, 11 of the major senatorial candidates were millionaires. The four who were not lost their bids for election."[38] A Ralph Nader study in 1975 revealed that twenty senators were millionaires; well over half of those who responded to Nader's inquiry had assets of $250,000 or more; only five had assets under $50,000. The "average" American that same year had assets of $4,000.[39] One would very likely look in vain for even one member of Congress representative of the average American. Legislators come from the ranks of business and the professions, law in particular. The main work force of the United States—factory workers, truckers, secretaries, etc.—goes virtually without any direct representation from its ranks.

But the presence of wealthy capitalists in high office is not the only argument used by Marxist critics. Michael Harrington, James O'Connor, and many neo-Marxists stress far more the "function" played by the state in behalf of free enterprise. If corporations complain of government regulations and taxes, these Marxist critics point to the many ways in which government subsidizes big business. James O'Connor, in *The Fiscal Crisis of the State*, argues that the state assists

---

[36]"The Communist Manifesto", in *The Marx-Engels Reader*, ed. Robert C. Tucker (New York: Norton, 1972), p. 337.

[37]G. Williams Domhoff, *Who Rules America?* (Englewood Cliffs, N.J.: Prentice-Hall, 1967), pp. 97-99, 105-7.

[38]Cited in *Detroit Free Press*, Parade sect., May 23, 1976, p. 4.

[39]Ibid. See also Richard Zweigenhaft, *"Who Represents America?"*, a study of the Ninety-second Congress, in *The Insurgent Sociologist*, vol. V, no. III (Spring 1975), pp. 119ff.

big business both by creating a climate for its accumulation of capital and by bearing much of the burden of social expenses (for example, education and health care) which would otherwise have to come from higher workers' wages. He illustrates government subsidy of private industry by reference to the automobile industry. Cars need roads, but private industry does not have to bear the cost of building them. The entire transportation budget from 1944 to 1961 was given to the construction of roads and highways. The federal government assumes 90 percent of the cost of interstate freeways and 50 percent of all other primary roads. Eighty percent of the funds earmarked for the redevelopment of Appalachia went into roads.[40]

The state subsidizes private industry, and hence private profits, in a variety of ways: through loans, as it did for Lockheed and Chrysler, through helping to finance land development and building, through tax exemptions for building depreciation and oil exploration, through funding research. By providing welfare it tempers the discontent created by unemployment. By assuming much of the cost of medical care it frees industry from paying higher salaries to cover these costs. It bears much of the expense for industrial pollution as well. The discontent of citizens demanding more benefits gets directed at the state, because it picks up expenses and responsibilities that private corporations escape.

Michael Harrington makes a similar case against "state management of the economy on behalf of the capitalists":

> Over the past three decades, the government has helped to build ten million units for the better-off and 650,000 units of low-cost housing for the poor. In 1969, the *Wall Street Journal* reported that there were $2.5 billion in subsidies, for the urban freeways, which facilitated the commuting of the privileged, and only $175 million for mass transit. All of this made good commercial sense even though it helped to perpetuate the social disaster of the disintegration of the central cities, the consequent isolation of the racial and ethnic minorities, the subversion of the passenger-rail system, and so forth.[41]

Government policies regarding farming reveal the same priorities. From 1940 to 1980 the number of farms in the United States decreased by 63 percent, and the size of the average farm increased by 156 percent. The "farmers" included ITT, Gulf + Western, Boeing, and other large corporations. But it was these giant agribusinesses which were the prime recipients of federal subsidy. In 1980, large farms with more than $40,000 a year in sales received $804 million of the federal government's $1,286 million subsidy payments. That same year, the poorest 33 percent of the farms received only 2 percent of subsidy payments.[42] Harrington,

[40]James O'Connor, *The Fiscal Crisis of the State* (New York: St. Martin's Press, 1973), pp. 105-6.

[41]Michael Harrington, *The Twilight of Capitalism* (New York: Simon & Schuster-Touchstone, 1976), p. 224.

[42]*Statistical Abstract of the United States,* 1981, pp. 660, 673. See also Douglas F. Dowd, *The Twisted Dream: Capitalist Development in the United States Since 1776* (Cambridge, Mass.: Winthrop, 1977), pp. 177-78.

again, directs his strongest criticism at government subsidy of oil companies which won multimillion-dollar subsidies and massive tax reductions by arguing that the defense and common good of the nation were at stake.

Charles Lindbloom, in *Politics and Markets,* presents a still different argument, focusing on the influence of big business on the state. Though a defender of a "market" economy and not a Marxist, Lindbloom believes that giant corporations are inconsistent with democracy. Business executives and not government officials, he argues, make most of the public policy decisions that affect the economic life of the nation. Their decisions, in turn, affect almost every aspect of life—jobs, homes, consumer goods, leisure. These executives determine income distribution, allocation of resources, plant locations, the pattern of work, the technologies to be used, what goods should be produced, the quality of goods and services, and of course executive compensation and status.[43] These major decisions are turned over to business leaders and taken off the agenda of government. Thus citizens have no vote at all on policies that affect every sphere of their welfare.

But these major decisions only begin to describe the public role of business leaders. Their influence on government is quite different than that of any other group in society. Public functions in the market system rest in their hands. For example, jobs, prices, production, growth, the standard of living, and the economic security of everyone is under their influence. Government officials cannot, consequently, be indifferent to how business performs its functions. Business leaders are not just representatives of one or more special interest groups; the whole welfare of society depends on what they do. They never get all they ask for or want, it is true. But whether they ask for subsidies for transportation and research, for aid in overseas promotion of business, for troops to protect investments in foreign countries, for tax reductions to stimulate investment, or for similar advantages, the state must respond.[44]

All citizen groups can compete in politics, but they depend on the use of their members' own incomes and energies. Business corporations can draw on extraordinary sources of corporate funds, organizations and personnel, and on special access to government. Business has myriad avenues by which to do its own "consciousness forming or raising." Through lobbying, through entertainment, through litigations, business uses its resources to confirm its position and gain approval. Roughly $60 billion per year is spent on advertising and other sales promotion. A large part of this is institutional advertising with a political content, such as Exxon's "Energy for a strong America." This matches all the funds spent on education or health in the country.[45] Few radical or dissenting journals

---

[43]Charles Lindbloom, *Politics and Markets: The World's Political-Economic Systems* (New York: Basic Books, 1977), p. 171.

[44]Ibid., pp. 172ff.

[45]Ibid., pp. 195, 214.

even exist to compete with dominant business views. The large, private corporation, Lindbloom concludes, does not fit into democratic theory and vision.

Social Consequences of Capitalism

To these major themes might be added a host of other issues, problems the Marxist considers directly related to the capitalist economic system. The inequality of women and their subservient role in society are for Marx consequences of private property and the division of labor. He viewed the family itself, with the husband dominating his wife and children, as the first form of property and as a "latent slavery."[46] Engels argued:

> . . . to emancipate woman and make her the equal of man is and remains an impossibility so long as woman is shut out from social productive labor and restricted to private domestic labor. The emancipation of woman will only be possible when woman can take part in production on a large, social scale, and domestic work no longer claims anything but an insignificant amount of her time.[47]

Lenin writes in a similar vein that "women are still in an actual position of inferiority because all housework is thrust upon them."[48] Needless to say, what the founders of Marxism had to say about the "woman question" has now become an open, sensitive, and pressing issue in the United States.

Social problems abound in the United States that are the direct consequence of subordinating social concerns to profit making. These problems are all too familiar, according to critic Felix Greene.[49] Capitalism has ravished the continent. The United States has killed off 85 percent of its wildlife and 80 percent of its forests; millions of acres of farmland have been misused and lost. Pollution is rampant. New York City dumps 200 million gallons of raw sewage into the Hudson River each day. Medical care for all citizens has been neglected. Three million children have untreated speech disorders. Crime and violence have come to be an almost accepted part of urban life. Armed robbery in Washington, D.C., runs 1,760 percent higher than in London; the number of homicides per year in Detroit is several times higher than for all of England. Drugs, inadequate housing, racial prejudice—the list goes on and on.

The charge that these problems are consequences of the free enterprise system is perhaps too facile an explanation. But the "face" of America is marred by serious social problems that make the charge difficult to dismiss. The United States prides itself as enjoying the highest standard of living in the world. The

[46]"The German Ideology," in Tucker, *Marx-Engels Reader*, p. 123.

[47]*The Woman Question: Selections from Marx, Engels, Lenin, Stalin* (New York: International Publishers, 1970), pp. 10–11.

[48]Ibid., p. 52.

[49]Greene, *The Enemy*, pp. 3–43.

average American enjoys far more material benefits than any people in history. But the Marxist critic questions even this achievement. How much of what we consume corresponds to *real* needs? Herbert Marcuse charges our consumer-propelled economy with the creation of mostly false "needs."[50] Advertisements keep us in a state of perpetual dissatisfaction with what we do have. Automobiles could be made to last for years, but that would reduce production and profit. So new "styles" become the selling point. Advertising seeks to convince us of our "need" for ever-drier deodorants, electric toothbrushes and combs, and automatic garbage compactors. We can no longer even be sure of what kind of vacation we would naturally like because advertisements have programmed us into what we *should* like.

invented by Advertisers Designer Jeans

60 billion/yr = to Amount spent on health care & education funding

The charges made by Marxists against our economic and political system are many. The wealth produced by industry profits owners and executives far more than workers. Financial investment multiplies the disproportionate distribution of wealth. Factory work stunts the capacities of workers engaged in it. Initiative, self-determination, and a voice in decision making are more possible in sales and management, but not in the labor force. Competitive self-interest characterizes work at every level. Poverty and unemployment become stigmatized as one's own fault. A wealthy, powerful elite controls the highest public offices. Laws favor the wealthy and protect their incomes by tax loopholes. Women are made subservient. Pollution, crime, drugs, racial discrimination, and false needs are by-products of an economic drive that considers only more and more goods and profits. The system stands condemned.

But has any system done a better job? Would communism provide a better way of life? The instinctive response of most Americans is probably "no." The Communist nations of the world have hardly achieved any utopia. Their economies still lag far behind our own. Their political regimes appear intolerably regimented and coercive. Anyone watching the persecution of Jews in the USSR or Soviet treatment of dissidents will hardly desire to live under a Soviet political system. The inefficiency and bureaucracy of the Soviet economy and the still-undeveloped state of the Chinese economy make them inadequate models for change in the economic system of the United States. Even severe struggles with inflation and unemployment are not likely to make most Americans eager to risk overthrowing their present political and economic system for socialism. But not being willing to trade places with Russians or Chinese should not be equated with not being willing to learn from them. For they have constructed economic systems that give priority to eliminating some of the social problems which beset our own.

Watching the achievements and failures of Marxist socioeconomic systems can tell us much about the aspirations and efforts of the peoples of the world. Observing people in Marxist societies tells us about both the perceptions of those people as to what system is most appropriate for them and the reality of how a collective socioeconomic system is able to work. Giving priority to eliminating

---

[50]Herbert Marcuse, *One Dimensional Man: Studies in the Ideology of Advanced Industrial Society* (Boston: Beacon Press, 1964), chap. 9, pp. 225-46.

poverty and increasing employment is a quite different goal for an economic system. Although it has its tradeoff costs, such goals certainly appeal to most people.

Highway System benefits wealthy —only consumers impt. to our type of society

Cooperative vs. Competitive Market System

Designing economic programs to deal with the problems of an unjust distribution of wealth and income is generally considered to be at the cost of efficiency and productivity. Government programs require planning and administrators. They are expensive and do not always achieve their intended goal. Moreover, such programs can have a negative effect on the incentive to work for both low- and high-income people.

On the other hand, critics accuse capitalism of not only objective exploitation and alienation of the worker but also of encouraging competitiveness and selfishness. While even the USSR and China now acknowledge the value of competition among production units, self-seeking and excessive competition among individuals can severely hinder the long-term efficiency of a firm and a society.

Two ideals of a democratic society, justice (or equality) and efficiency, are thus often placed in opposition to one another. That is, in the minds of most people to achieve more fully one means to sacrifice some of the other.[51] The ideals of *justice* are basic to any society, especially to a free, democratic one: [All men and women have a right to the basics of food and education; all men and women have equal opportunity to work and be treated fairly at work; all people are to be treated equally before the law; and there is no great disparity among families in income and wealth.]

The ideal of *efficiency* is a pragmatic goal of the United States. It includes the following convictions:[A more efficient and productive society yields more jobs and income for all; all individuals should work hard according to their abilities; rewards should be proportionate to an individual's work and merits; and people, material, and capital should be able to move freely.]

These two goals are basic for Americans. As a society we pride ourselves on being both a just and an efficient society. Although it is true that we have failed in one or the other from time to time, it is also true that both remain explicit and real goals for Americans. To move totally toward the achievement of one may be at the expense of the other. Yet we also know that it is unwise to undermine seriously either justice or efficiency. Both are essential to American society.

During the period from the 1960s through 1981, American society moved steadily toward more justice and equality. The civil rights movement, the women's movement, and affirmative action plans and their successes attest to that. It is often said that this has been at the cost of efficiency. Often corporate managers complain of a growing sense of "entitlement" among workers ("a job and a pro-

[51]See Arthur Okun, *Equality and Efficiency: The Big Tradeoff* (Washington, D.C.: Brookings Institution, 1975).

motion is owed to me"). Perhaps this is true to some extent, yet the evidence is mounting that lessened American productivity has much deeper roots than worker laziness and excessive government regulation. Although managers with a narrower viewpoint sometimes exclusively blame these two causes, they less often recognize that a more basic cause of the lack of productivity gains are their own attitudes, policies, and practices. In the current lessened American productivity we are witnessing the unhappy outcome of the drive for immediate, short-term, bottom-line results; this, in turn, often stems from executives who are more concerned about their own successful careers than about the long-term success of their firms.[52]

Currently, unemployment is high and productivity is not rising rapidly in the United States. We define productivity as output per person-hour. That is, productivity increases as the amount of labor to produce a good or service decreases. Interestingly, we do not define productivity as a function of capital or even energy used. Yet capital and energy are scarce and becoming more valuable. Perhaps we need new terminology (maybe capital productivity, energy productivity) to describe moving toward fuller employment and using less energy to produce the same goods. *Idedcgies / nerms / goals / values*

The notion that any modern economy can be "unregulated" is mistaken. Every economy operates according to a predetermined set of priorities and resulting rules.[53] The only relevant question is: On what priorities are the rules devised? For example, every society assesses taxes and provides subsidies in order to be of the greatest benefit to the people as a whole. That is, legislation, taxes, and other government activities *should be* are directed to the common good. *compromise*

Most government actions directed to the common good require that some individuals or groups must sacrifice some immediate benefits. For example, taxing people to pay for fire protection and parks is a cost to some who may never use the fire department or the park. Thus this demands a political decision that fire protection and parks are an important good for which all people should pay, whether or not they directly benefit from these services.

Such political decisions in a democracy require an objective, even-handed approach to looking at the common good. Legislative decisions are made that will infringe upon, and hence will not be popular with, certain segments of the population. These groups may be quite powerful, either because of their money, their influence, or both. Such legislative decisions are thus becoming harder to make, because of political action committees that contribute to a candidate's campaign, special interest groups, and other lobbyists. It is now more difficult for a congressperson to support legislation that would be for the long-term benefit of most people if it is a short-term cost for a powerful segment. For example, Congress has been unable to enact an energy plan that would effectively lower the amount of petroleum we use and hence must import. All acknowledge that the

---

[52]See, for example, Robert Hayes and William Abernathy, "Managing Our Way to Economic Decline," *Harvard Business Review* (July–August 1980), pp. 67–77.

[53]Lester C. Thurow, *The Zero-Sum Society* (New York: Basic Books, 1980), p. 128.

$50 billion or so that we spend annually for imported petroleum is a principal cause of inflation, but Congress does not have the courage to tax or otherwise provide incentives so that we would use less.

Enlightened self-interest can lead the enterprising entrepreneur to provide the products and services that people want, and to do so efficiently. Enlightened self-interest also tells the individual that during times of inflation, it is foolish to save. Yet continually pouring more money into the purchase of goods increases their cost and hence fuels inflation. Suffice it to say that enlightened self-interest must often be guided so that the common good is achieved—all the more so in contemporary society when so many of my actions infringe on others (for example, pollution, noise, and use of scarce resources).

It is charged that enlightened self-interest encourages individuals to become more selfish. An infant is born self-oriented, but as it grows it gradually comes to recognize the role and importance of other people. This realization comes gradually with maturity. Excessive stress on self-interest in adult life can stunt a person at an adolescent level of growth: a focus on me and mine. (These issues are discussed more fully in Chapters 4 and 6.)

This case for private ownership of large firms is justified primarily in the name of efficiency. The large disparities in income and wealth that we witness in the United States also are defended on the basis of efficiency: Money motivates people to work and to work harder. It surely has been our experience that the private sector *is* generally more efficient than the public sector. That large disparities in income and wealth also bring about greater efficiency is more difficult to establish. Moreover, it is here that we find one of the most clear-cut conflicts in basic American values: justice versus efficiency.

SUMMARY AND CONCLUSIONS

Karl Marx perceptively pinpointed the weaknesses of the capitalistic economic system. He and his followers have shown that capitalism possesses a series of undesirable characteristics. According to Marx, capitalism results in

1. Exploitation of the worker
2. Alienation of the worker
3. Imperialism: exploitation of other countries
4. Capitalist domination of the state

Although Marxists are at their best in criticizing capitalism, they also propose an alternate method for organizing a society. That system has been developed and tried in such countries as the USSR, the People's Republic of China, and Cuba.

An evaluation of communism for many Americans goes no further than concluding that "We have more and better consumer goods available, and more money with which to buy them. Moreover, we are free; they are not." True, but the Communist nations also possess much that we lack: greater cooperativeness, less unemployment, less disparity of wealth, greater equality of all—including women and the disadvantaged—and less crime, drugs, and violence.

Each system has its strengths and weaknesses. A bureaucratic, totalitarian system is hardly desirable to most Marxists. Unemployment, poverty, and crime are certainly not advocated by the defenders of free enterprise. But the comparison does raise the question of priorities and how they are formulated. Who decides what specific values and goals of a society are to be given priority? In the Communist nations, the party and the government set priorities, both economic and political. The system is devised precisely to encourage cooperation, to provide greater participation, and to eliminate unemployment. Through meeting these goals, the system also thus encourages production and economic growth. With free enterprise, conscious priorities are set only in the political sphere. Government can regulate and sometimes subsidize, but it generally does not set specific economic goals. Free enterprise advocates firmly defend this nonintervention as more efficient and effective. When it comes to priorities, in theory free enterprise recognizes only one: "Will it return a profit?" The system does not ask how important is the need the product fulfills; it has no method of rating products or services on any human scale of values.

Perhaps profits should be the sole concern of the corporation. But then who, if anyone, does set national economic priorities in the United States and sees that they are implemented? Do individual consumers have the vision to look to the long-term economic and social good of the majority of the people? Who decided that automobile travel was better than urban rapid transit systems? Who decided that cat food and cosmetics would have priority over food for the hungry of the world? As we will see in Chapter 5, it is not clear where this responsibility lies. Those advocating greater corporate responsibility have focused attention on the moral and social consequences of some business policies—energy and other resource use, toxic substances, product safety, plant closings. But the issue of national priorities goes beyond these.

Both efficiency and justice are important goals for Americans. Competition encourages flexibility and efficiency. A concern for others and cooperation undergird justice. However, paradoxically much of the current declining efficiency in the United States is attributed to a self-centered competition. In short, a value that we purposefully cultivated in the name of efficiency and success now results in making us less efficient and successful. Moreover, in the process we can become blind to the values of cooperation and justice. Perhaps at least this much can be learned from the Marxist critique of free enterprise and the goals Communist nations set for themselves: they can stimulate us to examine our own personal and national priorities. They can help us to see the limits and the inadequacies of our own ideology, so that we may improve. The remaining chapters of this book examine these contemporary issues.

DISCUSSION QUESTIONS

1. Describe the (a) origins and (b) characteristics of early American communal societies.
2. How do you respond to each of the seven questions posed at the beginning of the chapter?
3. What elements in a communal society allow it to last a generation or more?
4. What evidence does Karl Marx provide that capitalism exploits the worker? Is the argument valid? Does income tax rectify the inequity?
5. What evidence does Marx use to sustain his charge that capitalism alienates the worker? Evaluate this position for the United States in the 1980s.
6. Does capitalism bring about exploitation of other countries? Why or why not?   *imperialism*
7. What does Marx mean by "capitalist domination of the state"? Is this a valid charge?
8. To what extent do the four major problems of capitalism, as cited by Marx, stem primarily from capitalism or industrialization?
9. Americans think of Marxism as materialistic. Is it more materialistic than capitalism or free enterprise? In what ways do the goals that Marxism holds out for the average worker transcend or go beyond materialism?
10. Outline the comparative advantages of cooperative and competitive socio-economic systems. Does the current American interest in worker participation run contrary to competitive free enterprise?

CHAPTER FOUR
PERSONAL VALUES
IN THE ORGANIZATION

Man is by instinct a lover, a hunter, a fighter, and none of those instincts are given much play at the warehouse!

—Tennessee Williams, The Glass Menagerie*

collection of wild animals on display

oRgANIZational life great influence

The organizations and groups of which we are a part—from family to corporation—have a profound <u>influence</u> on our personal values and goals, although we are seldom explicitly aware of it. Personal values, a basic component of personality, are often accepted uncritically from parents, peers, teachers, television, and the film. During the working years, we often so identify with an organization that success within it becomes a measure of personal worth. Moreover, realization of the inadequacy of that measure often does not come until midlife, and brings with it profound anxieties, frustrations, and even serious physical ailments. *university & money makers*

Additional occasion for conflict stems from the fact that Americans in general, and especially business managers, show little social concern. As we will see later in this chapter, these managers show less concern about social conditions and less willingness to set aside personal gain for the sake of less fortunate people. These attitudes are in sharp contrast to the self-image most Americans have of themselves as generous, both personally and as a nation. Although we see ourselves as open-minded, empirical tests show that concern about others is not a primary value for us.

---

*Tennessee Williams, *The Glass Menagerie,* ed. Gilbert L. Rathbun of Random House. Quoted with permission.

[A major hypothesis of this book, and especially of this chapter, is that when such values are held uncritically and are not explicit, they contain the seeds of potential conflict and anxiety. Moreover, those in responsible positions who make decisions based on these uncritically held values are in danger of causing severe social disruption. We need look no further than the Nixon presidency and ITT for examples of what can happen to individuals and nations. There is here a paradox for organizational managers, since they conceive themselves as being objective, rational, and not led by personal whim. They are generally unaware of how strongly their unexamined personal values bias their decisions. Even more than most organizations, the business firm has carefully designed processes and structures for making decisions. A good manager insists on careful analysis of all the facts of a case before coming to a judgment. Market surveys, outside consultants, product planning groups, and computer analyses are indications of the high priority rational decision making has within the firm.

At the same time that the decision-making process is a source of pride to a manager, that manager is often unaware that the process itself rests on rarely examined assumptions. For beneath this structure lie certain presuppositions about the purpose of the corporation: to maximize profits, to expand market share, to enable the firm to survive and grow. These very ideological assumptions upon which the rational decision making is based are often accepted unquestioningly, much as we accept traditional cultural mores. *Red cross - charity*

Organizations develop a life and norms of their own. An organization's own struggle for survival and growth can give a superficial legitimacy to many activities that would not be undertaken under more careful and conscientious scrutiny. The needs of the organization then often conflict with the individual's personal values of honesty, integrity, and concern for others. This conflict may then trigger an individual's reflection on the consistency or inconsistency of these personal and organizational values. From an institutional point of view, the inadequacy of traditional business values and ideology often does not appear until the goals of the firm come into contact with the goals of the larger society. These latter issues will be discussed in greater detail in Chapter 6.

This chapter will examine the person and her or his values in the workplace. We will look at such issues as *Money markets*

institutional values help secure goals. Formative influence

1. The influence of organizational climates and expectations on the attitudes and values of the individual
2. Goals and motives of individuals, and how motives support and are affected by personal values
3. Sources of satisfaction and sense of accomplishment, as well as of stress, anxiety, and frustration, within the organization and how these contribute to personal health or illness
4. Methods for examining and making explicit and operative personal goals and values.

New members don't have much influence. Can't really

Each of these issues will be investigated with the aid of current research from the organizational and behavioral sciences. *Affect/change unless they compromise personal values to be 'congruent'.*

THE ORGANIZATION'S FORMATIVE INFLUENCE: SOCIALIZATION

Supphs Profits count.

A large organization exerts a powerful effect on its members and their values by means of the socialization process. Superiors' expectations, unwritten norms, and the career ladder have a profound influence on participants. Many of these values are introduced early in orientation and training programs, but they are amplified and solidified by exposure forty hours a week to the expectations of superiors and peers. When coupled with the perceived importance of success within the organization, this leads to unconscious changes in or solidification of values.

The organization has its own demands: Organizational norms, activities, and standards are directed to maintain the health of the organization. Health in turn translates into growth, which is measured by profitability, market share, or return on investment. Maturity and stability of the organization are not acceptable goals for the long term; chief executive officers have been fired for following such goals. Moreover, organizations have become all-embracing and affect almost every segment of our lives. Hence, as management researchers William Scott and David Hart put it, "because modern organizations have created and have largely defined the American value system, they must be considered the most important socializing agencies in America."[1] In such an environment, individual managers have little influence on the values and norms of the organization, unless they happen to be the chief executive officer. Because the organization has its own dynamism and is unquestioningly dedicated to efficiency and technological innovation, it has effective control over the lives of its members. Behavioral control is already being practiced in many segments of our lives, both knowingly (for example, drugs of various kinds) and unknowingly (subtle advertising appeals) by various "elites." Summing up their indictment, Scott and Hart say, "Thus, the modern organization is the essential feature of totalitarianism because it is the primary means of control."[2]

A bureaucratic form of organization is characterized by high productive efficiency but low innovative capacity. When tasks are predictable and can therefore be repeated and codified, they can be done quickly and efficiently. Nevertheless, that very stabilization of tasks and roles can bring rigidity. It is difficult for the organization designed for efficiency to remain open and innovative; its very success tends to solidify and reinforce past ways of doing things.

Organizations generally reappraise their goals and values only in the face of new demands from the outside. Without such challenges, they tend to con-

---

[1]William G. Scott and David K. Hart, *Organizational America* (Boston: Houghton Mifflin, 1979), p. 36. On socialization, see also Daniel C. Feldman, "The Multiple Socialization of Organization Members," *Academy of Management Review*, 6, no. 2 (April 1981), 309-18.

[2]Scott and Hart, *Organizational America*, p. 211. See also Richard D. Arvey and John M. Ivancevich, "Punishment in Organizations: A Review, Propositions and Research Suggestions," *Academy of Management Review*, 5, no. 1 (January 1980), 123-32.

tinue to operate in those ways that have proved effective in the past and become more rigid and less open as the years go by. At the same time, the organization is quite effective in selecting individuals and socializing them into persons who "fit well" into the system. The organization has a subtle but potent influence on its members' attitudes and values, as the sociologist Robert Merton puts it:

> The bureaucrat's official life is planned for him in terms of a graded career through the organizational devices of promotions by seniority, pensions, incremental salaries, etc., all of which are designed to provide incentives for disciplined action and conformity to artificial regulations. The official is tacitly expected to and largely does adapt his thoughts, feelings, and actions to the prospect of his career. But *these very devices* which increase the probability of conformance also lead to an overconcern with strict adherence to regulations which induce timidity, conservatism, and technicism. Displacement of sentiments from goals onto means is fostered by the tremendous symbolic significance of the means (rules).[3]

The organization develops a life of its own, protecting its own special interests, being jealous of its own position, power, and prerogatives. The corporation's way of doing things, especially when it has been successful in the past, can become rigid and ossified. The individual is expected to "learn IBM's way of doing things." Empirical studies show that managers tend to select for promotion subordinates who have values like their own.[4] Although we would expect these managers to make decisions that are objective and rational, there is evidence that personal likes and values play an important role.

When thousands of employees are organized to perform a certain productive task, it requires coordination among people and units of the organization. As these various relations and responsibilities are spelled out, either in writing or implicitly, there is correspondingly less discretion left to the individual. Even in decentralized companies, standard practices and procedures constrain new ideas and initiatives. Moreover, accepted goals and values become internalized by the individual employees. Deviant values are eliminated, either initially in the selection process or through socialization. It quickly becomes clear which values are accepted and which are not.

In the large organization, the competitive, achievement-oriented manager wants to be noticed quickly as a success. He or she therefore tends to focus on short-run efficiency and performance, as these can be more readily measured and will make good material for a report to top management. Hence corporate economic values become all-embracing and permeate personal and social values as well.

---

[3]Robert K. Merton, "Bureaucratic Structure and Personality," in *Organizations: Structure and Behavior*, 3rd ed., ed. Joseph A. Litterer (New York: Wiley, 1980), pp. 232–33.

[4]John Senger, "Managers' Perceptions of Subordinates' Competence as a Function of Personal Value Orientations," *Academy of Management Journal*, 14, no. 4 (December 1971), 415–23.

Money and Market as Goals

Corporate and material values influence much of Americans' lives. To foreign observers, it sometimes appears as if all Americans do is directed toward providing and acquiring material goods. The centrality of corporate life, advertising, and individualized suburban homes are but a few manifestations of the phenomenon. It is as if Americans really believed that "happiness is a new car or a new home." Economic goals and the corporation can have a profound influence on our political values as well. The loud and clear voice of industry, through the business round table, trade associations, and the individual firm, often has a decisive influence on both domestic and foreign policy. Economic values dominate when we threaten war if our oil supplies are cut off, and in many other of our international embroilments.

Karl Marx was the first to charge that an industrial society separates people from their work and alienates them. We examined Marx's critique in the last chapter. Here, we will see that work is not, as it happens, an attractive and rewarding activity for many Americans. Inquiries among assembly-line workers show that they generally find their work monotonous, impersonal, uncreative, unchallenging. An extensive study of assembly-line workers as early as the 1950s showed that nine out of ten of these individuals intensely disliked their immediate jobs.[5] The current high turnover, absenteeism, and tardiness in industry are attributed mainly to the fact that the work is so unattractive. Not only is there no incentive in the work, there is a positive aversion to it. On the assembly line a person is used like a single-purpose tool. The individual's actions are repetitive and paced from outside and thus demand little intelligence or imagination; the person is used as an addition to the machine. All this creates a distance between the workers and their work. They have little control, and the workplace is impersonal. Work values are material and not human: productivity and efficiency, even at the expense of pride, responsibility, and joy in one's work. Recent quality of work-life programs call for job redesign, job enrichment, and greater involvement (for example, quality control circles). These programs are getting considerable attention now in the United States, primarily because the lack of job satisfaction is reflected in lower productivity and poor quality. Such programs had been proposed for many years and a few experiments were undertaken, but the programs were not taken seriously until the bottom line dictated their importance.

The executive, too, is held to this same impersonal emphasis on productivity. Ironically, the goals and values communicated to the corporate executive by the corporation, and then to others, are not unlike those given the assembly-line worker. The manager's goals are productivity, return on investment, and a

[5]Charles R. Walker, "Human Relations on the Assembly Line," *Proceedings of Ninth Annual Industrial Engineering Institute*, University of California (February 1957), p. 50. See also the more complete study by Charles R. Walker and Robert H. Guest, *The Man on the Assembly Line* (Cambridge, Mass.: Harvard University Press, 1952). These same findings are supported and updated in Theodore V. Purcell and Gerald F. Cavanagh, *Blacks in the Industrial World: Issues for the Manager* (New York: Free Press, 1972), pp. 72-85.

larger share of the market. Managers have no choice in this, if they and their firm are to survive. The individuals who are attracted to and make it to the corporate executive suite have a high need for success. They must be able to make decisions unencumbered by emotional ties to persons or groups. They must always be ready to move to a new location and leave old friends and associations behind. They must have sufficient detachment from their friends and neighborhoods. In fact, for many, there is little point in making deep friendships or getting involved in local activities; it would only make the parting more difficult. In his study of the executive personality, William Henry concludes:

> The corporate executive is a special type, spawned on impersonality and hurried into the task of defending his individuality in the diffuse and open competition of nonfamily life. His energy to prove his competence again and again is extreme, and his need to re-create a safe and personalized nest is minimal. . . . Undeterred by other than the purely conventional in personal life, he is able without sense of loss to devote his entire life to the executive task.[6]

Those attracted to corporate executive work are people who do not depend on close personal relationships. They obtain their major satisfaction from completing a task. Their personal values set the tone of the organization; these values are communicated and transferred to others in the firm. It becomes clear that the successful ones are more task- than person-oriented.

Gamesman as a Winner

Having tested and interviewed some 250 managers in twelve large, high-technology companies, Michael Maccoby concluded that such people were not primarily interested in skills, power, or loyalty but rather in "organizing winning teams."[7] Hence, he characterized the contemporary successful manager as the "gamesman." The gamesman, Maccoby concluded, has developed many positive intellectual characteristics to aid in "winning the game" (for example, analysis, problem solving, and policy development), but at the same time has allowed his or her emotional life to atrophy. The gamesman is more detached and emotionally inaccessible than previous types in the corporate hierarchy.

Gamesmen do "not have a developed heart." They lack compassion and appreciation for suffering. In fact, Maccoby calls them "weak-hearted"; they cannot bear to look at suffering. In his terms a "strong-hearted" manager is able to empathize and to understand the suffering that may come from a particular business decision. The gamesman cannot understand or empathize; ironically, it is the strong-hearted that makes the best executive in Maccoby's judgment. Yet the more

[6]William E. Henry, "Executive Personality and Large-Scale Organizations," in *The Emergent American Society*, vol. 1, by W. Lloyd Warner, Dareb Unwalla, and James Trim (New Haven, Conn.: Yale University Press, 1967), p. 275.

[7]Michael Maccoby, *The Gamesman: The New Corporate Leaders* (New York: Simon & Schuster, 1976), p. 34.

[handwritten annotations at top: Jungle fighter / trouble shooter — Rile up company / Predatory view of Co. life cause conflict to solve conflict. great when needing cleaning up. Not good at top level executive mgt. Makes too many enemies]

prevalent type among younger managers is the weak-hearted gamesman.

Gamesmen also have a shallow notion of social responsibility. They are unaware of and hence unconcerned about the social and human effects their actions have on others. Theirs is the primitive notion that the growth of their organization will automatically benefit poor people. They refuse to consider any undesirable secondary effects. Although most of the gamesmen indicated that they wanted friendship and help from their friends, fewer than 10 percent said that helping others was a personal goal. This contrasts with more than half of a group of factory workers who mentioned helping others as a personal goal. Maccoby found managers in Mexico to be "more aware than Americans that their careers protect them from the poor, but even the Mexican executives are not aware that within their enclaves they are becoming more alienated from themselves." Around their houses they have built walls, and on the top of those walls they put broken glass or spikes.

Gamesmen set out to be "winners". Their alert, aggressive behavior does make them successful in focused tasks at work. However, the tradeoff is much of their affective life. The fatal danger of gamesmen is to be trapped in perpetual adolescence: striving to be a winner at the game during their adult life.[8]

Today many talented people do not find the corporation an attractive place to work. From their own experiences and those of relatives and neighbors, they see the problems as outlined above. Moreover, for more than fifteen years corporations and corporate leaders have not had the confidence of the American people. (This erosion of trust in American institutions and its significance will be examined in greater detail in Chapter 6.) Much of this erosion stems from the goals and the values of the business firm. It is a material goal of producing goods and services, most of which are valuable to society, but many of which are trivial and some harmful. Nevertheless, this is the organization's goal, and it has a powerful influence on the individual manager and often becomes his or her goal as well. Appropriating the goal to one's self increases loyalty and decreases dissonance and frustration.

[handwritten margin note: discord, frustrated noise]

The corporation requires few of the many and varied talents of its employees. Although executives have wider scope for their abilities, they are still constrained by accepted procedures and values. Their own values must be subordinated to those of the organization, which may be narrow, shortsighted, and even potentially self-defeating. Some have even closed their eyes to, or have actually themselves participated in, poor workmanship, bribery, incomplete and dishonest testing of products, lack of sensitivity to valid customer complaints, and more.[9] In this sort of environment, it takes a strong character to "blow the whistle." Few

[8]Ibid., pp. 109, 203. Samuel Culbert and John McDonough, in *The Invisible War: Pursuing Self-Interest at Work* (New York: Wiley, 1980), suggest that self-interest is the determining goal for all individuals in organizations. We should thus be willing to expose our goals *in a limited way*, while being alert to the values, goals, and self-interests of others in the organization.

[9]See the half-dozen cases of flagrant corporate evil-doing in Robert Heilbroner and others, *In the Name of Profits* (Garden City, N.Y.: Doubleday, 1972).

of us want to be heroes or martyrs; we are co-opted by the values of the organization that provides our livelihood.

The corporation provides a pragmatic, task-oriented climate. It supports similar values in the manager: winning personally and assembling a winning team. The worst fear of the manager is to be labeled a "loser." This highly competitive environment encourages aggressiveness, flexibility, and intelligence and discourages cooperation and concern for people. Is there thus a built-in conflict between the climate and goals of the organization and the needs of mature men and women?

Personal Growth
Within the Organization

Organizational psychologists have spent considerable effort in attempting to unravel the many threads of influence binding the organizational participant and her or his organization. Among the basic questions they ask is this: Is the corporation able effectively to pursue its corporate objectives and at the same time encourage the development of its members as persons? Social scientists demonstrate that an individual can grow toward full maturity and self-actualization only in an interpersonal atmosphere of complete trust and open communication.[10] These open, trusting interpersonal relationships are essential to that growth. Work relationships can seldom reach such openness and trust. Nevertheless, if the working climate inhibits personal growth, it will result in frustration and, eventually, a poor working environment. Managers are therefore concerned about the quality of these relationships within the organization.

Although not explicitly focusing on values and goals, psychologists and many corporation executives have become vitally interested in supporting the personal growth and maturity of their employees. Executives are especially concerned if it can be established that this will benefit the corporation in the long run, or at least not detract from the basic goal of producing a good product at a profit. Can the sort of supportive relationships that are necessary for personal growth be achieved in an organization that is primarily concerned with production and efficiency? Or is the corporation to be an organization set apart, where the necessary trust, openness, communication, cooperation, and strong interpersonal relationships must simply be set aside in the interests of the primary goals of the firm? Do the essential dedication to the task, production orientation, short time span, and hardheadedness of the industrial corporation necessarily rule out the conscious pursuit of more subtle human values?

The case for shared decisions and encouraging individual initiative and creativity has been building for a generation. The concern that many firms have for these issues is often indicated by the size of the staff and the budget devoted

[10]Herbert A. Shepard, "Changing Interpersonal and Intergroup Relationships in Organizations," in *Handbook of Organizations,* ed. James G. March (Chicago: Rand-McNally, 1965), p. 1125.

to them. Although encouraging shared decisions and individual growth within a firm goes under a variety of names, from personnel research to organizational development, it is significant that a corporation as productivity-oriented as General Motors has more than two hundred professionals working on what they themselves call organizational development. Firms face the prospect of losing some of their best talent if there is not sufficient opportunity for self-determination. In the long term, this loss also affects productivity. Chris Argyris shows that there is a conflict between the traditional view of the goals of an organization and a healthy human personality. Under the traditional formal principles of organization (chain of command, task specialization), introducing into it persons who are fairly mature and are thus predisposed to relative independence, initiative, and the use of their important abilities will cause a serious disturbance, according to Argyris. He says that the results of this disturbance are "frustration, failure, short time perspective, and conflict."[11] Argyris then outlines some of the adaptive behavior in which a person in such a restrictive organization will engage: (1) leaving the organization; (2) climbing the organizational ladder; (3) manifesting defense reactions, such as daydreaming, aggression, ambivalence, regression, or projection; and (4) becoming apathetic and disinterested in the organization, its makeup and goals. This then leads to employees' reducing their expectations of what they will achieve at work and to goldbricking, restricting quotas, making errors, cheating, and slowing down.[12]

In his seminal *Human Side of Enterprise,* Douglas McGregor contrasts two views of individuals and their desire to work.[13] The first, which he calls Theory X, outlines the traditional view that has heavily influenced management style and control:

1. People don't like to work and will avoid it if they can.
2. Therefore they must be coerced, controlled, directed, and threatened with punishment to get them to work.
3. People prefer to be directed, wish to avoid responsibility, have little ambition, and want security.

In contrast to the traditional view, McGregor presents and proceeds to argue in favor of his Theory Y:

1. Work is as natural to people as play or rest.
2. Individuals will exercise self-direction and self-control in the service of objectives to which they are committed.
3. Commitment to objectives is a function of the rewards associated with their achievement (especially satisfaction of ego and self-actualization).
4. People learn, under proper conditions, to accept and even ask for responsibility.

[11]Chris Argyris, *Personality and Organization* (Homewood, Ill.: Dorsey, 1962); see also his "Personality and Organization Theory Revisited," *Administrative Science Quarterly*, 18, no. 2 (June 1973), 141–67.

[12]Argyris, *Personality and Organization*, p. 235.

[13]Douglas McGregor, *Human Side of Enterprise* (New York: McGraw-Hill, 1960), p. 33.

These divergent views of the values and goals of people have a significant influence on the organizational climate and management style of an organization. Theory X provides the foundation for a formal, highly structured, control-oriented organization. One of the characteristic disadvantages of this sort of organization is goal displacement. Goal displacement is a bureaucratic process in which members of an organization tend to turn their procedures into goals. Petty organization officials tend to make adherence to the rules and preservation of their office the purpose of their work, and most often this is at the expense of the persons or process they are serving.

Although there is often noisy pressure from members of organizations for more participation and communication, their actions often belie their words. A *misrepresent* concern for an organization or a product over a long period does not seem to be a strong value among today's younger men and women. Their focus is on themselves and their careers. Witness the titles of recent best sellers: *Looking Out for #1, How to Prosper During the Coming Bad Years, Winning Through Intimidation.* Christopher Lasch chronicled this attitude in *The Culture of Narcissism:* a centering on self, concern with *my* life and *my* career.[14] Loyalties are shallow, and there is little concern with the old virtues for success: dedication, allegiance, and fidelity.[15]

Over the last few decades it does seem clear, however, that individuals are looking for more communication, more participation, and more opportunity for individual initiative within the organization. While these trends may be slowed or deflected by the "me generation" attitude and other external events, both executives and lower level members of organizations are well aware that providing satisfying and challenging work is essential to retaining talented people, improving their involvement in the product and process, and thus improving creativity and product quality. *no dissent in top lev. mgt.*

Dissent in the Organization

The importance of the individual and that individual's independent judgment have always been paramount, explicit values for Americans. But although we mouth the value of independent judgment, laboratory research indicates it does not hold the high priority we claim. In fact, the opinions and attitudes of the group have a definitive influence on the individual. Individuals are often willing to deny their own perceptions and better judgments because of the attitudes of their group. On the other hand, self-oriented competitiveness can undermine the cooperation and teamwork required in an organization.

One of the classic experiments in studying the influence of the group on the judgment of the individual was done by Solomon E. Asch.[16] Asch gathered groups of seven to nine college men for "psychological experiments in visual judg-

Asch — people go w/ crowd - line experiment —

[14]Christopher Lasch, *The Culture of Narcissim* (New York: Warner Books, 1979).

[15]Roy Rowan, "Rekindling Corporate Loyalty," *Fortune,* (February 9, 1981), pp. 54-58.

[16]Solomon E. Asch, "Opinions and Social Pressure," in *Science, Conflict and Society* (San Francisco: Freeman, 1969), pp. 52-57.

Fire / Ignore deviant even if right idea
Agreement most impt. to group.

100 Chapter Four

ment." The group was shown two cards simultaneously; one card bore a standard line, the other bore three lines, one of which was the same length as the one shown on the first card. Of the men in the group, all were "confederates" (instructed ahead of time to pick the same erroneous line), except one who was "naive" and was therefore the subject of the experiment. The question was: How often would a subject pick the right length of line even in the face of unanimous agreement by the rest of the group that it was another line? It was visually quite clear which line was the same length; ordinarily, mistakes would be made only 1 percent of the time. The subject was seated near the end of the group, so that most of the others would have responded by the time it was his turn to do so.

For our reputedly individualistic society, the findings are significant: When the subjects were exposed to the incorrect majority, 75 percent erred in the direction of the majority. Only 25 percent braved conflict with the group and held to their own perceptions. As Asch himself points out, when a majority of reasonably intelligent and educated young men will call black white when faced with the opinions of the group, it is obvious that we are losing much of the benefit of an individual's independent assessment of reality. The opinions, norms, and values of the majority can become a tyranny. We can see this readily in Nazi Germany or Soviet Russia but are often less able to see it in our own society.

In spite of their positive contributions, persons with an independent judgment are not always popular in the organization. This was established in experiments with problem-solving groups. A "deviant," a person whose values and attitudes did not coincide with those of the group, was placed in half the groups. In every case, the groups with a deviant had a better solution to the problem they were given than did the homogeneous groups. Each group was then asked to eliminate one member of the group before they received their next problem. In every case, the "deviant" was thrown out, and this in spite of the fact that it was fairly clear the deviant had significantly contributed to the work they were doing.[17] The group values harmony and "togetherness" more than challenge, new information, and perhaps irascibility. The suppression of dissent among those in working groups results in failure, often disastrous failure, as important information and options are not brought forward. Hence it is important to provide a vehicle for the expression of dissent.[18] On the other hand, additional experiments have shown that in groups, competitive behavior (the individual looking to her or his own success and satisfaction) often leads to disruption and inefficiency in the group's effort. Competitive behavior leads to greater efficiency when the job can be done on one's own and does not require the help of others.[19] Competition within the group often results in disruption and even obstruction.

[17]Elise Boulding, *Conflict: Management in Organizations* (Ann Arbor, Mich.: Foundation for Research on Human Behavior, 1964), p. 54.

[18]John D. Stanley, "Dissent in Organizations," *Academy of Management Review*, 6, no. 1 (January 1981), 13-19.

[19]Alexander Mintz, "Nonadaptive Group Behavior," in *Basic Studies in Social Psychology*, ed. Harold Proshansky and Bernard Seidenberg (New York: Holt, Rinehart & Winston, 1965), pp. 620-27.

In sum, the corporation tends to inculcate *[instill]* and thus perpetuate its own values. With other organizations, it shares the goals of survival and growth. These, plus the characteristic goals of long-term profit and return on investment, have a profound influence on the attitudes and values of its members. Members learn to accept the rules of the game as they are understood in their organization. Although creativity is a long-term benefit to the firm, it is not easily tolerated. The material goals of the firm often force individuals into judging the success of their work in numerical terms: number produced and dollars profit. The bias toward the concrete and measurable is satisfying, because it is objective and unarguable. But this bias can readily undermine more long-range and human values, such as creativity, trust, and openness.

[handwritten: Fitzgerald — kill the bearer of bad News. Cost control pentagon official now inspects bowling alleys. Amantype for govt defense contracts. is a whistle blower]

WHY PEOPLE WORK: INTERDEPENDENCE OF IDEOLOGY AND MOTIVATION

[handwritten: Money best motivator]

During the past decade, various theories of motivation have been quite popular with businesspeople. Executives have invested their own time in reading and company funds in leadership training programs based on various theories of what moves a person to act and work. To determine why they and their employees work is a bread and butter issue to managers. If we can find out, perhaps we can influence people to work more efficiently and effectively. Dozens of men and women have researched the motives that influence a person's work. Psychological theories of motivation and their implications are an important part of the knowledge and skills available to the professional manager. Hence, they are a core part of any business school curriculum.

When psychologists ask why people work, they inevitably touch on values. What sort of values move the employee, according to these specialists?[20] Most theories of motivation popular with businesspersons describe moving forces within the individual, but rarely or never explicitly discuss values, goals, or ideology. These theories generally implicitly presuppose traditional, accepted goals. In thus ignoring values and goals, and in that way seeming to hold that they are unimportant, motivational psychologists do business a disservice. This is especially so, since there is actually an intimate and complex, although seldom acknowledged, relationship between ideology and motivation.

Among the questions we might ask are these: To what extent do theories of motivation imply values and goals? Do they presuppose goals, or predispose one toward certain goals? Do these theories aid in a search for values and goals, or mask their absence? The greatly increased interest in motivation in the past

---

[20]For an overview of the literature on motivation, see Richard M. Steers, *Introduction to Organizational Behavior* (Santa Monica, Calif.: Goodyear Publishing Co., 1981), especially pp. 51-77 and 149-79.

Success means you know you have achieved something.

few decades has paradoxically coincided with, and perhaps partially caused, a decrease in interest in values and ideology. Ideology is, as we have seen, a product of deliberate reflection and articulation. But psychologists warn us to be suspicious of stated reasons for actions. It is too easy, they remind us, to be unaware of unconscious or subconscious motives that have a powerful influence on our activities. We may think we know why we do something, and respond with that answer when asked. But according to psychologists, that may not be the real reason at all. In sum, the search for acknowledged values and an explicit ideology is not aided by the many psychologists who imply that straightforward verbal statements are generally self-deceiving and invalid.

Need for Achievement and Power *key — motivation*

Dream test

David C. McClelland's work on the need for achievement is well known to students of organizations. He has pointed out that the success of a society and of the individual is most often positively correlated with a high need for achievement. A person's need for achievement, according to McClelland, can be measured; indeed, it can even be increased. He has designed programs for increasing the need for achievement of poor and disadvantaged people.[21] It is not to our purpose to go into the details of McClelland's work. In this instance, as with the others that follow, we must be content with a brief examination of the psychologist's explicit treatment of the relationship between motivation and values. Of the motivation theorists, McClelland treats the relationship most explicitly. He examines the long-range impact of a person's ideology on motivation. McClelland cites Max Weber's work[22] in showing how the Protestant ethic has contributed to attitudes supportive of modern capitalism. Protestantism encouraged independence and self-reliance. The church was no longer the central agency for communicating values; individuals were much more on their own.

Attitudes of independence, self-reliance, and the need for achievement are very much influenced by the way parents bring up their children. Indeed, it is understandable and appropriate that parents' ideals and values do have an effect on how they rear their children. McClelland is able to predict from the content of children's stories, fantasies, daydreams, and dreams a high or a low need for achievement. Since parents' own values and ideology influence the stories they tell or provide their children, they then in turn have a profound effect on their children's motivation. In experimental work, it was found that boys who showed a high need for achievement had mothers who expected their sons to master a number of activities early in life: Know their way around the city; be active and energetic; try hard for things for themselves; do well in competition; make their

Ring toss — ① Coward of failer — Standover peg/drop

[21]See David C. McClelland, "Achievement Motivation Can Be Developed," *Harvard Business Review*, 43, no. 4 (November–December 1965), 6–24; and "Black Capitalism: Making It Work," *Think*, July–August 1969, pp. 7–11.

[22]Max Weber, *The Protestant Ethic and the Spirit of Capitalism*, tr. Talcott Parsons (New York: Scribner's, 1958).

② uninterested throw general direction of Ring

③ higest Achever knows just where to stand to get most skillfully not too easy own friends.[23] On the other hand, the mothers of boys with low need for achievement reported that they restricted their sons more. These mothers did not want their sons to make important decisions by themselves or to make friends with other children not approved of by their parents. *parents stress independence*

McClelland theorizes that the Protestant Reformation encouraged a new character type possessing a more vigorous and independent spirit. This self-reliance was then passed on in families and especially through child-rearing patterns. Furthermore, McClelland follows Weber in maintaining that it is precisely this self-reliance that forms the foundation for modern capitalism. He cites evidence that the need for achievement is increased as an effect of an ideological or religious conversion, whether that conversion be Protestant, Catholic, or Communist.[24] In the wake of the reflection and forced reassessment a conversion entails, a felt challenge and resulting need for achievement emerge. According to McClelland, religion, ideology, and values are inextricably intertwined with motivation, and especially the need for achievement; and this relationship is especially close when these values are reassessed and changed. *money impacts as a symbol. car & house &*

In modern society, the need for achievement is generally exercised in the marketplace. McClelland cites Florence of the late Middle Ages as an example of the need for achievement being expressed in art, and thus in something other than economic development. In modern societies, however, business seems to be the major outlet for this need. McClelland's practical criterion for the success of the achiever today, and hence his implicit goal, is generally economic growth. In this fashion McClelland seems to accept rather unquestioningly the traditional business ideology and the prevailing social norm: that economic growth is the best final goal of a people.

McClelland denies that the businessperson with a high need for achievement is motivated by money. Nevertheless, he does hold that achievement is measured in money terms.[25] He notes that money is a *symbol* of success. An increase in salary, which is often demonstrated to friends and neighbors by a more expensive car and a larger home, is the reward that comes to those who have achieved; it is the sure sign of success, at least in the eyes of corporate superiors. Some further observations by Erich Fromm on money as a measure of personal success will be examined later in this chapter.

People with a high need for achievement are more likely to be successful where they can be their own boss. One who begins a business, an entrepreneur, typically is expressing a high need for achievement. Given the fact that 80 percent of new jobs are created in firms with less than 100 employees, it seems clear that American business, and indeed the United States as a whole, depends heavily on individuals with a high need for achievement.

[23]David C. McClelland, *The Achieving Society* (Princeton, N.J.: Van Nostrand, 1961), pp. 46–50.

[24]Ibid., pp. 406–17.

[25]Ibid., pp. 232–37.

[handwritten: top mgt. need power / control not Achievment learn to control]

In more recent years McClelland has turned his attention to the need for power or influence. The need for power is the desire to have impact, to be strong or influential. McClelland found that top managers in companies possess a high need for power, even more than their need for achievement. This need for power must be "disciplined and controlled so that it is directed" toward the benefit of the institution as a whole and not toward the manager's personal aggrandizement."[26]

[handwritten: Need for Affiliation not good]

Managers with a high need for power, who do not exercise it with self-control, can be very disruptive: "They are rude to other people, they drink too much, they try to exploit others sexually, and they collect symbols of personal prestige such as fancy cars or big offices."[27]

People with a high need for being liked by other people (need for affiliation) do not make good managers, since they are overly concerned with pleasing their subordinates. Special treatment given to one person is resented by others in the work group as being unfair.

The Self-Actualizing Person *[handwritten: Maslow hierarchy of Needs]*

Abraham H. Maslow was the principal proponent of a school of humanistic psychology that sees motivation as arising from a hierarchy of needs. Maslow maintained that his theory of motivation was based on observations of healthy, mature persons. He found that as "lower needs" (food, water, safety, security) were gratified, they ceased to be motivators. The person then moved on to "higher needs" (belongingness, love, self-esteem, and self-actualization), so that ". . . a healthy man is primarily motivated by his needs to develop and actualize his fullest potentialities and capacities."[28]

Of the various human needs, Maslow is quick to point out that some of the higher needs are not always strong. In spite of the fact that in the long run they can be vital for the individual, their importance is not often seen by those who do not have enough to eat or a roof over their heads. In Maslow's words, "The human needs for love, for knowledge or for philosophy, are weak and feeble rather than unequivocal and unmistakable; they whisper rather than shout. And the whisper is easily drowned out." For individuals to arrive at their own internalized personal values, to say nothing of their own philosophy and religion, demands that their lower needs be somewhat satisfied.

Maslow consistently maintains that as individuals become more mature and accepting, they will move correctly toward establishing their own values. He concludes that a firm foundation for a value system is automatically furnished by open acceptance of one's own self, "of human nature, of much of social life, and of

---

[26]David C. McClelland and David H. Burnham, "Power Is the Great Motivator," *Harvard Business Review*, 54, no. 2 (March–April 1976), 101.

[27]Ibid., p. 103.

[28]Abraham H. Maslow, *Motivation and Personality* (New York: Harper & Row, 1954), pp. 35–58.

nature and physical reality." A society made up largely of self-actualizers is characterized by more free choice and nonintrusiveness. Under these conditions, "the deepest layers of human nature would show themselves with greater ease."[29] Maslow goes on to describe the personal characteristics of the people he has examined—those whom he calls self-actualizers. They tend to be "strongly focused on problems outside themselves"; they are problem-centered rather than ego-centered. Most often these mature, self-actualized individuals have "some mission in life, some task to fulfill"—a task outside themselves that enlists most of their energies. Significantly, especially for our purposes, these tasks are generally nonpersonal or unselfish; they are directed primarily toward the good of others. Furthermore, self-actualizers "are ordinarily concerned with basic issues and eternal questions of the type that we have learned to call philosophical or ethical."[30] Their major concerns are not ego-centered, trivial, or petty; they have a wider breadth of concerns, larger horizons. They seem to have a stability that enables and encourages them to address the larger ethical and social issues.

The possession of basic, root values is described a bit later in more detail. Self-actualizers "are strongly ethical, they have definite moral standards, they do right and do not do wrong." They are less confused about their basic values. It is easier for them to distinguish right from wrong, although these values do not always coincide with those of the accepted, conventional, surrounding culture. Maslow holds that as persons grow and mature, they will become less selfish and more concerned with other people and larger problems. Their values will become clearer, more explicit, and highly ethical. Indeed, although Maslow finds that these people are not always theists, and most have scant loyalty to an institutional church, they are nevertheless the sort of people who a few centuries ago "would all have been described as men who walk in the path of God or as godly men."[31]

Maslow gives values and goals an important place. Further, he is convinced that ethical values will emerge as the individual matures, and that this process is rather automatic. In so describing the process, Maslow implies that the development of internalized ethical principles and unselfish goals can *only* be accomplished as a person matures. He therefore has little room for a value system, asceticism, or a "spirituality" that seeks explicitly to develop unselfish, highly ethical principles and goals. Given Maslow's view, we would have to wait for a significant number of people to become self-actualizers before unselfish goals and policy could be developed. It is doubtful whether the problems that face our contemporary world can wait for this maturity to come about, or whether such maturity will *ever* characterize a significant number of the major world leaders and policymakers.

The above motivation models involving need for achievement, need for power, and need for self-actualization continue to generate research and to be useful in managing people. Meanwhile, theories of motivation that are designed

[29]Ibid., pp. 276-78.
[30]Ibid., pp. 159-60.
[31]Ibid., pp. 168-69.

to take into account a wider variety of personality traits, attitudes, needs, and values, have developed. They are called expectancy/valence or path-goal theories.[32] It is not to our purpose to go into the details of these theories. However, it is noteworthy that an individual's personal attitudes and values are tracked and given weight in these theories. Again, we notice the close relationship between motives and personal values.

All of the above theories of motivation take into account the attitudes and values of the individual. The values and goals of the organization within which the individual is working are not as clearly considered. Psychologists may respond that the goals of the firm are beyond their concern and competence. This may be true enough, yet there can be little doubt that an organization's goals and values will have considerable influence on the individual participant's motivations. If purposes and values are in conflict, it will lead to frustration for the person and various inefficiencies for the organization. Moreover, our traditional neglect of values and goals leaves the impression that they are unimportant. In reality, we have taken organizational goals for granted; and now we find ourselves in the awkward position of wanting to probe these goals, yet having few tools and little expertise for doing so.

Unexamined Assumptions

More than a decade ago, after having worked with Maslow, Douglas McGregor began to dig into the accepted ideology, the conventional assumptions, that lay beneath the literature on management and motivation. He was incisive in penetrating the "let's be practical; theorizing has no place in management" mentality and in demonstrating that "it is not possible to reach a managerial decision or take a managerial action uninfluenced by assumptions, whether adequate or not."[33] The assumptions and implicit goals and values are there. The relevant question is whether or not these assumptions and implicit goals and values are examined for their adequacy. McGregor pinpoints one of the most glaring deficiencies of this self-imposed managerial blindness: "The common practice of proceeding without explicit examination of theoretical assumptions, leads, at times, to remarkable inconsistencies in managerial behavior."[34]

It is not easy to cast a cool, clear eye on our own assumptions and values. All of us engage in various shortcuts in our perceptions of our own values and those of others. Rationalization, stereotyping, and other mechanisms block our ability to perceive these values in ourselves and in others.[35] Sometimes these barriers also block our ability to reflect on the goals and the values of the organization. We convince ourselves, for example, that the growth of the organization

---

[32]For a summary of these views, see John B. Minor, *Theories of Organizational Behavior* (Hinsdale, Ill: Dryden Press, 1980), pp. 133-50.

[33]McGregor, *Human Side of Enterprise*, p. 7.

[34]Ibid.

[35]Steers, *Introduction to Organizational Behavior*, pp. 115-23.

benefits people and thus automatically compensates for damage done to others. Or, more to the point here, we may think that businesspeople are wasting their time speculating on abstract values and goals. They are irrelevant to successful performance, and it is better to be about the work before us.

On the other hand, it has become clear that there is no such thing as "value-less" management. Proceeding to carry out the unexamined goals of the organization without explicit awareness of what values undergird those goals is to have chosen a way of acting; it is precisely to have made decisions on the basis of a value. This value is to accept without question the values of the organization. Rather than being value-free, decisions are supported by value judgments made by default. For example, that the present goals of the organization are acceptable; that in a conflict with the larger society or with another organization, loyalty demands that I pursue the good of my organization. The Firestone 500 tire debacle, the Watergate coverup, Gulf + Western's fanfared introduction of a battery for electric automobiles that fizzled—all bear testimony to the shortsightedness and ultimate inefficiency of this sort of "value-free," loyal, and blind management.

SOURCES OF SATISFACTION AND PRESSURE TO PERFORM

We have examined how the structure and environment of the organization affect the values and goals of the manager. In this section, we will focus on the business manager as a person and on her or his values.

In a classic empirical study of the backgrounds, education, and attitudes of business executives by W. Lloyd Warner and James Abegglen,[36] the authors found that the executive is best characterized as a mobile person, able to leave and take up a new job in a new community rather easily:

> The mobile man must be able to depart: that is, he must maintain a substantial emotional distance from people, and not become deeply involved with them or committed to them; and he must be an energetic person and one who can focus his energy on a single goal.[37]

These top managers are not particularly sensitive to the needs of other people. Even though their own success is often built on decisions that result in considerable loss to others, this does not seem to disturb them. They do not set out to hurt others, but the fact that others are hurt does not seem to bother them; they do not allow themselves to become "distracted into personal duels, for they do not allow themselves to become so involved with others." Successful executives

[36]W. Lloyd Warner and James Abegglen, *Big Business Leaders in America* (New York: Atheneum, 1963).

[37]Ibid., pp. 81–82.

upper mid class domineering moms — Affection is reward *praise love* by Achievement
CAN never do enough — praise worth by Actions.

108   Chapter Four

". . . are not men who know guilt. The distractions of consideration for others, of weighing the potential damage to others of a contemplated move, do not enter into their calculations."

Mobility and lack of consideration for others enable them to approach managerial decisions dispassionately. This objectivity, combined with their other more obvious talents, contributes to making them successful. But their success does not allow them the satisfaction one might expect. There is rarely time to relax, to look back on one's successes, ". . . for an essential part of the system is the need for constant demonstration of one's adequacy, for reiterated proof of one's independence."[38]

What sort of a background is it that would give a person these qualities of mobility, lack of involvement with others, and the need constantly to demonstrate personal adequacy? The researchers found that these executives tended to have strong, demanding mothers and weak or even absent fathers. Although mothers of these successful executives are seen as even-tempered and hardworking, they are also stern, rigid, moralistic, and controlling. They hold out high standards of achievement and parcel out their love as reward for success. At the same time, the fathers are distant from their children; they are not supporting and reinforcing. These executives see their fathers as rather unreliable figures. They also could not identify with their fathers; it was their mothers who held out goals of achievement. According to Warner and Abegglen, if they were to win their mothers' love and others' respect, they must prove themselves; they must be successful at what they are doing. They can never be fully sure that they have achieved. The overwhelming majority of the families of these executives are upper or middle class: 76 percent of the managers' fathers were owners, executives, professionals, or white-collar workers. They are conservative in their politics. Moreover, when they have any involvement with community activities, it tends to be with conservative movements—Chamber of Commerce, boys' clubs, conservative charities.

Warner gathered his material in 1950, but a survey twenty years later showed many of the same attitudes, especially on political and social issues.[39] The more recent survey showed that just short of 80 percent of the chief executives call themselves Republicans, and 80 percent are Protestant. Only 9 percent are Catholics, nowhere near their 23 percent of the total population. Blacks and women, of course, are hard to find in executive suites. Most of these top managers have grown up in middle-class or upper-middle-class homes.

When chief executives were asked what they would look for in their successors, surprisingly they did not give high priority to such attributes as youth or the ability to get along well with people of different races and classes. They are generally looking for men who are very much like themselves in background and attitudes. Organizations and their attitudes tend to be self-perpetuating. The

[38]Ibid., p. 83.

[39]Robert S. Diamond, "A Self-Portrait of the Chief Executive: The Fortune 500 Yankelovich Survey," *Fortune*, (February 1970), pp. 180-81, 320-23.

ordinary struggle for growth and survival urges people and organizations to seek "their own kind."

Selling of Self   *CAReeRism —*

Although these goals and values are influenced by background, education, and age, they are also heavily affected by an individual's estimate of what sort of personal values will "sell" in the marketplace. The market concept of value, what a person will be able to obtain when he puts his body into the employment market, has a considerable influence on notions of self-worth.[40] Today we call this careerism.

The individual begins to be concerned about how well he or she "sells," or appears to a prospective employer, what sort of package he or she appears to be. The individual then becomes less concerned with personal goals of achievement, satisfaction, and happiness; attention is focused on pleasing someone else, rather than on determining one's own values and goals. The more the person sees self-esteem as largely dependent on monetary value in the market, the less control that individual has over his or her own life. Individual notions of personal adequacy are determined by unpredictable and insensitive market forces. One is not valued for the person one is, but rather for what one can fetch in the marketplace. When such an individual receives an increase in salary, it is less the money itself that delights him than the fact that someone has recognized that he is worth more and is willing to pay for it. Without the salary increase, the person might sink into depths of lowered self-esteem and even self-pity. *Remain flexible*

Furthermore, since the market can be the principal determiner of self-worth and since value in the market is subject to many changing, unpredictable forces and fads, the individual must remain flexible. Her present value may collapse, simply because there are too many with the same talents on the market. She must then be able to shift to a new career. This phenomenon encourages an individual to maintain flexibility and maximum exposure. No matter how much she may like her present work or locale, it is to her advantage not to sink deep roots. If she becomes known as a one-talent person, her value, and hence her self-esteem, will be severely limited. This situation does not encourage developing expertise, loyalty or settling into and becoming involved in a community.

This notion of self-worth makes the individual totally dependent on others for his or her own self-esteem. Self-worth stems not from accomplishments, interests, or loves but rather from the impersonal forces of the employment market—in this case, from company superiors. This is the "other-directed" person. The heavy influence of a changing external environment on personal values contributes to making Americans practical and pragmatic. They will rarely dispute

[40]Erich Fromm, "Personality and the Market Place," in *Man, Work, and Society: A Reader in the Sociology of Occupations*, ed. Sigmund Nosow and William Form (New York: Basic Books, 1962), pp. 446–52.

outside reading Gayle Shehe 'Passages'
? – 45 time for reassessment
time to think about success is early & get Established

principles for their own sake; they find martyrdom to be the ultimate folly. Thomas More's beheading under Henry VIII makes superb drama in *Man for All Seasons*; Americans find the episode quaint and moving, but difficult to understand and perhaps even smacking of fanaticism or some other aberration. Indeed, the businessperson finds disputes over principles time-consuming and unproductive and will rarely allow himself or herself to be caught up in ideological battles. The shallow soil in which the principles and values of most Americans are rooted was graphically demonstrated in the ability of the Chinese to "brainwash" American prisoners of war after the Korean conflict.[41] Most were astonished at the prisoners' lack of deep convictions and the ease with which expert Chinese propagandists could undermine them. Explicit, articulated principles and values are not often a part of an American's baggage. This enables us to be flexible and pragmatic, but it also allows us to float and to become more victims of events and the environment than masters.

Mid-Life Identity Crisis

It is this same lack of internalized personal values and goals that enables a person to undertake a career or a life without much personal clarification of goals and examination of alternatives. This then often leads to the much-publicized "mid-life identity crisis." Not many months go by without still another article on people who have opted out of the corporation.

John Z. DeLorean quit his job as vice president and group executive in charge of all General Motors car and truck divisions in North America. DeLorean felt that the GM committee system was too unwieldy; it dispersed authority and responsibility, and as a result he felt that no one could move aggressively. His case is by no means unique. The *Wall Street Journal* ran a series of articles on scores of men who left well-paid corporate jobs to do something quite different at a fraction of their former pay. These men found their work in the corporation to be confining and deadening and most turned to a simpler and less structured life. Typical of them is Ross Drever, fifty-two, who quit as director of Amsted Industries' research division at a $50,000 salary. He now spends his time working a cranberry bog in Three Lakes, Wisconsin. He says, "I have a lot of suits and shoes I'll never use again."

These managers felt they were giving too many hours to an activity that gave them little satisfaction. They yearned for a simpler life. They made the radical, lonely change; they left comfortable jobs, homes, and friends to carve out a new life. The increasing number of these men and women that we hear about tells us some people are beginning to examine their own life values and goals and are willing to act on the values they find.

However, the mid-life identity crisis can be traumatic: to family, to fellow

---

[41]See Edgar H. Schein, "Reaction Patterns to Severe, Chronic Stress in American Prisoners of War of the Chinese," *Journal of Social Issues*, 13 (1957), 21-30.

Don't brood on death — prepare is all you can do, will

workers, and to the person experiencing it. The classic symptoms occur to a person who is roughly around the age of forty. He or she looks about and asks if this is the way one would choose to lead the rest of one's life. The clear realization presses that time is running out; there may be only two or three decades of healthy work life left. On some occasions the person experiencing the mid-life transition panics and seeks a dramatic change. That individual sometimes breaks all connections with the past, leaving spouse and children behind, and goes off to a different part of the country with different friends. This sort of radical break can cause much hurt and disruption, to families surely, but also to neighbors, co-workers, and other relatives, too. Suffice it to say that such a reaction is one born of desperation and is not a mature one. These sharp mid-life breaks also tell us that too few of us have sufficiently probed our own goals in order to chart our own course. Too often we leave it to opportunity, to "significant others," or to accepted norms to determine our career and our life goals for us.

Stress and Illness

As in any culture, self-esteem is highly dependent on the feedback a person receives from others. That feedback can be either positive or negative. In the American culture, those who gain the esteem of their peers are considered to be successful. Such people are typically competent, goal-oriented, conscientious, ambitious, and hardworking.[42] These are qualities we have previously identified with the Protestant ethic. The culture, through its family life, schools, churches, government, and business, is able to communicate its values to the individual. A culture does this in order to give itself direction and integrity. Otherwise it cannot develop; legal systems and economic growth become difficult or impossible. Without this socialization process, it is not even possible to know what one person may expect of another in everyday dealings.

Although broader cultural expectations are not as strong in the United States now as they were a decade ago, the route to success in business is more agreed-upon. Those who make it up the corporate ladder generally adhere to a variation of what we have called the Protestant ethic. People who are not successful, according to those norms, are often judged inferior by others; this is a source of stress. Additional job-related stress is caused by conflict and confusion over a person's responsibilities.[43] Stress is also caused when the job calls for actions or policies that are at variance with an individual's values and ethics. In these cases, either a compromise is reached or something is sacrificed. Each situation causes its share of anxiety and frustration.

Those who are judged successful according to the prevailing norms of be-

[42]See H. J. Wahler, "Winning and Losing in Life: A Survey of Opinions About Causes," *Mental Hygiene*, 55, no. 1 (January 1971), 94.

[43]Thomas V. Bonoma and Gerald Zaltman, *Psychology for Management* (Boston: Kent, 1981), pp. 128-41.

What me worry!?! (handwritten)

you need to chill dude! (handwritten, left margin)

ing competent, ambitious, and hardworking may by that very fact suffer anxieties. Earlier we have seen how successful corporate managers are those who are mobile; they are able to leave their present jobs and homes in order to move on to better positions. Psychologists tell us that anxiety is caused by moving from the known to the unknown. Having mastered one environment, it is unsettling to be asked to move to a new one. It is true that the challenge of life and that which encourages us to grow as persons often involves moving into the unknown. Nevertheless, when much of life consists of being uprooted every few years, leaving behind not just the confidence built in mastering a job but relatives, friends, and knowledge of the community, it can undermine willingness to commit oneself to a new job or neighborhood. Such persons may be forced in upon themselves, depending more on their aggressiveness and individuality than on the help and cooperation of co-workers, friends, and neighbors. When they choose to grow in this fashion, they force their families to undergo the same cyclic trauma of arriving and departing, along with the pain and anxiety it involves.

The unknown, and even more the uncontrollable, produce anxieties. Ulcers and stress usually result when there are two conflicting demands on the individual. Neuroses have been experimentally induced in animals exposed to ambiguous stimuli. After the same or very similar stimuli, the animals were sometimes rewarded and sometimes not, or sometimes rewarded and sometimes punished. Gastric ulcers were produced in laboratory rats who spent one month in a special cage. During 47 hours of every 48-hour period, they had to endure an electric shock every time they went to the food box or the water cup. They needed the food, but also feared the shock. Furthermore, they were never sure they would get a shock along with their food. They developed ulcers. The conflict of wanting the food yet risking considerable pain, plus a lack of control over the situation, produced the ulcers. Control rats, which were simply deprived of food and water for 47 of the 48 hours, did not develop ulcers.[44]

Cats, which were first fed and then shocked following the same buzzer, exhibited a wide variety of aberrant physical activities, such as restless roving, clawing at wire cages, butting the roof with their heads, and ceaseless vocalizing—all indicating a high degree of anxiety. These cats were then given the opportunity to drink milk that had been laced with alcohol. Half the animals quickly learned that the alcohol relieved the symptoms of their anxiety, and they invariably chose the 5 percent alcohol mixture served in a distinctive cocktail glass. The cats preferred the alcohol as long as their tensions persisted and they remained neurotic. When the animals experienced uncontrollable psychic pain, they sought relief in periodic withdrawal, and their neurotic symptoms disappeared under the influence of the alcohol.

Individuals will attempt to escape from the pain of uncertainties and not being able to control their immediate environment. That escape can be healthy

---

[44]Bernard Berelson and Gary A. Steiner, *Human Behavior: An Inventory of Scientific Findings* (New York: Harcourt, Brace & World, 1964), pp. 276-79.

or can result in suppression and postponing the facing of the issues that caused the problem. The stress that ensues can bring on ulcers, high blood pressure, heart attack, and even cancer. On the other hand the same situation can lead us to reflect on our own position and our values and goals. The latter posture could enable us to emerge from a stressful situation healthier and in greater control of our own lives.

Job-related stress has taken on new importance for businesspeople.[45] Stress and the illness, absenteeism, and health-care costs that are related to it are becoming immense expenses for the firm. In addition, in a few notable court cases, firms have been held responsible for work-related stress. However, not all stress is bad for the individual or for job performance. In fact a moderate amount of stress correlates with better job performance; the "fight-or-flight" response releases a moderate amount of stimulants to enable a person better to achieve the objective. A large amount of stress causes poor job performance. Exercise and relaxation are advocated to reduce stress.[46] Taking quiet time, reflection, meditation, and prayer are old tried and true techniques that are being rediscovered. They are found to be quite effective in enabling individuals to deal with normal stress and, in the process, to become more mature persons.

Decision Making vs. Sensitivity

Use facts not feelings for best decision

Another aspect of the tension that is brought to bear on businesspeople is the conflict between the characteristics that are rewarded on the job and those that make for a good spouse and parent. Much has been said about this, and here we will discuss but one example. The typical manager is aggressive, decisive, and fact-oriented. He or she makes decisions, not on the basis of intuition or feelings, but rather on the basis of facts and clear, defensible reasoning. The mobile manager is one who does not become too involved with people and is not unduly influenced by human feelings. This talent of looking only to the articulated and measurable facts of the case does not work nearly so well when the manager is at home with spouse and children. When one's spouse asks to go to a movie, it is not necessarily because the spouse is enraptured with the particular film; it may simply be a desire to be alone together for a few hours away from house and children.

It is sometimes equally difficult for the fact-oriented businessperson to determine what a son is saying beneath the flurry of words and argument. He has trained himself to look for the facts, and so he takes the words at face value. Furthermore, he can often be impatient with his children for not saying what they

---

[45]John M. Ivancevich and Michael T. Matteson, "Optimizing Human Resources: A Case for Preventive Health and Stress Management," *Organizational Dynamics*, Autumn 1980, 5-55; also Saroj Parasuraman, "An Examination of the Organizational Antecedents of Stressors at Work," *Academy of Management Journal*, 24, no. 1 (March 1981), 48-67.

[46]Herbert Benson and Robert Allen, "How Much Stress Is Too Much?" *Harvard Business Review*, 58, no. 5 (September-October, 1980), 86-92.

[handwritten: aggressive, competitive, impatience, restless, higher heart ailment risk — Type A]

really mean. He finds it impossible to sift through the sentences to determine what his wife, son, or daughter is really saying—often enough nonverbally. Moreover, in his impatience he is often unable to be open enough to encourage them to communicate what they are really thinking and feeling. He is sometimes aware of this inability and conflict, and this causes additional tensions and anxieties.

This sort of person has been called a "Type A" personality, characterized by impatience, restlessness, aggressiveness, competitiveness, having many irons in the fire, and being under considerable time pressure. Sixty percent of managers in the average organization are Type A. The Type A manager is two to five times more likely to have heart disease or a fatal heart attack as other managers. Interestingly enough, it has been shown that Type A managers have the talents and attitudes that enable them to rise in the organization. However, the top managers, chief executive officers, are generally not Type A; they are more patient and willing to examine the long-term ramifications of decisions.[47]

Authority *[handwritten: following orders is essential w/in organization]*

Following orders within an organization is essential to any organization's success. But to what lengths will a person go in following orders, when those orders seriously conflict with her or his own moral values? Evidence of a person's willingness actually to do harm to another individual when instructed by authority to do so was provided by a series of controversial laboratory experiments.[48] Subjects were told that they were to engage in experiments in memory and learning. The subjects were placed at a shock generator with thirty intervals marked from 15 volts (slight shock) to 450 volts (danger—severe shock). Another person (a confederate), who was strapped in a chair with electrodes on his wrists, could be seen in an adjoining room through a glass partition. The subject was then instructed to shock the learner, increasing the intensity for every wrong answer the learner gave. As the shock level rose, the learner cried out in increasing pain, yet almost two-thirds of the subjects administered the highest level of shock.

The subjects would become nervous, agonize, and rationalize, but nevertheless administer the highest level of shock under the auspices of authority. The experiment has been criticized as being unethical. Indeed, it did play with people's consciences. However, it also gives us frightening evidence of what one human being is willing to inflict on another when it seems to be legitimized by some authority. Obedience in this experiment drops if the subject is in the same room as the learner, or if the subject must actually touch the learner to administer the shock. The more impersonal the situation, the more willing is the subject to do harm to another.

Not infrequently, a lower level manager is instructed to do something that violates that individual's ethics. The above experiments show that about 60 percent of us will perform actions at serious variance with what we see is right, if

---

[47]Steers, *Introduction to Organizational Behavior*, pp. 353-56.
[48]Stanley Milgram, *Obedience to Authority* (New York: Harper & Row, 1974).

someone in authority instructs us. Yet this sort of obedience has its cost in tension, anxiety, stress, and the resulting physical ailments. Modern organizations are designed to produce results in an impersonal fashion. Layoffs, pollution, and exploitative advertising are the direct result of decisions of executives and the policies they formulate. These activities are more readily condoned when the executives do not view the victims of the policy, and they can thus feel that they themselves did not directly bring about the undesirable result. In the minds of some executives, the system demands that they act impersonally if they are to see to it that the firm survives and grows.

EXAMINING PERSONAL VALUES

One solution to the problem of ambiguous, conflicting personal goals and values is to make an explicit attempt to clarify them. A scale that has been used for measuring personal values for more than a generation is the Allport-Vernon-Lindzey value scale. It attempts to discriminate personal values according to six potentially dominant personality characteristics: theoretical, economic, aesthetic, social, political, and religious.[49]   *love of beauty*

The authors administered the value test to business students in college, who came out significantly higher on economic and political values and significantly lower on aesthetic, religious, and social values, as compared with college students as a whole. The same scale was administered to those who had returned for the Advanced Management Program at the Harvard Business School. The predominant values these individuals espoused were economic, theoretical, and political (see Table 4-1). For the population as a whole, these same values tended to average out at around 40 on the scale.

TABLE 4-1   Personal Values in Business

VALUE	SCORE	
	BUSINESS STUDENTS	BUSINESSPERSONS
Economic	46	45
Theoretical	43	44
Political	46	44
Religious	34	39
Aesthetic	39	35
Social	33	33

Sources: For students, Gordon Allport, Philip Vernon, and Gardner Lindzey, *Study of Values* (Boston: Houghton Mifflin, 1931), p. 14; for businesspersons. William D. Guth and Renato Tagiuri, "Personal Values and Corporate Strategy," *Harvard Business Review,* 43 (September-October 1965), 126.

[49]Gordon Allport, Philip Vernon, and Gardner Lindzey, *Study of Values* (Boston: Houghton Mifflin, 1931).

Economic values are primarily oriented toward what is useful and practical. Theoretical values are primarily concerned with discovery of truth. Political values are characterized by an orientation to power—influence over people. The religious person is one "whose mental structure is permanently directed to the creation of the highest and absolutely satisfying value experience." The aesthetic person is primarily interested in the artistic aspects of life—form and harmony. The highest value for the social person is love of people.

When we compare the relative strengths of the six values for the business-people and the business students, the dominance of economic, theoretical, and political orientations is characteristic of both groups, and there is a significant gap between them and the lower three value orientations. Social values are the lowest by a wide margin for both businesspersons and business students. Religious values are stronger for the older businessperson, whereas aesthetic values are stronger for students.

More recently, the values of managers from three continents and five countries—Australia, Japan, Korea, India, and the United States—were measured and compared by George W. England.[50] The value systems of these managers in widely spread cultures were more similar than different. Among the minor differences, the Japanese were more pragmatic and more homogeneous in their values, and Indian managers were more moralistic.

More interesting for our purposes were the significant differences between the values of younger and older managers. The values of business as a whole may change as the values of younger managers become predominant. England found that across all the countries, compared with their senior peers, younger managers tended to

1. Place less importance on organizational goals
2. Place less importance on co-workers and more on themselves ("me" mentality)
3. Place less importance on trust and honor
4. Place more importance on money, ambition, and risk
5. Be slightly more pragmatic

The picture that emerges is that of the "gamesman"—a person who is primarily concerned with his or her own life and career and less concerned with the organization, trust, honor, and other people.

The Allport and other value scales were originally designed as research tools to learn more about personalities and their values. These scales are now also widely used by interviewers and guidance counselors to determine the attitudes and potential vocational interests of students and employees. This use of the scale as an indicator of a person's compatibility with a future career underscores two of its principal limitations. The first of these is that the test measures only *relative*

---

[50]George W. England, "Managers and Their Value Systems: A Five-Country Comparative Study," *Columbia Journal of World Business*, Summer 1978, p. 35.

values. One person could possess exactly the same value *profile* as another, yet possess each value much more strongly. A second problem in using any test as a career indicator is that, based on profiles of successful businesspeople, counselors often advise students who have relatively high social values to stay out of business. It is true that, according to the scales of those businesspeople who have previously taken the test, social values are lowest. But to give career advice merely on the basis of how past persons in that career have scored is at best heuristic and at worst prevents new values and creativity from entering a career or profession. It discourages young people with higher social values from entering business and hence perpetuates and rigidifies an old pattern.

Who school counselors advise to go into business and who they advise to stay away can have an immense influence on the values and goals of business itself. High school counselors have generally had little if any contact with business life beyond casual work to help pay for their college educations. Most have no direct experience of working in a corporation, and surely not of entrepreneurial activities. As a result, their attitudes toward business are often stereotyped and negative. Nevertheless, these counselors have considerable influence on young people's career choices.

The value profile of the businessperson has for generations been more pragmatic, materialistic, and self-centered than that of the average American. Concern for people was the lowest value of managers a generation ago, and this same lack of concern for others carries through among younger managers. Recent value probes of younger managers show them to be even more concerned with themselves and less with the organization or with other people. Speaking candidly, this does not present an encouraging picture for business, which now recognizes the need for planning for the long term and being sensitive to other people's needs as well as one's own. If the values of the younger manager have thus shifted, it promises a more competitive, "me-first," selfish society. It will make cooperation and participation even more difficult. Individuals will be interested primarily in themselves and their own careers and less with the product they produce or with other people.

Personal Experience Gives Values and Direction

live & learn

In previous generations, children growing up in a family would witness their father and mother doing work in or near the home. They would see, not only the skill, effort, and challenge required in work, but also the joy of accomplishment. Since commercial work is generally done away from home today, the young person growing up in a family rarely has direct contact with it, and so hears only secondhand, and generally negative, comments on work and business. All Americans, and perhaps especially young people, are influenced by the media in their attitudes. Here again, most TV and film writers have no direct experience with business. The result is often caricature. There is rarely, if ever, a TV program or film that presents work and business in even an objective light, let alone a favorable one. Consider business as pictured in literature, on television, and in films. The businessperson is generally portrayed as shallow, grasping, narrow, and petty, concerned only with status and position.

Thus the biased perceptions of the TV writer are exaggerated on film and are passed on. While the values tests we have seen support some of this stereotype, these same probes show older managers developing stronger religious and social values, and the chief executive having a much more balanced set of values. Yet these latter facts are almost never pictured in the media. In this way, biased perceptions have a powerful influence on all of us—especially the young and most impressionable.

Measuring Personal Values

The Allport-Vernon-Lindzey value scale is only one of several instruments for measuring personal values. Another scale for measuring those values has been developed which asks an individual to rank eighteen final and eighteen instrumental values (see Tables 4-2 and 4-3) in order of importance for her or him.[51] Among the terminal values, Americans tend to rank at the top a world at peace, family security, and freedom. At the top of the instrumental values are honest, ambitious, and responsible. The scale was administered to university business school teachers, and they tended to rank "a sense of accomplishment" significantly higher than do Americans in general. On the instrumental scale, the business educators ranked "capable" higher than did American men and women in the general population.

A third psychological investigation of the relationship between personality and career values tends to support these findings. Professional students in the fields of business, engineering, law, medicine, and theology show distinctive personality patterns when asked in a forced-choice test to rank their own personal values.[52] MBA (masters of business administration) students are significantly differentiated from other professional students in more often describing themselves as (1) able to inspire confidence and enthusiasm and willing to accept leadership responsibility; (2) feeling self-confident and adequate to cope with life's problems; and (3) being businesslike in dealings with others, avoiding personal emotional involvement, and being keenly ambitious and strongly competitive.

On the other hand, MBA students rank significantly lower than other professional students in such values as (1) a concern about others and willingness to set aside personal gain and advantage in order to help others; (2) strong involvement in working toward improvement of social conditions such as poverty,

[51]Milton Rokeach, *The Nature of Values* (New York: The Free Press, 1973). Copyrighted and quoted with permission of the Free Press. Copies of the Rokeach Value Survey can be purchased from Halgren Tests, 873 Persimmon Avenue, Sunnyvale, CA 94087.

[52]K. N. Kunert, "The Psychological Concomitants and Determinants of Vocational Choice" (unpublished doctoral dissertation, University of California, Berkeley, 1965).

Less Appreciation of esthetics

prejudice, social injustice; ③ appreciation of esthetic and cultural values as cru-
cial to development of character and personal maturity. The graduate business
student also shows that she or he is at home in new and challenging environments. Compared to other professionals, MBA students see themselves as
dynamic, competitive, mobile, pragmatic. They have strong loyalties to family
and also to the job. They see their own self-worth as being measured by what
they accomplish in the competitive marketplace, not by what they can contribute
to the welfare and happiness of those with fewer advantages. This picture of the
values of business-oriented students corroborates the value profiles presented previously. For a variety of reasons, the values and goals of business students differ
significantly from the values of other professional students—and, indeed, from
those of the population as a whole.

Yet another survey of working people found six distinct sets of working
values: conformist, manipulative, sociocentric, existential, tribalistic, and
egocentric.[53] The authors found that the first four of these value sets were most
common among contemporary managers. The conformist set described the older,
lower-level, and less well-educated manager. Managers who were highly
manipulative were found most often among the better-educated, high-income
workers in large retail organizations in the northeastern United States. Those with
high sociocentric values tended to be well-paid, well-educated presidents of
organizations who are over sixty years old. High existential values (clear goals,
able to work by oneself) were found most often among upper middle managers
with relatively short service. The findings demonstrate that value orientations of
managers vary considerably, according to job responsibility, sex, age, location,
education, type of industry, size of community, and a variety of other factors.

One paradox of this study is worth giving special attention: Presidents tend
to have sociocentric values, that is, they allow the development of friendly relationships between people. For them, "working with people toward a common
goal is more important than getting caught up in a materialistic rat race."[54] Ironically, sociocentric managers are significantly underrepresented in jobs just two levels
below the president. Therefore, the values that get a person to within sight of
the top job are not the values that will bring her or him along further. Put another
way, for those searching about the organization for potential successors to the
chief executive officer, they will find few potential candidates in some of the best
preparatory slots in the organization: two levels down from the president: plant
manager, director, and other similar positions.

The above variations underscore the need not to stereotype the values of
the businessperson. We have seen earlier the problems that develop when we
make decisions based on stereotypes: (1) The biases tend to perpetuate themselves—that is, they are self-fulfilling; (2) they tend to steer persons of differing

[53]Vincent S. Flowers and others, *Managerial Values for Working* (New York: AMACOM, 1975).
[54]Ibid., p. 2.

TABLE 4-2   Final Values

_____	A COMFORTABLE LIFE (a prosperous life)
_____	AN EXCITING LIFE (a stimulating, active life)
_____	A SENSE OF ACCOMPLISHMENT (lasting contribution)
_____	A WORLD AT PEACE (free of war and conflict)
_____	A WORLD OF BEAUTY (beauty of nature and the arts)
_____	EQUALITY (brotherhood, equal opportunity for all)
_____	FAMILY SECURITY (taking care of loved ones)
_____	FREEDOM (independence, free choice)
_____	HAPPINESS (contentedness)
_____	INNER HARMONY (freedom from inner conflict)
_____	MATURE LOVE (sexual and spiritual intimacy)
_____	NATIONAL SECURITY (protection from attack)
_____	PLEASURE (an enjoyable, leisurely life)
_____	SALVATION (saved, eternal life)
_____	SELF-RESPECT (self-esteem)
_____	SOCIAL RECOGNITION (respect, admiration)
_____	TRUE FRIENDSHIP (close companionship)
_____	WISDOM (a mature understanding of life)

Source: Milton Rokeach, _The Nature of Values_ (New York: Free Press, 1973), p. 145. Adapted with permission of Macmillan, Inc. Copyright© 1973 by The Free Press, a division of Macmillan Publishing Co., Inc.

values away from business as a career; and (3) they often present an erroneous description of businesspeople. Hence, it is important not to fall into the stereotype trap. It is even more important for each individual, whether business-oriented or not, to examine his or her own personal values.

Examining One's Own Values

Planning for a career and for life itself can be much more solidly based if an individual is able to clarify and articulate her or his own goals and values. Milton Rokeach's two value scales can aid in this examination. Each person is asked to arrange the values "in order of their importance to YOU, as guiding principles in YOUR life." The values are then ranked from 1 to 18, the most highly valued to the least important. The two scales are given in Tables 4-2 and 4-3.[55]

A more pointed aid for individuals attempting to formulate their own personal goals has been developed in an experiential, organizational psychology context.[56] The authors suggest that each individual write out his or her major goals according to six categories: career satisfaction, status and respect, personal relationships, leisure satisfactions, learning and education, and spiritual growth. Then,

[55]Rokeach, _Nature of Values._

[56]David A. Kolb, Irwin M. Rubin, and James M. McIntyre, _Organizational Psychology: An Experiential Approach_ (Englewood Cliffs, N.J.: Prentice-Hall, 1971), pp. 273-93. See also Sidney B. Simon and others, _Values Clarification_ (New York: Hart, 1972).

TABLE 4-3   Instrumental Values

_____	AMBITIOUS (hardworking, aspiring)
_____	BROADMINDED (open-minded)
_____	CAPABLE (competent, effective)
_____	CHEERFUL (lighthearted, joyful)
_____	CLEAN (neat, tidy)
_____	COURAGEOUS (standing up for your beliefs)
_____	FORGIVING (willing to pardon others)
_____	HELPFUL (working for the welfare of others)
_____	HONEST (sincere, truthful)
_____	IMAGINATIVE (daring, creative)
_____	INDEPENDENT (self-reliant, self-sufficient)
_____	INTELLECTUAL (intelligent, reflective)
_____	LOGICAL (consistent, rational)
_____	LOVING (affectionate, tender)
_____	OBEDIENT (dutiful, respectful)
_____	POLITE (courteous, well-mannered)
_____	RESPONSIBLE (dependable, reliable)
_____	SELF-CONTROLLED (restrained, self-disciplined)

Source: Milton Rokeach, _The Nature of Values_ (New York: Free Press, 1973), p. 146.
Adapted with permission of Macmillan, Inc. Copyright© 1973 by The Free Press, a division of
Macmillan Publishing Co., Inc.

with regard to each individual goal, the individual determines (1) the relative importance of the goal, compared to other goals; (2) how easy it would be to achieve
the goal, compared to other goals; and (3) whether pursuing this goal involves
a conflict with other goals. When finished, the individual has a much clearer picture of what her or his own major goals are, how important they are, their ease
of attainment, and whether conflicts will likely arise in their pursuit.

Readers might rank their goals on the two 18-item scales and also state their
major goals according to the six categories, and then compare the two lists. Do
the values support the major goals, or do they conflict? Are some personal values
in conflict with career goals? How does my present work compare with my values
and goals? Does this explain any satisfaction or dissatisfaction with my present
job? What implications does this examination have for my future career and life
plans? These questions have been raised and answered by graduate business
students in brief papers in the author's classes. A vast majority indicated that the
exercise was a great aid to them in clarifying their own values and goals.

Helping Behavior and Life Values

It is not merely businesspeople and business students who hold social values
in relatively low esteem; their attitudes reflect the values of much of American
culture. As laboratory experiments have shown, individuals in American culture
are heavily influenced by the values and activities of others. Norms of right and
wrong are inculcated by family, neighborhood, and environment in every culture, but the attitudes of bystanders in the immediate vicinity also have an un-

duly large influence on Americans. Several laboratory experiments were prompted by the murder of a young woman in New York City. She was stabbed to death in full view of many apartment dwellers. Later investigation showed that at least thirty-eight people saw or heard the attack, but not one tried to help; no one even phoned the police. This story shocked the country, and some researchers decided to try to determine what elements influence helping behavior.

In one experiment, several individuals were placed in adjoining rooms connected by an intercom phone.[57] The subjects were led to believe that there were one, two, or five other persons present in successive experiments. In reality, the subject was the only person involved. During a discussion on a topic of current interest over the intercom, one "participant" suffered what seemed to be an epileptic seizure; that person choked, stuttered, and called out for help. The greater the number of persons the subject thought were present, the less likely he would be to help, and he would be slower to help. Apparently, the subject would think he could leave it to others. If he thought he was the only person present, the more likely he was to feel the responsibility and respond to the need.

Similar results were obtained when individuals were placed in a room and asked to fill out a questionnaire. Subjects were alone in the room, with two other subjects, or with two confederates who were instructed to remain impassive. After a few minutes, smoke began to pour into the room through a small wall vent. Results of this experiment again showed that the greater the number of individuals present, the lower the frequency of prosocial behavior. When the subject was with two passive confederates, she reported the apparent fire only 10 percent of the time.

These experimental studies show that individuals will act in a more socially responsible way when they feel the responsibility directly. When another unknown person is present, they are not as apt to stick their necks out. Nevertheless, these and other studies show that people *will* help others, even if they don't expect anything in return. Furthermore, subjects will tend to respond more quickly and in a more responsible fashion if they have been successful in similar earlier efforts, and also if they have been the recipients of help themselves in the past.

Before concluding, it is important to note some recent findings on the values of Americans. Periodic surveys of values over the last few decades by the University of Michigan's Institute of Social Research show significant new values emerging.[58] As people achieve a degree of economic security, their attention and values turn toward nonmaterial needs: the need for challenging and significant work, for the respect and approval of friends, for identification with the community, and for a stimulating and fulfilling life. That this shift is especially true of the young, well-educated, and affluent has special significance for business values. These

[57]Robert A. Baron and Robert A. Liebart, *Human Social Behavior* (Homewood, Ill.: Dorsey, 1971), especially p. 492.

[58]Angus Campbell, *Sense of Well-Being in America: Recent Patterns and Trends* (New York: McGraw-Hill, 1981).

personal needs are being carried into the working place. Moreover, as these people become managers themselves, they will undoubtedly seek to reshape the work environment so that it can satisfy these needs. This will be essential if the organization is to attract the young, educated, and talented people it needs.

A more focused survey of the values of American managers was done by the American Management Association. Consistent with earlier surveys, Warren Schmidt and Barry Posner found that American managers continue to be pragmatic—very concerned with efficiency and productivity. Interestingly, female managers seem to emphasize these values even more than do male managers. Furthermore female managers are more career oriented than their male counterparts: 60 percent of women managers say that they get more satisfaction out of their career than their home life, whereas only 37 percent of male managers feel this way.[59] Also important for our purposes, 61 percent of all managers responded that an improvement in the quality of life in the United States will come by means of a return to basic values—emphasizing individual initiative and responsibility. To improve the quality of life, these managers judged that a return to basic values was more important than technological advances (7 percent chose this), political leadership (12 percent) or a new cooperative value system (19 percent).[60] The changing values of managers and organizations of the future will be discussed in greater detail in Chapter 7.

SUMMARY AND CONCLUSIONS

Our values are heavily influenced by business and the corporation. During the working day our supervisors' expectations and socialization influence our behavior. In the evening, the corporation, its products, and its values are sold to us through television's advertisements and programming.

Successful businesspeople generally are ambitious, achievement- and power-oriented, disciplined, and adaptable. Younger managers are intent on being "winners," even at the expense of not having empathy for others. The business manager ingests many of these values when he or she joins the firm. The prevailing values of competition, the free market, and opposition to government intervention are imbibed early. Hence managers' goals are largely determined for them: success *within* the firm. Moreover, when they are in policymaking positions their goal becomes success *for* the firm. Just as the rules of the game were set by some-

---

[59]Warren H. Schmidt and Barry Z. Posner, *Managerial Values and Expectations: The Silent Power In Personal and Organizational Life* (New York: American Management Association, 1982), pp. 52-53.

[60]Ibid., pp. 28-29. For a more comprehensive assessment of the effect of managerial values on corporate policy and strategies, see Dalton E. McFarland, *Management and Society* (Englewood Cliffs, N.J.: Prentice-Hall, 1982).

one else early in life, so too the economic rules of the game come from outside and are accepted. Perhaps largely because of this uncritical early acceptance, we find many mid-career identity crises. Individual managers no longer find themselves able to make someone else's or the system's goals their own. They begin to probe their own personal values and goals. This can be an opportunity for deeper personal convictions, or it can be a time of panic and irresponsibility. Reflection on one's own values and goals, sensitivity to others, and prayer can lessen the trauma of this transition.

Potential conflicts that pit the good of the firm against the good of the individual or the larger society are often resolved by the free market ideology. That ideology says that the more successful the firm is (as measured in dollar terms), the better off individuals and the larger society will be. It says further that pollution and decaying cities are a small price to pay for real increases in personal income and gross national product. These are the basic, unarguable criteria of a healthy, successful society. Moreover, dissent within the organization is not encouraged.

The emphasis on success and winning has an additional price. It can bring on stress and serious physical ailments. Particularly prone to heart attacks, ulcers, and other illnesses are the 60 percent of managers who are Type A: impatient, aggressive, restless, and pressured. Their ambition, task orientation, and quick action allow them to move up rapidly in the organization. Yet these same qualities are ultimately a barrier to getting to the top. Top management is generally patient, has the ability to listen and weigh alternatives, and to work with and through other people.

Evidence is accumulating that, despite occasional setbacks, people's goals are changing. Individuals are looking for more than salary and status as goals. They want challenging work, the respect and approval of their friends, ability to identify with their community, and a stimulating and fulfilling life. The business firm may be able to provide much of this, if its senior executives utilize some wisdom as they engage in careful corporate planning.

DISCUSSION QUESTIONS

1. Since Americans often claim to be "value-free," what is the benefit in inquiring about values?

2. Is it acceptable for a firm to attempt to socialize its members? How does it do so? Are there any problems with such socialization?

3. Outline the pros and cons of making salary and status goals. Do Americans "sell themselves"? Are you concerned with making yourself "more marketable"?

4. Do business managers tend to be more interested in people, power, or tasks? Are executives more conformist or innovative? What do the Solomon Asch experiments on the influence of the group tell us?

5. What characterizes the upbringing of men with a high need for achievement? What in a culture encourages a high need for achievement? Are those elements present in contemporary U.S. culture?

6. What are the symptoms of the mid-life identity crisis? How can the effects of the mid-life transition be moderated?

7. What causes anxieties and stress? What physical ailments do these anxieties lead to? What do the experiments with rats and cats tell us? What role does alcohol play?

8. Business executives tend to have less social concern than others. What processes tend to perpetuate this?

9. What is the effect of authority on any other person's willingness to inflict pain or even danger of death? Describe the experiments on this subject. Do parallel situations occur in an organization? How so?

10. Under what circumstances is an individual more likely to come to the aid of another person? Describe the results of these experiments.

CHAPTER FIVE
ETHICS IN BUSINESS

[handwritten annotations:]
economic & political
People willing to sacrifice freedom for stability

Freedom is expendable, stability is indispensable. — *Analog ist of when*
—Arnold Toynbee *mers. face*

i.e. curfew in crisis
freedom is new idea to human history
free to accumulate & hold assets
rep. form of gov't. / Bill of personal/political rights
gov. enters economic. free. / 1st ten amendments basic

No human institution can long exist without some consensus on what is right and what is wrong. Managers recognize the need for ethical norms in their daily dealings. Decisions made at every level of the firm are influenced by ethics, whether these be decisions which affect quality of work, employment opportunity, safety of worker or product, truth in advertising, use of toxic materials, or operations in third world countries. An increasing sense of the importance of ethical norms among executives is demonstrated by the facts that

1. Almost three-quarters of U.S. firms now have a code of ethics.[1]
2. More than 100 boards of directors of large firms have established an ethics, social responsibility, or public policy committee of the board.[2]

The material in this chapter owes much to several years of work with Manuel Velasquez, S.J., and Dennis Moberg of the University of Santa Clara, Santa Clara, California.

[1]According to a survey by Opinion Research Corporation, 73 percent of the larger corporations in the United States now have a written code of ethics. See *Chronicle of Higher Education*, August 6, 1979, p. 2.

[2]"Business Strategies for the 1980's," in *Business and Society: Strategies for the 1980's* (Washington, D.C.: U.S. Department of Commerce, 1980), pp. 33-34.

3. Speeches of chief executive officers and annual reports more often allude to the importance of ethics in business decisions.[3]

Managers understand that without ethics the only restraint is the law. Without ethics, any business transaction that was not witnessed and recorded could not be trusted. If government regulation and legislation are perceived to be unneeded and burdensome, then each manager must possess a set of internalized and operative ethical criteria for decision making. Or, as some have put it: "Shall we be honest and free, or dishonest and policed?"

NEED FOR ETHICS
IN BUSINESS

great esp. now.
E F Hutton – hold money float
collect interest
Gen Dyna. overchay navy
defense contract
Fortune 500

A significant minority of large American firms have been involved not only in unethical activities but also in illegal activities. During the 1970s, 11 percent of the largest U.S. firms were convicted of bribery, criminal fraud, illegal campaign contributions, tax evasion, or some sort of price fixing. Firms with two or more convictions include Allied, American Airlines, Bethlehem Steel, Diamond International, Firestone, Goodyear, International Paper, J. Ray McDermott, National Distillers, Northrop, Occidental Petroleum, Pepsico, Phillips Petroleum, Rapid-American, R. J. Reynolds, Schlitz, Seagram, Tenneco, and United Brands. Those that lead the list with at least four convictions each are Braniff International, Gulf Oil, and Ashland Oil.[4] Perhaps Gulf and Ashland will suffer the same punishment meted out to Braniff!

Most of the major petroleum firms illegally contributed to Richard Nixon's reelection committee in the mid-1970s: Gulf, Getty, Standard of California, Phillips, Sun, Exxon, and Ashland. The chairman of Phillips personally handed Richard Nixon $50,000 in Nixon's own apartment. Many firms were also involved in multimillion-dollar foreign payments: Exxon, Lockheed, Gulf, Phillips, McDonnell Douglas, United Brands, and Mobil.[5] The presidents of Gulf, American Airlines, and Lockheed lost their jobs because of the unethical payments. Other presi-

[3]For example, Reginald Jones of General Electric, who was selected by his fellow CEOs as the best CEO, has often made a strong case for ethics. See, for example, Reginald Jones, "Managing in the 1980's," address at Wharton School, February 4, 1980, p. 5. See also Richard J. Bennett, chairman of Schering-Plough, "A New Compact in the Age of Limits," address at Fordham University, November 5, 1981.

[4]Irwin Ross, "How Lawless Are Big Companies?" *Fortune*, December 1, 1980, pp. 56–64. See also Robert K. Elliott and John J. Willingham, *Management Fraud: Detection and Deterrence* (New York: Petrocelli Books, 1980).

[5]Marshall B. Clinard and Peter C. Yeager, *Corporate Crime* (New York: Free Press, 1980); and "Drive to Curb Kickbacks and Bribes by Business," *U.S. News & World Report*, September 4, 1978, pp. 41–44.

dents just as guilty—Northrop, Phillips, and Exxon—were excused by their boards. Firms based in the United States are, of course, not alone in engaging in unethical behavior. Sixteen executives of two large Japanese electronics firms, Hitachi and Mitsubishi, were indicted for stealing trade secrets from IBM.[6]

bad for business in long run — Reputation

Corporate Pressure and Fraud

Embezzlement, fraud, and political backbiting are most often due to personal greed. Bribery, price fixing, and compromising product and worker safety generally stem from the pressure for bottom line results. In a study of managers at several firms, 59 to 70 percent "feel pressured to compromise personal ethics to achieve corporate goals."[7] This perception increases among lower level managers. A majority felt that most managers would not refuse to market off-standard and possibly dangerous products. On the more encouraging side, 90 percent supported a code of ethics for business and the teaching of ethics in business schools.

This pressure and organizational climate can influence the ethical judgments of individual managers. What the manager finds unethical in another setting or before taking this job is more readily considered acceptable behavior once the job is taken. Two recent research studies question whether American executives have a sufficient sensitivity to ethical issues, and whether their work environment works against such a sensitivity. Public affairs officers in firms have the direct responsibility for dealing with a wide variety of stakeholders: customers, suppliers, local community, and shareholders. These officers are a principal conduit through which the firm is informed of new social concerns. Evidence shows that even though these public affairs officers spend more time with these various stakeholders, they tend to be poor listeners. In fact, according to this study, the more contact company officers have with external publics, the less sensitive they become to their concerns.[8]

Another study was in an ethically sensitive area: corporate political activities. It was found that the more involvement a company officer had in these activities, the less likely he or she would be alert to ethical issues. The more involved the manager was, the more dulled became her or his conscience. There are many ethically debatable areas with regard to a firm's political activities, and this evidence shows that those who are most involved in these activities are precisely those who are less sensitive to the moral and ethical issues involved. The more involved manager is more likely to declare a debatable activity to be ethi-

---

[6]"IBM Data Plot Tied to Hitachi and Mitsubishi," *Wall Street Journal*, June 23, 1982, p. 4.

[7]Archie Carroll, "Managerial Ethics: A Post-Watergate View," *Business Horizons*, April 1975, pp. 75–80; and "The Pressure to Compromise Personal Ethics," *Business Week*, January 31, 1977, p. 107. See also "Some Middle Managers Cut Corners to Achieve High Corporate Goals," *Wall Street Journal*, November 8, 1979, pp. 1, 19.

[8]Jeffery Sonnenfeld, "Executive Differences in Public Affairs Information Gathering," *Academy of Management Proceedings*, 1981, ed. Kae H. Chung, p. 353.

cally acceptable and is also more likely to declare as gray an activity that fellow managers would declare ethically unacceptable.[9]

Laboratory research has shown that unethical behavior tends to rise as the climate becomes more competitive, and it increases even more if such behavior is rewarded. However, a threat of punishment tends to deter unethical behavior. Whether a person acts ethically or unethically is also very strongly influenced by the individual's personal ethical values and by informal organizational policy.[10]

These instances of unethical behavior of managers point to the need for (1) a sensitive and informed conscience, (2) the ability to make ethical judgments, and (3) a corporate climate that rewards ethical behavior and punishes unethical behavior. Technical education does not bring with it better ethics, as we have seen, for example in Nazi Germany. In fact, as society becomes more technical, complex, and interdependent, the need for ethics increases dramatically. When encounters are person to person, there exists the built-in sanction of having to live with the people one has lied to. In the large, complex organization, or when one deals with people over the telephone or via a computer, ethical sensitivities and decision-making abilities are far more important.

more tech a society need more ethics

Enlightened Self-Interest and Ethics

Some advocates of free enterprise argue that if managers pursued enlightened self-interest, this would bring about greater honesty. The long-term reputation of the firm and of its products demands better ethics. This argument will be discussed in greater detail in the next chapter, but for now let us acknowledge that it will take the manager a long way in the direction of being more ethical.

There is strength in such a simple and straightforward position. However, there are also serious problems with this view: "Enlightened" is an elastic term, and does not mean the same thing for everyone. Also, even with the best possible understanding of "enlightened," self-interest can easily slip into selfishness. Our normal human selfish personal interests (original sin, if you will) pull us in this direction, and this view is often encouraged by a free enterprise, self-interest ideology and by many conservative groups.

Hence the necessity of altruism: looking also to the benefits and harm that accrue precisely to others, plus the willingness to sacrifice some personal benefits for the sake of others. Thus some altruism will provide a floor, a buttress, and a personal disposition. In many instances enlightened self-interest is a shortcut as a method of solution; but as with all shortcuts, it cannot handle all cases and it is easily lost. In addition, in espousing the enlightened self-interest ideology,

[9]Steven N. Brenner, "Corporate Political Actions and Attitudes," *Academy of Management Proceedings*, 1981, pp. 361-2.

[10] W. Harvey Hegarty and Henry P. Sims, Jr., "Unethical Decision Behavior: An Overview of Three Experiments," *Academy of Management Proceedings*, 1979, p. 9.

Altruism [handwritten]

one feels compelled to justify every move a manager makes by pointing out how it will increase the profitability of the firm. Perhaps the justification is important for many shareholders. But it freezes one into a certain mind set, and such a doctrinaire position makes ethics difficult or impossible. Instances will arise when treatment of others, perhaps outside the firm, will be at a net cost to me or my firm. Thus most popular forms of free enterprise ideology do not permit consideration of others for their own sakes, and are so close to falling over the cliff into amorality or immorality that they are a precarious perch at best. Moreover, many do fall, as we have already seen.

When considering the ethics of a situation, each person takes a basic stance toward other people. There are five possible ways one can consider oneself in regard to others:

1. Self alone   *Rude-egoist New Yorkers* [handwritten]
2. Self first   *Sophist-* [handwritten]
3. Self equally with others   *Reasonable see others as equal* [handwritten]
4. Others first   *Parents mostly - put kids 1st* [handwritten]
5. Others alone   *Saints remarkable so few exist* [handwritten]

A person choosing option 1 is an egoist, and 2 is more enlightened in one's self-interest. An equitable consideration of others, as in the golden rule ("Do unto others as you would have them do unto you.") begins with 3. Numbers 4 and 5 are generous forms of altruism. A good mother takes at least option 4 in her attitude toward her child. Option 5 describes a selfless, generous, saintly sort of person (for example, Mother Theresa of Calcutta). It is hard to find many of these folks in any era.

Taste, Bias, and Culture   *Nowadays difficult to develop mores* [handwritten]

Even though managers recognize the importance of ethics, in the popular mind ethics is hard to distinguish from taste, bias, or particular cultural background. Difficult ethical dilemmas are resolved arbitrarily, for there seem to be no objective values or criteria that can be used to help judge the issues. Moreover, experts in ethics often differ among themselves, thus encouraging the popular notion that ethics is not an objective discipline and no common norms can be derived.

The need for some ethical criteria that can be useful to managers is almost universally recognized; yet it is also quite clear that developing these criteria is no easy task. We are faced with different value systems, varying perceptions of facts, and different judgments on tradeoffs. Moreover, even if we can develop adequate ethical decision-making criteria, this will not automatically make decision making easy. Ethical issues are not as easily supported by measurable data as are financial (return on investment) or marketing (share of market) questions. Nevertheless, a developed sensitivity and an understanding of ethical principles can provide a basis for correct ethical judgments and better insurance against a

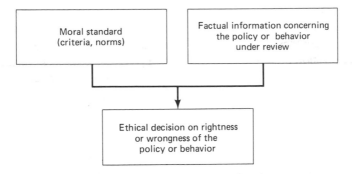

FIGURE 5-1 Elements of ethical decision making

serious ethical blunder (ITT's attempt to overthrow the government in Chile, Lockheed's bribery of foreign officials); and will generally enable a firm to be a better producer, employer, and citizen and thus a more trusted and valued member of society.

From the above we can conclude:

1. Some sense of what is right and wrong, plus some ethical criteria for making judgments, are essential to any sort of human society and thus also to business operations.
2. However, these ethical norms and criteria are not easily derived, and even when arrived at, there will be disagreements on the facts of the case, the relevant criteria, and the various tradeoffs.

Thus both the importance of the task is recognized, as well as the difficulty of accomplishing it. The process of ethical decision making is presented schematically in Figure 5-1.[11]

Young People and Morals   *Immoral Acts are Rampant*

Some believe that young people instinctively act ethically, and so there is less need for a formal study of their ethical norms. Facts, however, suggest otherwise. A large-scale study of 3,180 young people in Illinois over a six-year period revealed some startling facts. One-third of all fourteen- to eighteen-year-olds had been involved in a serious crime. Thirteen percent admitted taking part in a robbery, 40 percent acknowledged keeping stolen goods, and 50 percent admitted shoplifting. Moreover, many of the conventional "predictors" for criminal behavior did not hold true. Except for the most violent behavior, the delinquent was just as likely to be a girl as a boy, to be white as black, to come from a small town

Some blame goes on older generation

[11]The flow chart is adapted from Manuel G. Velasquez, *Business Ethics: Concepts and Cases* (Englewood Cliffs, N.J.: Prentice-Hall, 1982); the five personal ethical options are adapted from Garth Hallett, *Reason and Right* (South Bend: Notre Dame Press, 1984). On the influence of culture on ethics, see William C. Frederick, "Embedded Values: Prelude to Ethical Analysis," University of Pittsburgh Working Paper, WP-446, 1982.

as an inner city, to come from an intact home as a broken home. The influence of the peer group was found to be the most important influence on young people, with parents less influential. In fact, in 80 percent of the cases, parents did not know about the offenses their children had committed. One research team member spent two years with youths in a wealthy Chicago suburb and reported a "near vacuum of morality enclosed by the perimeter of the edict to achieve. . . . Anything that jeopardizes their occupational future is bad. The rest really doesn't matter." To repeat: The juvenile delinquent is just as likely to come from an intact, suburban, middle-class family as from a poor, broken, inner-city home.[12]

There is considerable unethical behavior in colleges and universities, also. A study that examined ethics on campuses found a significant and apparently increasing amount of cheating by students in academic assignments; a substantial misuse by students of public financial aid; theft and destruction of valuable property by students, most specifically library books and journals; inflation of grades by faculty members; competitive awarding of academic credits by some departments and some institutions for insufficient and inadequate work; and inflated and misleading advertising by some institutions in search of students.[13]

In sum, the need for ethics in business is clear. The daily news stories of unethical and illegal activities remind us of the need for accepted norms. Most business executives and managers are ethical—probably 80 or 90 percent. However, many of these same businesspeople cannot intelligently discuss ethical problems and hence cannot defend their instinctive judgment. American managers do not know the terminology, the concepts, or the models for approaching ethical questions. This chapter will provide some of these concepts and models. The next section will examine how moral development takes place; thus each of us will be able to find ourselves at a particular stage of moral development. The section following will introduce some of the classical ethical criteria: rights, justice, and utilitarianism.

MORAL DEVELOPMENT OF
THE PERSON

Moral development is the increased ability of a person to distinguish between right and wrong. A person's ability to make moral judgments and to engage in moral behavior increases with maturity. An infant is naturally self-centered and is interested in its own survival. As that child grows more mature, she begins to take other peoples' needs into her calculations in making moral judgments and acting.

Moral development has been observed by scholars for centuries, and they

---

[12]"Kid Crime: Host of Juveniles Admit Serious Acts," *Detroit Free Press*, January 24, 1977, pp. 1, 2. See also "Why Are They Cheating?" *Wall Street Journal*, June 10, 1980, p. 20.

[13]"Ethical Conduct Needs Improving," *Higher Education in National Affairs*, April 20, 1979, p. 1.

worked w/ kids

have classified the stages of development in various ways. John Dewey and earlier philosophers noted the fact of development and proposed theories to explain it.[14] Child psychologist Jean Piaget was the first to obtain data from observation and interview, but he limited his observations to children.[15] During the last twenty-five years the psychologist Lawrence Kohlberg has expanded Piaget's observations and model to span the lifetime of moral development.[16] Table 5-1 compares Kohlberg's stages of moral development with those of other researchers.

Kohlberg organizes moral development into three levels, each of which in turn contains two successive stages of development. Let us now examine these stages of moral development.[17]

Kohlberg worked 25 yrs to develop moral model

Definition of Stages of Moral Development

how age affects moral development

Level I: Preconventional   At this level a child is able to respond to rules and social expectations and can apply the labels "good," "bad," "right," "wrong." The child sees these rules, however, as something imposed from outside and largely in terms of the pleasant or painful consequences of actions or the power of those who set the rules. The child views situations from his or own point of view. The child does not yet have the ability to identify with others, so its point of view is largely one of self-interest. *good & bad no meaning or understanding why*

Stage 1: Punishment and Obedience Orientation   The child does the right thing to avoid punishment or to obtain approval. There is little awareness of the needs of others. The physical consequences of an act determine its goodness and badness, regardless of the wider impact of consequences. *to teach good behavior teach that bad behavior not rewarding*

Stage 2: Naively Egoistic and Instrumental Orientation   The child is now aware that others also have needs and begins to defer to them in order to obtain what he or she wants. Right actions are those which satisfy one's own interests. Right is what is fair, an equal exchange, a deal. Human relations are viewed as like those of the marketplace. *not center of universe*

learn manners please & thankyou - do whats necessary to receive

Level II: Conventional   Maintaining the expectations of one's family, peer group, or nation is viewed as valuable in its own right, regardless of the consequences. The person does not merely conform to expectations but is loyal to those groups and tries hard to maintain and justify that order. The person is now able

learned & maintain peer group norms who ever they identify with

[14]John Dewey, "What Psychology Can Do for the Teacher," in *John Dewey on Education: Selected Writings*, ed. Reginald Archambault (New York: Random House, 1964).

[15]Jean Piaget, *The Moral Judgment of the Child* (Glencoe, Ill.: Free Press, 1948).

[16]Lawrence Kohlberg, "The Cognitive-Developmental Approach to Moral Education," in *Readings in Moral Education*, ed. Peter Scharf (Minneapolis: Winston Press, 1978), pp. 36-51.

[17]Based on Kohlberg's description of the stages.

TABLE 5-1 Moral Development and Ethical Theory: An Overview

STAGES OF MORAL DEVELOPMENT[a]			ETHICAL THEORY CORRESPONDING TO STAGES OF MORAL DEVELOPMENT[b]
JEAN PIAGET	JOHN DEWEY	LAWRENCE KOHLBERG	EDWARD STEVENS
0. Premoral		0. Premoral	Group A
1. Heteronomous (age 4–8)	I. Preconventional	I. Preconventional	1. Social Darwinism
		1. Punishment and obedience orientation	2. Machiavellianism
2. Autonomous (age 8–12)		2. Naively egoistic and instrumentalist orientation	3. Objectivism (Ayn Rand)
	II. Conventional	II. Conventional	Group B
		3. Interpersonal concordance: "good boy—nice girl" orientation	4. Conventional morality
		4. Law and order orientation	5. Legalistic ethics
	III. Autonomous	III. Postconventional, autonomous, principled	6. Accountability model of ethics
		5. Social contrast orientation	Group C
		6. Conscience and principle orientation	7. Pragmatism
			8. Marxism
			9. "Economic humanism"

[a]Adapted from Lawrence Kohlberg, "The Cognitive-Development Approach to Moral Education," in *Readings in Moral Education*, ed. Peter Scharf (New York: Winston Press, 1978), pp. 36–37.
[b]Adapted from rough congruence presented by Edward Stevens, *Business Ethics* (New York: Paulist Press, 1979).

to identify with another's point of view, and assumes that everyone is similar in point of view. The person conforms to the group's norms and subordinates the needs of the individual to those of the group.

Stage 3: Interpersonal Concordance: "Good Boy—Nice Girl" Orienta-tion   Good behavior is that which pleases or helps close family or friends and is approved by them. Right action is conformity to what is expected; it uses stereo-types of what is majority or "natural" behavior. Behavior is frequently judged by intention: "He means well." One earns approval by being a "good boy" or a "nice girl."

Stage 4: Law and Order Orientation   Right behavior consists in doing one's duty, showing respect for authority, and maintaining the social order for its own sake. Loyalty to the nation and its laws is paramount. The person now sees other people as individuals, yet part of the larger social system which gives them their roles and obligations. This stage grows out of experiencing the inadequacy of Stage 3.

Level III. Postconventional, Autonomous, or Principled   The person no longer simply accepts the values and norms of the groups to which he or she belongs. There is a clear effort to find moral values and principles that impartially take everyone's interests into account. The person questions the norms and laws that society has adopted and redefines them so that they make sense to any ra-tional individual. Proper laws and values are those to which any reasonable per-son would commit herself, whatever status she holds in society or whatever society she belongs to.

U.S. Constitution

Stage 5: Social Contract Orientation   The individual is aware that people hold a variety of conflicting personal views, but even relative rules must be up-held in the interests of the social contract. Laws are agreed upon, and must be followed impartially, although they can be changed if need be. Some absolute values are held regardless of differing individual values and even majority opin-ion, such as life and liberty. Utilitarianism, "the greatest good for the greatest number," is the characteristic ethical norm. This stage is the "official" morality of the U.S. government and the Constitution.

Stage 6: Conscience and Principle Orientation   Right action is defined by a decision of conscience in accord with universal ethical principles which are self-chosen because of their comprehensiveness, universality, and consistency. These ethical principles are not specific, concrete moral codes like the Ten Command-ments, but are universal moral principles dealing with justice, public welfare, the equality of human rights, respect for the dignity of individual human beings, and the belief that persons are ends in themselves and should not be used as means. The person's motivation for doing right is a belief in the validity of universal moral principles and a personal commitment to them.

Logic and Climbing the Stages

Kohlberg has found that these stages follow an invariable sequence. Individuals do not move on to a higher stage until they have passed through each of the lower stages. However, not all people get to the higher stages; some remain stuck at a lower stage for their entire lives. Kohlberg finds that most Americans never do reach the later stages, but remain at stage 3 or 4.[18] For example, Kohlberg finds that Richard Nixon as president never got beyond moral stage 3 or 4. He never really understood the U.S. Constitution, which is a document built upon stage 5 thinking.

To the idea that schools should be value-free and not concerned with moral development, Kohlberg responds that this is nonsense. All teaching, and hence schools, communicate values. The only relevant point is: What are the values that are being communicated? Choosing to be value-free is a value system in itself that is propagated. In recent years, numerous groups, including public school systems, have asked Kohlberg to develop a scheme for encouraging moral development. He has done so, in Pittsburgh and in Cambridge, Massachusetts, and with some success.

Kohlberg also found that moral judgment is the single most important factor in moral behavior. It is impossible to move up the stages without the ability to confront various options and to make intelligent and informed judgments as to the rightness and wrongness of each. Moral judgment in turn depends upon moral reasoning, and this in turn demands the ability to reason logically. Thus Kohlberg points out how a person's ability to reason logically sets a limit to the moral stage that can be achieved. If persons are unable to reason logically, they will be restricted to a lower stage of moral behavior. On the other hand, people's logical reasoning is most often more advanced than their moral reasoning, so for most, reasoning does not pose a constraint.

Kohlberg's theories have been challenged in a variety of ways,[19] but even the challengers agree that moral development takes place in something of the fashion he describes. Moreover, no other individual has studied moral development in as much detail and has proposed as useful a theory as has Kohlberg. Thus, at present, Kohlberg has the most accurate and useful general theory of moral development.

An innovative book on business ethics uses Kohlberg's levels of moral development as an outline. Edward Stevens proposes that many popular ethical theories stem from one of Kohlberg's levels.[20] For example, Stevens finds that

---

[18]Kohlberg, "Cognitive-Developmental Approach," p. 38.

[19]See, for example, some of the points made in Thomas Lickona, ed., *Moral Development and Behavior: Theory, Research and Social Issues* (New York: Holt, Rinehart & Winston, 1976); Howard Muson, "Moral Thinking: Can It Be Taught?" *Psychology Today*, February 1979, pp. 48-68, 92; and Thomas Lickona, "What Does Moral Psychology Have to Say to the Teacher of Ethics?" in *Ethics Teaching in Higher Education*, ed. Daniel Callahan and Sissela Bok (New York: Plenum Press, 1980) pp. 103-32.

[20]Edward Stevens, *Business Ethics* (New York: Paulist Press, 1979).

both social Darwinism (see Chapter 1) and Ayn Rand's objectivism flow from a primitive, preconventional view of moral development (see Table 5-1).

Let us now move on in an attempt to sharpen our abilities to do moral reasoning.

ETHICAL MODELS FOR BUSINESS DECISIONS

The previous section chronicles the developing moral maturity of the individual: sensitivity to moral issues, breadth of vision, willingness to take into consideration the needs of others, along with one's own needs in making moral judgments. Now we examine ethics. Ethics is a system of moral principles and the methods for applying them; ethics thus provides the tools to make moral judgments. It encompasses the language, concepts, and models that enable an individual to effect moral decisions.

Mature ethical judgments are not always easy to make. The facts of the case are not always clear-cut; the ethical criteria or principles to be used are not always agreed upon even by the experts themselves. Hence, ethics seems to most businesspeople, indeed to most Americans, to be subjective, amorphous, and ill-defined and thus not very useful. Just as with politics and religion, there is often more heat than light in discussion. This lack of confidence in ethics is unfortunate, since without some commonly agreed-upon ethical principles, it is everyone for him- or herself, and trust, which is basic to all business dealings, is undermined.

Dilemmas to Decisions

Let us begin our examination of ethical decision making by assessing a case that was first judged by 1,700 business executive readers of *Harvard Business Review*. This case was a portion of a classical large-scale study of business ethics by Raymond C. Baumhart, S.J.:[21]

> An executive earning $30,000 a year has been padding his/her expense account by about $1,500 a year.

First some background: An expense account is available for legitimate expenses that are incurred in the course of one's work. If the employee has to use personal funds, without reimbursement, that person might cut back on important business trips or not order vital equipment. Moreover, it is not fair to ask a person to personally pay the bills for what are legitimate business expenses.

---

[21]Raymond C. Baumhart, S.J., *Ethics in Business* (New York: Holt, Rinehart & Winston, 1968), p. 21. For an updating of Baumhart's findings, see Steven Brenner and Earl Molander, "Is the Ethics of Business Changing?" *Harvard Business Review*, 55 (January-February 1977), 57-71.

To return to the case, how ethical is it to pad one's expense account? On numerous occasions over the years hundreds of other managers have been asked to judge the case, and the results have been substantially the same. Speaking for themselves, 85 percent of these executives think that this sort of behavior is simply unacceptable. Perhaps more important, almost two-thirds of the group think that their business colleagues would also see such behavior as unacceptable under any circumstances.

Why would padding an expense account be considered wrong by these executives? The expense account is not a simple addition to one's salary. It is designed to cover the actual expenses that are incurred by employees in the course of doing their work.

Pocketing a company pencil or making a personal long-distance phone call from the office may seem relatively trivial. Perhaps. However, fabricating expenses up to 5 percent of one's salary is not trivial; it is a substantial violation of justice. The executive is taking more compensation than he is entitled to. Presumably the executive's salary is ample enough compensation for his work, and the extra $1,500 is not intended as direct compensation nor is it recognized by law as such.

Circumstances are often cited that might seem to mitigate the injustice. Some would say, "Many others are also doing it," or "My superior knows about it and says nothing." In the cited study, only about a quarter of the executives thought that their peers would justify such actions on these counts. A mere handful (about 10 percent) said that they themselves thought that it would thus be acceptable. Why are these circumstances not truly extenuating?

The fact that others are doing something can never in itself justify my action. It might give me pause and bring me to reflect more deeply on my own conscience and principles. Even though superiors ordered an action and others did it was no legal defense for concentration camp officers at the post-World War II Nuremberg war crimes trials. Even less so is it an ethical defense. Although ethics can be influenced by conditions, a moral principle is not determined by voting.

In this case, as in many others, we must acknowledge that it would be of benefit to me if I could rationalize adding 5 percent to my salary. To have that extra $1,500 would be in my self-interest. Focusing primarily on my self-interest can lead me to be less objective in my search for the right action and may make me more prone to look for excuses to do that which is of benefit to me.

Justice calls for a fair distribution of the benefits and burdens of society. In this case, we are concerned with benefits: When is it ethical to take funds from an expense account? Presuming that the executive's family is not starving because of his abnormally low salary, justice maintains that the expense account be used for expenses, not as a supplement to salary. Ignorance and coercion can lessen responsibility. However, in this case, the person could hardly claim that he did not know what an expense account was, or was coerced into taking the money.

If I can get away with it, why should I not pad my expense account? Is there really any basic difference between the executive who is ethical and one who isn't? A basic assumption that almost all businesspeople would support is that a businessperson should be ethical. That is, individuals should try to do good and avoid evil, not only on the job, but in all aspects of one's life. It is only because of the understanding that most businesspeople are ethical, trustworthy, and truthful that the business system can succeed. If most businesspeople were not ethical, it would be almost impossible to purchase supplies, sell goods or securities, or do most of the transactions in the manner in which we are accustomed in modern society.

Admittedly there can be a short-term financial advantage for an embezzler or a supplier who takes $10 million and delivers defective goods. It is because of individuals like this that we have laws, courts, and jails. Yet we also know that not all unethical acts can be regulated, nor are they all fully punished (in this life anyway). If a large percentage of businesspeople took advantage of business partners, did not pay their bills, and such, the business system could not survive.

Ethical Theories

Ethical criteria and ethical models have been the subject of considerable thinking over the centuries. Of all the ethical systems, businesspeople feel most at home with utilitarian theory—and not surprisingly, as it traces its origins to Adam Smith, the father of both modern economics and utilitarian ethics. Jeremy Bentham[22] and John Stuart Mill[23] more precisely formulated utilitarianism a bit later. Utilitarianism evaluates behavior in terms of its consequences. That action which results in the greatest net gain for all parties is considered moral.

Rights theories focus on the entitlements of individual persons. Immanuel Kant[24] (personal rights) and John Locke[25] (property rights) were the first to present developed theories of rights. Justice theories have a longer tradition, going back to Plato and Aristotle in the fifth century B.C..[26] Theoretical work in each of these traditions has continued to the present.[27] For an overview of these three theories—history, strengths and weaknesses, and when most useful—see Table 5-2.

---

[22]Jeremy Bentham, *An Introduction to the Principles of Morals and Legislation* (1789) (New York: Hafner, 1948).

[23]John Stuart Mill, *Utilitarianism* (1863) (Indianapolis, Ind.: Bobbs-Merrill, 1957).

[24]Immanuel Kant, *The Metaphysical Elements of Justice* (1797), tr. J. Ladd (New York: Library of Liberal Arts, 1965).

[25]John Locke, *The Second Treatise of Government* (1690) (New York: Liberal Arts Press, 1952).

[26]Aristotle, *Ethics*, tr. J. A. K. Thomson (London: Penguin, 1953).

[27]For example, John Rawls, *A Theory of Justice* (Cambridge, Mass.: Belknap, 1971). See two books of readings: Thomas Donaldson and Patricia Werhane, *Ethical Issues in Business* (Englewood Cliffs, N.J.: Prentice-Hall, 1979); and Tom Beauchamp and Norman Bowie, *Ethical Theory and Business* (Englewood Cliffs, N.J.: Prentice-Hall, 1979).

TABLE 5-2 Ethical Models for Business Decisions

DEFINITION AND ORIGIN	STRENGTHS	WEAKNESSES	WHEN USED
UTILITARIANISM			
"The greatest good for the greatest number": Bentham (1748–1832), Adam Smith (1723–1790), David Ricardo (1772–1823)	1. Concepts, terminology, methods are easiest for businesspersons to work with; justifies a profit maximization system. 2. Promotes view of entire system of exchange beyond "this firm." 3. Encourages entrepreneurship, innovation, productivity.	1. Impossible to measure or quantify all important elements. 2. "Greatest good" can degenerate into self-interest. 3. Can result in abridging person's rights. 4. Can result in neglecting less powerful segments of society.	1. Use in all business decisions, and will be dominant criteria in 90%. 2. Version of model is implicitly used already, although scope is generally limited to "this firm."
THEORY OF JUSTICE			
Equitable distribution of society's benefits and burdens: Aristotle (384–322 B.C.), Rawls (1921-).	1. The "democratic" principle. 2. Does not allow a society to become status- or class-dominated. 3. Ensures that minorities, poor, handicapped receive opportunities and a fair share of output.	1. Can result in less risk, incentive, and innovation. 2. Encourages sense of "entitlement."	1. In product decisions usefulness to all in society. 2. In setting salaries for unskilled workers, executives. 3. In public policy decisions: to maintain a floor of living standards for all. 4. Use with, for example, performance appraisal, due process, distribution of rewards and punishments.
THEORY OF RIGHTS			
Individual's freedom is not to be violated: Locke (1635–1701)— property; Kant (1724–1804)— personal rights	1. Ensures respect for indvidual's property and personal freedom. 2. Parallels political "Bill of Rights."	1. Can encourage individualistic, selfish behavior.	1. Where individual's property or personal rights are in question. 2. Use with, for example, employee privacy, job tenure, work dangerous to person's health.

Be∆t for All

Utilitarianism +able p140 -143

Utilitarianism judges that an action is right if it produces the greatest utility, "the greatest good for the greatest number." It is very much like a cost-benefit analysis applied to all parties who would be touched by a particular decision: That action is right that produces the greatest net benefit, when all the costs and benefits to all the affected parties are taken into consideration. Although it would be convenient if these costs and benefits could be measured in some comparable unit, this is not always possible. Many important values (for example, human life and liberty) cannot be quantified. So it is sufficient to state the number and the magnitude of the costs and benefits as clearly and accurately as possible.

The utilitarian principle says that the right action is that which produces the greatest net benefit over any other possible action. However, this does not mean that the best act is that which produces the greatest good for the person performing the action. Rather, it is the action that produces the greatest summed net good for all those who are affected by the action. Utilitarianism can handle some ethical cases quite well, especially those that are complex and affect many parties. Although the model and the methodology are clear, carrying out the calculations is often difficult. Taking into account so many affected parties, along with the extent to which the action touches them, can be a calculation nightmare.

Hence several shortcuts have been proposed that can reduce the complexity of utilitarian calculations. Each shortcut involves a sacrifice of accuracy for ease of calculation. Among these shortcuts are (1) adherence to a simplified rule (for example, the Golden Rule, "Do unto others as you would have them do unto you"); (2) for ease of comparison, calculate costs and benefits in dollar terms; and (3) take into account only those directly affected by the action, putting aside indirect effects. In using the above decision-making strategies, an individual should be aware that they are simplifications and that some interests may not be sufficiently taken into consideration.

A noteworthy weakness of utilitarianism as an ethical norm is that it can advocate, for example, abridging an individual's right to a job or even life, for the sake of the greater good of a larger number of people. This, and other difficulties, are discussed elsewhere.[28] One additional caution in using utilitarian rules is in order: It is considered unethical to opt for the benefit of narrower goals (for example, personal goals, career, or money) at the expense of the good of a larger number, such as a nation or a society. Utilitarian norms emphasize the good of the group; it is a large-scale ethical model. In this sort of calculation, an individual and what is due that individual may be underemphasized. Rights theory has been developed to give appropriate emphasis to the individual and the standing of that individual with peers and within society.

[28]Gerald F. Cavanagh, Dennis J. Moberg, and Manuel Velasquez, "The Ethics of Organizational Politics," *Academy of Management Review*, 6 (July 1981), 363-74; and the more complete treatments in Manuel Velasquez, *Business Ethics: Concepts and Cases* (Englewood Cliffs, N.J.: Prentice-Hall, 1982), pp. 46-58; and Richard T. DeGeorge, *Business Ethics* (New York: Macmillan, 1982), pp. 47-54.

Rights of the Individual   ~~table 143 -140~~

A right is a person's entitlement to something.[29] Rights may flow from the legal system, such as the U.S. constitutional rights of freedom of conscience or freedom of speech. The U.S. Bill of Rights and the United Nations Universal Declaration of Human Rights are classical examples of individual rights spelled out in some detail in documents. Legal rights, as well as others which may not be written into law, stem from the human dignity of the person. Moral rights have these characteristics: (1) They enable individuals to pursue their own interests, and (2) they impose correlative prohibitions and/or requirements on others. That is, every right has a corresponding duty. My right to freedom of conscience is supported by the prohibition of other individuals from unnecessarily limiting that freedom of conscience. From another perspective, my right to be paid for my work corresponds to a duty of mine to perform "a fair day's work for a fair day's pay." In the latter case, both the right and duty stem from the right to private property, which is a traditional pillar of American life and law. However, the right to private property is not absolute. A factory owner may be forced by law, as well as by morality, to spend money on pollution control or safety equipment. For a listing of selected rights and other ethical norms, see Table 5-3.

Judging morality by reference to individual rights is quite different from using utilitarian standards. Rights express the requirements of morality from the standpoint of the individual; rights protect the individual from the encroachment and demands of society or the state. Utilitarian standards promote society's benefit and are relatively insensitive to a single individual, except insofar as that individual's welfare affects the overall good of society.

A business contract establishes rights and duties that were not there before: The right of the purchaser to receive what was agreed upon, and the right of the seller to be paid what was agreed. Formal written contracts and informal verbal agreements are essential to business transactions.

Immanuel Kant recognized that an emphasis on rights can lead one to focus largely on what is due oneself. So he formulated what he called his "categorical imperatives." As the first of these, Kant said, "I ought never to act except in such a way that I can also will that my maxim should become a universal law." Another way of putting this is: "An action is morally right for a person in a certain situation if and only if the person's reason for carrying out the action is a reason that he would be willing to have every person act on, in any similar situation."[30] As a measure of a difficult judgment, Kant asks if our reason for taking this action is the same reason that would allow others to do the same thing. Note that Kant is focusing on a person's motivation or intention, and not on the consequences of the action, as is true of utilitarianism.

---

[29]Velasquez, *Business Ethics*, p. 29. See also Thomas Donaldson, *Corporations and Morality* (Englewood Cliffs, N.J.: Prentice-Hall, 1982).

[30]Immanuel Kant, *Groundwork of the Metaphysics of Morals*, tr. H. J. Paton (New York: Harper & Row, 1964), pp. 62-90. See also Velasquez, *Business Ethics*, p. 66-69.

TABLE 5-3 Some Selected Ethical Norms

UTILITARIAN

1. *Organizational goals* should aim at *maximizing the satisfactions* of the organization's constituencies.
2. The members of an organization should attempt to attain its goals as *efficiently* as possible by consuming as few inputs as possible and by minimizing the external costs which organizational activities impose on others.
3. The employee should use *every effective means* to achieve the goals of the organization, and should neither jeopardize those goals nor enter situations in which personal interests conflict significantly with the goals.

RIGHTS

1. *Life and safety:* The individual has the right not to have her or his life or safety unknowingly and unnecessarily endangered.
2. *Truthfulness:* The individual has a right not to be intentionally deceived by another, especially on matters about which the individual has the right to know.
3. *Privacy:* The individual has the right to do whatever he or she chooses to do outside working hours and to control information about his or her private life.
4. *Freedom of conscience:* The individual has the right to refrain from carrying out any order that violates those commonly accepted moral or religious norms to which the person adheres.
5. *Free speech:* The individual has the right to criticize conscientiously and truthfully the ethics or legality of corporate actions so long as the criticism does not violate the rights of other individuals within the organization.
6. *Private property:* The individual has a right to hold private property, especially insofar as this right enables the individual and his or her family to be sheltered and to have the basic necessities of life.

JUSTICE

1. *Fair treatment:* Persons who are similar to each other in the relevant respects should be treated similarly; persons who differ in some respect relevant to the job they perform should be treated differently in proportion to the difference between them.
2. *Fair administration of rules:* Rules should be administered consistently, fairly, and impartially.
3. *Fair compensation:* Individuals should be compensated for the cost of their injuries by the party that is responsible for those injuries.
4. *Fair blame:* Individuals should not be held responsible for matters over which they have no control.
5. *Due process:* The individual has a right to a fair and impartial hearing when he or she believes that personal rights are being violated.

Source: Quoted and adapted from Manuel Velasquez, Gerald Cavanagh, and Dennis Moberg, "Organizational Statesmanship and Dirty Politics: Ethical Guidelines for the Organizational Politician," *Organizational Dynamics*, (Fall, 1983).

Kant's second categorical imperative cautions us against using other people as a means to our own ends: "Never treat humanity simply as a means, but always also as an end." An interpretation of the second imperative is: "An action is morally right for a person if and only if in performing the action the person does not use others merely as a means for advancing his or her own interests, but also both respects and develops their capacity to choose for themselves."[31] Capital, plant, and machines are all to be used to serve men and women's purposes. On the other hand, individual persons are not to be used merely as instruments for achieving one's interests. This rules out deception, manipulation, and exploitation of other people.

Justice   ~~table 143 -140~~

Justice requires all persons, and thus managers too, to be guided by fairness, equity, and impartiality. Justice calls for evenhanded treatment of groups and individuals (1) in the distribution of the benefits and burdens of society, (2) in the administration of laws and regulations, and (3) in the imposition of sanctions and means of compensation for wrongs a person has suffered. An action or policy is just in comparison with the treatment accorded to others.

Standards of justice are generally considered to be more important than utilitarian consideration of consequences. If a society is unjust to some group of its members (for example, apartheid treatment of blacks in South Africa), we generally consider that society unjust and condemn it, even if the results of the injustices bring about greater productivity. On the other hand, we seem to be willing to trade off some equity, if the results will bring about greater benefits for all. Standards of justice are not as often in conflict with individual rights as are utilitarian norms. This is not surprising, since justice is largely based on the moral rights of individuals. The moral right to be treated as a free and equal person, for example, undergirds the notion that benefits and burdens should be distributed equitably. Personal moral rights are so basic that they generally may not be traded off (for example, free consent, right to privacy, freedom of conscience, right to due process) to bring about a better distribution of benefits in a society. On the other hand, property rights may be abridged (for example, graduated income tax, tax on pollution) for the sake of a more fair distribution of benefits and burdens.

Distributive justice becomes important when there are not enough of society's goods to satisfy all needs or not enough people to bear the burdens. The question then becomes: What is a just distribution? The fundamental principle is that equals should be treated equally, and unequals treated in accord with their inequality. For example, few would argue that a new person who is hired for the same job as a senior worker with twenty years' experience should receive the same pay as the experienced worker. People performing work of greater responsibility or working more difficult hours would be eligible for greater pay. However, it is clear that pay differentials should be related to the work itself, not on some arbitrary bias of the employer.

Having said all of the above does not determine what is a fair distribution of society's benefits and burdens. In fact quite different notions of equity are generally proposed. A classic difference is the capitalist model (justice based on

---

[31]Kant, *Groundwork*; Velasquez, *Business Ethics*, p. 68.

contribution) versus the socialist ("from each according to abilities, to each according to needs"). A more recent contribution to justice theory has been the work of John Rawls.[32] Rawls would have us construct the rules and laws of society as if we did not know what role we were to play in that society. We do not know if we would be rich or poor, male or female, African or European, manager or slave, handicapped or physically and mentally fit. He calls this the "veil of ignorance." The exercise is intended to try to rid ourselves of our status, national, and sexist biases. Under such circumstances each of us would try to design the rules of society to be of the greatest benefit to all, and not to undermine the position of any group. Thus Rawls proposes that people generally develop two principles:

1. Each person is to have an equal right to the most extensive liberty compatible with similar liberty for others.
2. Social and economic inequalities are to be arranged so that they are both reasonably expected to be to everyone's advantage and attached to positions and offices open to all.

The first principle is consonant with the American sense of liberty and thus is not controversial in the United States. The second principle is more egalitarian, and also more controversial. However, Rawls maintains that if people are honest behind the "veil of ignorance" they will opt for a system of justice that is most fair to all members of that society.

SOLVING ETHICAL DILEMMAS   *figure p.146*

Any human judgment is preceded by two steps: gathering data and analyzing the data. Before any ethically sensitive situation can be assessed, it is essential that all the relevant data be at hand. As an aid to analysis, the three classical norms—utility, rights, and justice—have been offered. For a schematic diagram of how ethical decision making can proceed, see Figure 5-2. The diagram is simplified, but nevertheless it can be an aid in our handling of ethical problems.

Let us apply our scheme to the case of an executive padding her expense account. For our purposes, we will accept the limited data as provided in the case. Applying the utility criteria, we would judge that although padding the expense account satisfies the interests of the executive doing it, it does not optimize the concerns of others: shareholders, customers, more honest executives, and people in other firms in similar situations. It also adds to the expense of doing business. Hence, it seems that utility would not allow for such padding. The rights of individuals are not so involved here: The executive has no right to the extra

[32]Rawls, *A Theory of Justice*.

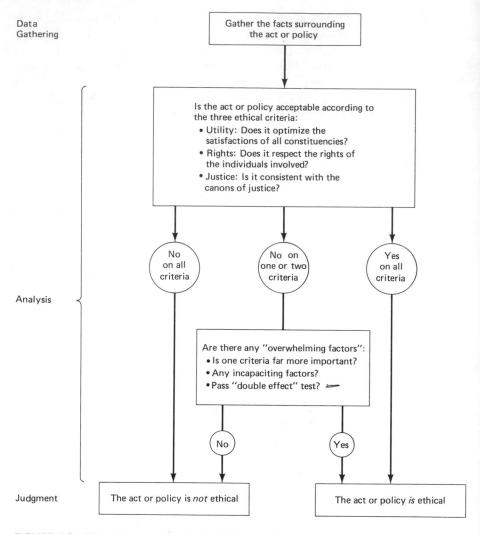

Data Gathering

Analysis

Judgment

Gather the facts surrounding the act or policy

Is the act or policy acceptable according to the three ethical criteria:
- Utility: Does it optimize the satisfactions of all constituencies?
- Rights: Does it respect the rights of the individuals involved?
- Justice: Is it consistent with the canons of justice?

No on all criteria

No on one or two criteria

Yes on all criteria

Are there any "overwhelming factors":
- Is one criteria far more important?
- Any incapaciting factors?
- Pass "double effect" test?

No

Yes

The act or policy is *not* ethical

The act or policy *is* ethical

FIGURE 5-2 Flow diagram of ethical decision making

Source: Adapted from Manuel Velasquez, Gerald F. Cavanagh, and Dennis J. Moberg, "Organizational Statesmanship and Dirty Politics: Ethical Guidelines for the Organizational Politician," *Organizational Dynamics* (Fall, 1983).

money, although we might make the case that the shareholders' and customers' right to private property is being violated. With regard to justice, salary and commissions are the ordinary compensation for individuals. Expense accounts have a quite different purpose.

In this instance, most managers responding to the case held that it was unethical for the executive to pad her expense account. John Rawls would maintain that any one of us would set the rules in this fashion, given the fact that we would not know what role we ourselves would have in the society. Hence, we conclude that padding one's expense account is judged unethical on all three ethical norms, so it is clearly wrong. Notice that this agrees with the judgment of 73 percent of the executives who were asked.

On the other hand, the *Wall Street Journal* recently described an entrepreneur who sells blank official-looking receipts of fifty different plausible but fictitious restaurants. The individual can then fill out the receipts as he likes and can submit them to his firm for reimbursement. And he has the receipts to prove the purchase of the meal! What would we say of the ethics of selling such receipts? Of purchasing them and using them?

Model Aids Solution

Let us examine another case:

> Brian Curry, financial vice president of Digital Robotics Corporation, is about to retire and has been asked to recommend one of his two assistants for promotion to vice president. Curry knows that his recommendations will be acted upon. He also knows that, since both assistants are about the same age, the one not chosen will find future promotions unlikely. Debra Butler is the most qualified for the position. She is bright and outgoing and has better leadership ability. Moreover, her father is president of the largest customer of Digital, and Curry correctly reasons that they will more likely keep this business with Butler as an officer of Digital. On the other hand, Charles McNichols has been with the company longer, has worked seventy-hour weeks, and has pulled the company through some very difficult situations. He did this because he was told he was in line for the vice presidency. Nevertheless, Curry recommends Butler for the job.

Using our schema to examine this case, utility would conclude that the selection of Debra Butler would optimize the satisfaction of top management, most of the workers, because she is a better leader, and shareholders and customers, for the same reason. The only cost is that to McNichols. Justice would conclude that because the promotional decision was made on relevant capabilities, it did not violate fair treatment. On the other hand, McNichols had been told that he would get the job, and worked extra hours because he thought the job would be his. He is being used in a fashion to which he did not consent. His rights are violated. Moreover, in being promised the job, and then having the promise broken, he is not being treated with fairness and equity.

Thus utility accepts the appointment of Butler as morally acceptable, since there will be a net gain in satisfaction. However, because of the promise made earlier to McNichols and his resultant extended work weeks, his rights are being violated. We can then ask if there are any "overwhelming factors" that ought to be taken into consideration (see Figure 5-2).

Overwhelming Factors

"Overwhelming factors" are data from the situation which may, in a given case, justify overriding one of the three ethical criteria: utility, rights, or justice. Overwhelming factors can be examined when there is a conflict in the conclusions drawn from the ethical norms. The first of the overwhelming factors are incapacitating factors. That is, if there are any elements that coerce an individual into a certain posture, then that individual is not held to be fully responsible. Managers at a H. J. Heinz plant felt great pressure from top management to show a profit. They could not do as well as was expected, so they began to juggle the books. While this meant cumulative overstatement of profits of $8.5 million, the managers who did the falsification would probably be judged less unethical than the top management that brought the unrelenting pressure to bear. Even though the act of falsifying the books was objectively unethical, the plant manager did not bear full responsibility because he was pressured by superiors.[33]

Second, the manager might not be able to utilize the criteria because she does not possess full information. She might think that another employee is embezzling from the bank. However, to report the employee to superiors might ruin the individual's reputation. So, even though stealing is a violation of justice, in this case there is not yet sufficient information to utilize the criteria. Finally, the manager may be sincerely uncertain of the criteria or their applicability in this particular case.

To return to the appointment of a financial vice president case: While utility would clearly call for recommending Debra Butler for the vice president's position, justice would call for considering McNichols' claim on the position more strongly. McNichols has worked harder, having considered this to be proportionate to the future promised reward. Moreover, since the position has been promised to him, fair treatment would call for some special consideration. Justice would probably say that, under these special circumstances, McNichols should get the position.

Because there is now a conflict between these two norms, it is necessary to see if any overwhelming factors should be taken into account. There seems to be little coercion involved, certainly no physical coercion. Curry made his decision freely. There might have been psychological coercion, however, if Debra Butler's father had mentioned the possible promotion to top management at Digital. Even without his mentioning it, the situation may still have caused psychological pressure for Curry.

The ultimate solution of this case would depend on a number of factors: How much better a manager would Butler be than McNichols, and how would this affect the firm's performance and the jobs of others at Digital? Exactly what sort of promise was made to McNichols? Was it clear and unequivocal? If the

---

[33]"Some Middle Managers Cut Corners to Achieve High Corporate Goals," *Wall Street Journal*, November 8, 1979, pp. 1, 19.

promise was more in McNichols' mind, and if Butler's performance would be judged to be significantly better than McNichols', then Curry could ethically recommend Butler. However, some sort of compensation should be made to McNichols.

Another kind of overwhelming factor occurs when criteria come to differing conclusions on the same case. The so-called "principle of double effect" can be useful here. When an act has both a good effect and a bad effect (for example, appointing Butler and not appointing McNichols), one may morally perform the act under three conditions: (1) One does not directly intend the bad effect (Curry is not trying to backstab or get back at McNichols); (2) the bad effect is not a means to the good end but is simply a side effect (the nonappointment of McNichols is not a means to Butler being appointed); and (3) the good effect sufficiently outweighs the bad (Butler's performance would be significantly superior to McNichols'). So this case passes the test of the double effect. Hence, in sum, Curry may ethically recommend Butler for the vice presidency.

Case of the Flammable Crib

Let us examine another case, this one on the issue of product safety and quality:

Assume you are president of a firm which manufactures baby cribs. You have the option of installing either of two pads: a less expensive one which meets what you feel to be too lenient federal safety requirements regarding flammability (a requirement which you are quite sure was established as a result of pressure from your industry) and one which is safe but somewhat more expensive. Assume that the safe pad will not bring a higher price for the crib.

Would using the more flammable pad be unjust to purchasers? Initially, it would seem that there is no injustice here—all purchasers of baby cribs are being treated the same. A possible source of injustice, however, would be to the consumer, who is presuming that he is purchasing a safe and not flammable baby crib. When examining rights, this becomes even clearer: The consumer presumes that his baby will be safe and that the product being sold has sufficient safeguards. The fact that the firm meets federal safety requirements does not settle the question, since the president is convinced that these are too lenient and were only set because of pressure from the industry. At stake are the lives of infants who might be burned. In fact, statistics tell us that some infants will be burned needlessly. As with sleepwear and toys, special precautions must be taken with infants and young children, since they cannot protect themselves. Although they don't smoke in bed, they nevertheless cannot put out a fire once it has begun from whatever source.

Applying the utilitarian norm demands weighing the costs and benefits of the two pads to all parties. The cheaper pad would result in lower cost to the consumer and probably better enable the firm to meet the lower price of its competitors. The cost of the lower priced pad would be the cost of the infants who would be burned because the cheaper pad was used. On the other hand, the safer pad could be advertised as such, and it might establish the firm as a manufacturer of safe children's goods. Presuming that there is a significant difference in the flammability, and thus the number of children's lives saved, utility would probably call for installing the safer pad. Since there are no ethical criteria that would call for the installation of the cheaper pad, we can then judge that ethics would ask the president to call for the safer, even though more expensive, pad.

This judgment is also the judgment of corporate executives. In a survey of chief executive officers, 94 percent would use the safe pad, even though it is more expensive.[34] Perhaps these executives are using a shortcut ethical test of a possible action: Would I do it if I knew that the decision was to be featured on this evening's TV news? Can my decision bear the sharp scrutiny of a probing reporter?

Loyalty and Whistleblowing

This final case, where the stakes are very high, will demand careful analysis and additional criteria:

> A worker in the design department of an airplane manufacturing firm is convinced that the latch mechanism on a plane's cargo door is not sufficiently secure and that the door has to be redesigned in order to ensure against the possibility of a crash. He presents his supervisor with the information and is told that the Federal Aviation Administration has given the legitimate approvals and that he should not "rock the boat." He goes to the president of the firm and gets the same answer.

Would that worker be justified in taking this information to the news media? The question is an extremely important one. The lives of hundreds of passengers might argue for going to the news media. On the other hand, the reputation, and hence perhaps the financial viability of the firm are also to be weighed. A mistake in either direction could be disastrous. Thus it is important to do the ethical analysis very carefully.

The most obvious right endangered here is the right to life and safety. If indeed the designer is correct that the faulty latch mechanism puts the plane in danger of a crash, then the lives of the passengers would assume paramount importance in our calculations. While the designer owes loyalty to his employer, nevertheless justice would also maintain that future passengers should not unknowingly bear the burden of the danger to their lives due to the faulty cargo door latch design.

Utilitarians would total up the costs and benefits to all parties affected. Redesign and recall of finished planes would cost the firm millions of dollars. More immediately, taking the issue to the ill-informed media would result in a serious erosion in reputation for the firm. On the other hand, presuming 300 people

---

[34]"Business Executives and Moral Dilemmas," *Business and Society Review* (Spring 1975), 55.

aboard a plane that crashes, how much are 300 lives worth? Utilitarians, too, would undoubtedly conclude that the designer would be justified in taking the issue outside the firm. Interestingly, even 69 percent of the corporate executives who responded to the question thought that the designer was justified in breaching loyalty and taking the issue to the media.[35]

When to Blow the Whistle

Since opportunities for whistleblowing are becoming more common, and the stakes are becoming bigger,[36] it is important to give some attention to the special conditions that would allow whistleblowing. This outline is based on the excellent analysis of Sissela Bok.[37]

To be legitimate, whistleblowing should fulfill several criteria:

1. The purpose should be moral: to benefit the public interest.
2. What is protested should be of major importance and should be specific.
3. The facts of the case must be certain; they should be checked and rechecked.
4. All other avenues for change within the organization must be already exhausted.
5. The whistleblower should be above reproach—that is, not gaining some advantage through revealing the information; ideally the individual should openly accept responsibility for whistleblowing.

Let us examine these criteria. The first demands that the purpose of whistleblowing should not be to attract attention, to seek revenge, or some other self-serving motivation. The revelation should be for the common good. Second, the situation must be important enough to consider whistleblowing, which could be a serious breach of ethics. Much is at stake, and the action should not be taken lightly. Third, it is obvious that the facts of the case must be certain and be double-checked. The fourth criterion demands that superiors and all others in the organization who might be able to rectify the situation have been informed and that they still refuse to do anything. This would include going to the president or even the board before going to an outside party. If a federal regulatory agency is involved, and all internal avenues have been tried, the agency is preferred to the news media. The fifth criterion indicates that the whistleblower should not benefit from the revelation. If one's career is benefited or one makes money from a book exposing the situation (ex-CIA agents), one's motives are immediately suspect. Moreover, these self-serving elements can unconsciously enter into one's own deliberations. To compensate for possible personal bias, a person should seek

---

[35]Ibid., p. 52.

[36]Alan F. Westin, ed., *Whistle Blowing* (New York: McGraw-Hill, 1980).

[37]Sissela Bok, "Whistleblowing and Professional Responsibilities," in *Ethics Teaching in Higher Education*, ed. Daniel Callahan and Sissela Bok (New York: Plenum Press, 1980), pp. 277-95. See also Kenneth D. Walters, "Your Employees' Right to Blow the Whistle," *Harvard Business Review*, 53 (July-August 1975), 26-34.

considerable external advice, so that he or she doesn't resort to whistleblowing as a result of being ill-informed and with a partial view. The potential whistleblower should also be aware of all the arguments for and against whistleblowing before going to the outside parties. The whistleblower should ideally be willing to accept responsibility for providing the information. Anonymous informers are justifiably not often trusted. Granted this takes courage, since a person's job may be on the line, yet this criterion can also be a test of one's motives.

Let us apply the criteria to the aircraft designer. The purpose of blowing the whistle would be the public interest: to prevent an airplane crash and to save hundreds of lives. The facts of the case should be checked. In this case we have no assurance that the designer is an engineer, or even a mentally stable engineer. Or whether he has checked his calculations with others who would be in a position to affirm or correct his estimates. The whistleblower has already gone to his own supervisor and to the president. The Federal Aviation Administration has not found the design problem. However, before going to the media, the designer should find out if the FAA is aware of the latch difficulty. This could accomplish the public purpose without the public splash which could severely damage the reputation of the manufacturer and the business of airlines using the plane. Since the whistleblower has not yet acted, we cannot be sure he will identify himself, although he probably would do so. In the same vein, we know nothing of the character of the designer. More than likely, however, there would be no personal advantage forthcoming from this whistleblowing.

So if we grant that the whistleblower has the correct facts, he would be justified in going to an external agency. This case is not distant from the real world. Had someone noted and protested the cargo door latch problem on the DC-10, the Turkish airliner taking off from Paris several years ago would not have crashed with the loss of more than 300 lives.

A serious deterrent to whistleblowing is the well-known fact that most whistleblowers are penalized, by firing, demotions, or at least by being shunted off to an unimportant job. They are labeled as ones who "rock the boat" or "fink" on fellow employees. A series of recent court decisions has begun to provide some protection for whistleblowers. Employees now cannot be fired for whistleblowing, at least in some restricted cases.[38]

On the other hand, as any practicing manager or management theorist will tell you, when whistleblowing becomes necessary, it is the result of management failures. The moral problem itself would not have arisen, for example, with more adequate design, clearer expectations on the job, or whatever. More immediately, whistleblowing is necessary only when supervisors do not listen to subordinates and their legitimate concerns. Too often management is willing to suffer shoddy products and practices in order to show higher quarterly profits or perhaps merely to maintain the status quo. In short, whistleblowing is necessary when an organization is not performing as intended, or has poor management, or both.

---

[38]"Armor for Whistle-blowers," *Business Week*, July 6, 1981, p. 97.

PR people become desyntasied to human needs
easy to not be truthful — poor listeners
Job is to always put Company in best light.

Ethics in Business   153

ETHICS
IN BUSINESS SCHOOLS

The difficulties in assessing the above cases stem in part from our lack of familiarity with ethics and the classical ethical traditions. Very little formal ethics is taught in contemporary American universities. In fact, the competitive, individualistic environment of American universities and professional schools works against helping students develop an ethical sense. The president of Johns Hopkins University, Steven Muller, maintains that the principal failing of universities today is that, "We fall short in exposing students to values. We don't really provide a value framework to young people who more and more are searching for it." He goes further:

> The failure to rally around a set of values means that universities are turning out potentially highly skilled barbarians: people who are very expert in the laboratory or at the computer or in surgery or in the law courts, but who have no real understanding of their own society.[39]

This was not always the case. Ethics, or moral philosophy as it was then called, was the vital center of the curriculum of American universities throughout the nineteenth century. It was the most important course, was required of all senior students, and was generally taught by the college president himself.[40] This course was intended to integrate all the student had learned, bringing together in a cohesive whole the entire college experience and preparing the individual for the working world. More specifically, this course was designed to sharpen the students' ethical sensitivity and to enable them to deal better with the ethical problems they were about to face.

It was assumed by educators of the nineteenth century and before that no nation could survive and prosper without common social and moral values. For a society such as ours, which is so fragmented—in ethnic backgrounds, in university disciplines, in differing allegiances—it was generally recognized to be even more important to provide some structure whereby students could unify their learning: "The entire college experience was meant above all to be an experience in character development and the moral life, as epitomized, secured, and brought to focus in the moral philosophy course."[41]

Needless to say, ethics has fallen from this exalted position in the college curriculum. Indeed, today only a small minority of college graduates have taken an ethics course. Few even recognize the ethical language that we used in the

[39]Steven Muller, "Universities Are Turning Out Highly Skilled Barbarians," *U.S. News & World Report*, November 10, 1980, p. 57.

[40]Douglas Sloan, "The Teaching of Ethics in the American Undergraduate Curriculum, 1876-1976," in *Ethics Teaching in Higher Education*, ed. Daniel Callahan and Sissela Bok (New York: Plenum Press, 1980), p. 2. This book contains several additional insightful and very helpful essays on the teaching of ethics.

[41]Ibid., p. 7.

last section: utilitarianism, justice, rights, and common good. The term "common good" (that is, looking to the best interests of all people in a society) has almost fallen out of our vocabulary. While we sometimes now talk of public policy or public interest, common good has deeper roots in ethical discourse, embraces much more, and is a more sophisticated term. The fact that it is no longer a subject of discussion or an articulated goal for our society is another early warning signal that we are badly in need of new ethical discourse. At present there is a glimmer of new interest in ethics in some undergraduate colleges.

Business Curriculum

Business school curricula are generally oriented to preparing the individual for work within the organization. The business school accrediting association, the American Assembly of Collegiate Schools of Business (AACSB), nevertheless mandates that about half of undergraduate business school course work be in the college of liberal arts. To our purpose here, it rarely contains work in ethics for the business student. Among graduate schools of business, only 16 percent offer formal ethics courses.[42] Moreover, when ethics is offered, it is not required. Fewer than 10 percent of the students in schools that offer ethics courses enroll in them. Hence only a very small fraction of MBA graduates have any formal education in ethics. Thus the business school graduates have no formal training in a discipline that is vital to their future. *Must be why their such hard asses.*

In a related move, corporate executives and the AACSB have taken a strong stand for almost twenty years on the necessity of business students being acquainted with public policy issues that face the corporation. As a result of these demands, 82 percent of business schools report that they offer a separate public policy course.[43] These courses consider a multitude of ethical issues: job discrimination, advertising, toxic wastes, product safety, and foreign operations. This course is required in more than half of the MBA programs.[44] The rationale is simple: No businessperson can begin a career without more understanding of how business deals with government, consumers, and society. Both in the entry-level job and as the manager moves up the ladder, these issues are of great importance. Even a brief look to the future verifies that these issues will become more important in the coming decades. We will see more of this in the last chapter.

Ethical issues arise often in this public policy or business and society course. Unfortunately, they are seldom treated in any depth. The problem is that the

[42]"Few Business Schools Offer Ethics Courses," *Chronicle of Higher Education*, August 6, 1979, p. 2.

[43]Rogene A. Buchholz, *Business Environment/Public Policy: A Study of Teaching and Research in Schools of Business and Management* (Washington, D.C.: American Assembly of Collegiate Schools of Business, 1979), p. 16.

[44]Charles W. Powers and David Vogel, *Ethics in the Education of Business Managers* (Hastings, N.Y.: Hastings Center, 1980), pp. 30-31. See also Clarence C. Walton, "To Break the Pentameter—Ethics Courses? Implications for Business Education," *Proceedings: 1979 AACSB Annual Meeting*, pp. 31-60.

business school teacher has little ability to draw on the rich ethical traditions available. Discussions, then, become a sharing of opinions or a voting on what is right, rather than a rational exploration of the most ethical alternative.

very HARVARD (59-70%) many corp. exes felt pressure Review to commit crime was greater

Harvard Business School and Ethics

Job pressure shouldn't influence business

Harvard University provides an illustrative case history of efforts to introduce social policy and ethics into the business school curriculum. For decades business schools in general have been charged with being exclusively concerned with teaching competition, control, and the techniques of success. Harvard Business School, the "West Point of capitalism," has been a special target of this criticism.[45] As early as 1971, a series of discussions were held at the school among faculty, administrators, and graduate students. Position papers were written by faculty to prepare for this inquiry. Among the important questions raised was the legitimacy of the school itself if it continued to ignore issues basic to the survival of the corporation and the business school. In his colorful and precise style, Theodore Levitt stated the problem, "The Harvard Business School, where such things aren't supposed to happen, is headed for a crisis of legitimacy." He indicted the school because it taught only skills and techniques and nothing about values.

A new need for clarifying goals and values has arisen because the accepted rationale has dissolved. This disintegration has occurred on two levels: the disappearance of delayed gratification for the individual and the questioning of traditional capitalism itself. The old postponement of gratification and delayed personal satisfaction is, especially among younger workers, "almost totally gone when it comes to sex, automobile ownership, sartorial possessions, travel, and social power." Everything must be had now. There is a narcissistic concern with self and "looking out for number one." Upon closer examination, we find that this "me-first" attitude is more consistent with traditional enlightened self-interest than is delayed gratification. In addition, "the moral legitimacy of traditional capitalism is under siege. Everything that goes with it is under jeopardy. . . . The spiritual cement has let go, the moral legitimacy of this beautiful machine is under question."[46]

In merely responding to challenges on a stopgap basis and continuing to teach competitiveness and techniques, the business school thus "confesses its own lack of self-esteem. It stands for nothing. . . . Opportunism and pragmatism are its style. Integrity is a word in the dictionary."[47] Yet even good business schools get caught up in running without a clear purpose and contribute to the "American way"—compete for the sake of competing, achieve for the sake of achiev-

---

[45]See, for example, Peter Cohen, *The Gospel According to the Harvard Business School* (Garden City, N.Y.: Doubleday, 1973).

[46]Theodore Levitt, "Crisis and Legitimacy on the Wrong Side of the River," *Committee on the School and Society in the 70s* (Boston: Harvard Business School, 1971), pp. 22-24.

[47]Ibid., p. 26.

ing. And they who do achieve are honored; they are the smartest, the cleverest, the richest, and that is the goal of any American, is it not?

The current president of Harvard, Derek Bok, has long been an advocate of placing more ethics in the university curriculum.[48] For almost a decade he has been urging the Business School at Harvard to introduce ethics into the MBA program. He devoted most of his President's Report in 1979[49] to the importance of reexamining the curriculum at the Business School and introducing additional material on human resources, corporate planning, business and government, and corporations and society. This last component includes business and society and business ethics.

A task force of corporate top executives examined Harvard's curriculum in the light of Bok's priorities. Its conclusions were generally favorable to the school with the exception of the ethics component. The task force reported that the faculty found business ethics difficult to define and even more difficult to teach, "But after 50 years of recognizing the importance of the subject, we believe it is time for the faculty to stop grappling and act."[50] With the encouragement of this group of executives, a new dean and three new ethically trained faculty have been able to formally bring ethics into the curriculum of the Business School.

Graduate business schools in urban areas with close ties to businesspeople have generally gone farther in integrating these new social and ethical questions into the curriculum. We have seen that record above. Faculty and students at business schools in small towns and rural areas, such as most of the land-grant universities, are not faced with problems of the employment of minorities, toxic waste disposal, or the need for management attention to longer term results, as they walk out of their classrooms. Hence, these small-town universities are farther behind in attempting to address these issues.

A traditional role of the university is to transmit the best elements of a culture and also to be a critic of that culture. One of the university's major concerns has therefore always been philosophy and values. A university can hardly claim to be a university if it does not encourage its students to probe their own values and goals and those of their society and if the university itself does not have a clear sense of what *it* stands for. If a business school in turn restricts itself to passing on the tools and techniques of achieving material success and neglects this larger and more important role, it aids society little more than does a barber college.

usually ethics were taught by univ. pres. after 1800

[48]Derek Bok, "Students Need to Grapple with 'Significant Ethical Problems,'" *U.S. News & World Report*, February 21, 1983, p. 83; see also "Can Ethics Be Taught?" *Change Magazine* (October 1976), pp. 26-37.

[49]Derek Bok, "The President's Report," *John Harvard's Journal* (May-June 1979), 73-84. See the summary and background, Walter Kiechel III, "Harvard Business School Restudies Itself," *Fortune*, June 18, 1979, pp. 48-58.

[50]"School of Business at Harvard Receives a Good Report Card," *Wall Street Journal*, January 28, 1980, p. 6.

Some schools strayed away from business values

A CODE FOR CORPORATE PERFORMANCE

W. Michael Blumenthal, chairman of Burroughs Corporation and former chair of Bendix and secretary of the U.S. Treasury, argued for several years for a code of ethics for business. After encouraging uncompromisingly ethical behavior as CEO of Bendix, Blumenthal became so convinced of its importance for business that during 1976 and 1977 he launched a nationwide effort among fellow CEOs to develop a national code of business conduct. Blumenthal proposed that top executives form a professional association, much as those for medical doctors and lawyers, formulate a code of ethics, and then set up a review panel for self-monitoring. He and other CEOs felt that this was a better alternative to additional legislation. To set up the code itself, Blumenthal proposed that corporate executives form a group that would include not only businesspeople but also clergy, statesmen, philosophers, and lawyers in order to obtain as wide an opinion as possible. Blumenthal maintained that the code would provide a benchmark for ethical business performance and a vehicle for restoring confidence in business by improving performance and not merely the image of business.[51]

Blumenthal found that CEOs shared his concern. Indeed, many had developed excellent codes for their own firms. Records show that about 75 percent of all U.S. firms have their own code of ethics. Among the largest companies in the United States, the percentage that have ethical codes rises to 90 percent.[52] However, there is little agreement among company officers as to what sort of issues the code should address. It was precisely on this uncertainty that Blumenthal's idea foundered. CEOs were in favor of a universal code of business ethics, but when it came to the specifics of what that code should cover, there was far less agreement.

Managers Want a Code of Ethics

Blumenthal was by no means alone in proposing a code of ethics. More than two decades ago, what remains as still the most carefully done empirical study of business ethics called for a code of ethics for business as one of its major conclusions. Raymond Baumhart's inquiries of almost 2,000 business managers revealed that more than two-thirds thought a code of ethics would raise the ethi-

---

[51]W. Michael Blumenthal, "New Business Watchdog Needed," *New York Times*, May 25, 1975, sec. F., p. 1; also "R$_x$ for Reducing the Occasion of Corporate Sin," *Advanced Management Journal*, 42 (Winter 1977), 4-13.

[52]Bernard J. White and B. Ruth Montgomery, "Corporate Codes of Conduct," *California Management Review*, 23 (Winter 1980), 80-87; also Paul M. Hammaker, Alexander Horniman, and Louis Rader, *Standards of Conduct in Business* (Charlottesville, Va.: Center for the Study of Applied Ethics, 1977), pp. 6-10.

we need Altruism in business All S types

cal level of business practice.[53] More than three-fourths thought that a code would be welcomed by the business community as a help in defining the limits of acceptable conduct, although an even greater number conceded that such a code would not be easy to enforce. What emerged from Baumhart's study is that most businesspeople would like a code of ethics to help them clarify their own ethical standards and decisions. In many instances, they did not *know* what was ethical and so felt they needed help. Cases of overseas bribery (Exxon, Bell Helicopter, Lockheed, ITT, Northrup), cases of using privileged information for private gain (Texas Gulf Sulfur, Penn-Central Railroad), and other trangressions have made the problem even more pointed.

When a code is designed for a firm, the CEO is most often the initiator. Although about three-fourths of all firms have a code, 58 percent reported that their code was only four years old or less.[54] The large-scale discussion of ethics in business over the last decade has had considerable influence on companies designing a code.

Two firms that have developed model ethical codes and systems of monitoring them are Caterpillar Tractor and Weyerhaeuser. Caterpillar's code is distributed to all managers worldwide, and annually these managers must report to the home office "any events or activities that might cause an impartial observer to conclude that the code hasn't been fully followed."[55] Its provisions are highly ethical: "The law is a floor. Ethical business conduct should normally exist at a level well above the minimum required by law. . . . We intend to hold to a single high standard of integrity everywhere. We will keep our word. We will not promise more than we can reasonably expect to deliver, nor will we make commitments we don't intend to keep."[56] Weyerhaeuser not only established a code of ethics but also set up a Business Conduct Committee (BCC). This group is charged with promulgating the code, answering questions on borderline cases, helping to develop and update the code. The BCC is made up of a small representative group of managers and workers.[57]

A growing number of firms have set up ethics committees within their boards of directors: Emerson Electric, Norton Company, Metropolitan Life, Kaiser Aluminum, U.S. Trust, and Consolidated Natural Gas of Pittsburgh. These committees are charged with overseeing the activities and policies of their firms and seeing that the firms adhere to their code and the boards' charges. The establish-

---

[53]Raymond C. Baumhart, S.J., "How Ethical Are Businessmen?" *Harvard Business Review*, 39 (July–August 1961), 166–71. See also his *Ethics in Business*.

[54]Survey done by National Opinion Research Center for Ethic Resource Center, Washington, D.C., 1980.

[55]"Business' Big Morality Play," *Dun's Review* (August 1980), 57.

[56]*A Code of Worldwide Business Ethics* (Peoria, Ill.: Caterpillar Tractor Company, 1977), p. 8.

[57]Earl A. Molander, "Weyerhaeuser's Reputation—A Shared Responsibility," in *Responsive Capitalism: Case Studies in Corporate Social Conduct* (New York: McGraw-Hill, 1980), pp. 224–37.

ment of codes and board committees and the institutionalization of methods of making the firm ethical are a growing movement.[58]

Both ethical codes and the issue of governance focus on providing some sort of social control of the corporation. The market promotes efficient and flexible, but not necessarily ethically and socially sensitive, performance.[59] The boards of directors and top management bear primary responsibility in both areas. It is essential that the board and management step up to the task, and, if necessary, structure the firm so as to ascertain better the ethical climate of the organization and to enable them to guide policies, decisions, and behavior. However, while codes, structures, and monitoring can encourage ethical decisions, it is even more important to have ethical people in the firm who want to make ethical judgments, know how to, and are not afraid to do so.

Managing Corporate Ethical Performance

It is not easy to manage ethical behavior within the firm.[60] The difficulties have been outlined in previous sections of this chapter: Ethical standards are difficult to establish, communication of those standards is not always clear (codes are only a beginning), and monitoring activities of a large corporation is a complex task. Executives and observers of the large corporation agree that several organizational factors can encourage unethical behavior:

1. Statements of corporate objectives, evaluation systems, and organizational climate that hold profit as the corporation's sole objective
2. Acceptance by management of the law as the only standard for corporate policies and actions
3. Ambiguous corporate policies, such that middle managers can presume that the policy is formulated as "window dressing" for external constituencies and not really to be observed
4. Inadequate management controls to implement and monitor compliance with affirmed company policies, such that lower level managers can violate the standards in pursuit of greater sales and profits for personal advantage
5. Failure of management to understand the ethical concerns of the public, resulting from isolation and the lack of two-way communication with external stakeholders

[58]Theodore V. Purcell, S.J., "The Ethics of Corporate Governance," *Review of Social Economy*, 60 (December, 1982), pp. 360-70.

[59]These issues were well and authoritatively described in the American Assembly Conferences: "The Ethics of Corporate Conduct" in 1977 and "The Corporate Governance in America" in 1978. Books of preparatory papers on each subject were prepared. See, respectively, Clarence Walton, ed., *The Ethics of Corporate Conduct* (Englewood Cliffs, N.J.: Prentice-Hall, 1977); and William R. Dill, ed., *Running the American Corporation* (Englewood Cliffs, N.J.: Prentice-Hall, 1978).

[60]For this material I thank Kirk O. Hanson, "Note on Corporate Ethical Behavior," Graduate School of Business, Stanford University, 1979.

Unethical behavior is especially troublesome for corporate management, since the unethical act can get considerable publicity. The public may then think of all firms as unethical, because of the actions of a few. A lack of open discussion by businesspeople reinforces this view. As Irving Kristol put it, "The business community as a whole remains strangely passive and silent before [unethical behavior]. This disquieting silence speaks far more eloquently to the American people than the most elaborate public relations campaign. And it conveys precisely the wrong message."[61]

SUMMARY AND CONCLUSIONS

Businesspeople want to be ethical; they generally have good instincts that lead them to the most ethical decision. Nevertheless, there has been a current rash of bribery, stealing trade secrets, and overseas political payments. In many of these cases, managers say that they could not distinguish the right action from the wrong action. Generations now growing up have even less moral ability. The media and advertising have taught them that ethics is relative, and they surely have not developed in school their abilities to make ethical judgments.

Businesspeople and educators alike lament the lack of formal ethics in the college curriculum. It wasn't always that way; in earlier centuries ethics held a commanding position in the lives of college students. It is a paradox that businesspeople have learned precise decision rules for inventory, financing, and other business problems but have almost no models for handling ethical decision making. If actions come to reflect knowledge, business behavior could become an ethical jungle. Theories of moral development show that this sort of behavior is more typical of young children than of mature men and women.

Ethical models and norms can be developed, learned, and exercised by the businessperson and thus made more accurate and useful for business decisions. The ethical principles presented here have been used to solve several ethical dilemmas. The decision rules are then expanded to handle cases of greater difficulty and with conflicting norms. Among the better business schools, social policy is well integrated into the curriculum; business ethics is still rather peripheral, but is growing in importance. Finally, most firms have developed a code of ethics for their own operations, with varying commitment and success.

DISCUSSION QUESTIONS

1. *What events of the last decade underscore the need for business ethics? List the ways that firms have responded positively to this need.*

[61]Irving Kristol, cited in Ibid, p. 5.

2. What is the principal limitation of free enterprise ideology ("enlightened self-interest") as a basis for moral action? On which state of moral development would Kohlberg place enlightened self-interest? Why?

3. What is the principal difference between utilitarian norms and rights? Do an individual's intentions have any role in utilitarianism? Do intentions have a role in rights theory? Explain.

4. What does John Rawls add to traditional justice theory? How does this compare to utilitarianism?

5. Outline the criteria necessary for whistleblowing. If you were an insider in the Nixon administration and knew of the "dirty tricks," the corporate payments to the reelection committee, and the attempted cover-up, would you feel that such actions justify blowing the whistle? Apply the criteria.

6. How many students take a course in ethics in the United States? Have you had such a course? What is the advantage to you of such a course? What is the disadvantage to you and others of not having ethics taught?

7. What are the arguments in favor of a voluntary code of ethics for a firm? What ensures that such a code is implemented? What are the advantages and disadvantages of a voluntary code of ethics for all firms? Is legislation the only other alternative?

8. Compare Caterpillar's and Weyerhaeuser's strategy and experience in implementing a code of ethics.

9. Assess the following case:

> Assume you own a large building in a major city. The real estate assessor offers, for a fee, to underestimate the value of your property and save you substantial sums in real estate taxes. Assume that this is a usual practice in this city.

Do you pay the fee?

10. Assess the following case:

> Frank Waldron is a second-year MBA student at Eastern State University. Although he has had many job offers, he continues to go through interviews arranged by the university placement office. He reasons that the interview experience will be valuable and may even turn up a better offer. In fact, Frank has discovered a way to make money from job interviews.
>
> On one occasion, two firms invited him to New York City for a tour of their home offices. He managed to schedule both firms on the same day and then billed each of them for his full travel expenses. In this way he was able to pocket about $500. When a friend objected that this was dishonest, Frank replied that each firm had told him to submit an expense account, so that he was not taking something he had no right to. One firm had not even asked for bills, which he interpreted to mean that it really intended to make him a gift of the money.

CHAPTER SIX
FREE ENTERPRISE
AND THE CORPORATION:
PEOPLE AND POLICIES

Actions speak

Practical men, who believe themselves to be quite exempt from any intellectual influences, are usually the slaves of some defunct economist.

—John Maynard Keynes*

The activities and policies of a firm are the best demonstration of its underlying values. We are able to tell much about a person by watching that individual's actions. This is also true with a business firm: Its actions and policies flow from the complex of values within that firm. The activities of individual firms and business as a whole tell us their basic ideology and values(Actions tell us more about business values than do executive speeches or advertising self-promotions.)

To gain perspective, recall from Chapter 2 the traditional Protestant ethic values that have characterized business in the United States. The Protestant ethic urges the individual to hard work, self-control, self-reliance, perseverance, saving and planning ahead, and honesty and observing the "rules of the game." What remains of these traditional values? What values characterize business today? Is that value system one that will support stability and long-term growth for the United States and its citizens, as did the Protestant ethic for so many generations? Or, on the contrary, are there inconsistencies in our contemporary value system such that it works against the stability and growth of business? Or, from

---

*John Maynard Keynes, *General Theory of Employment, Interest and Money* (New York: Harcourt Brace Jovanovich, 1965). Quoted with permission.

162

TABLE 6-1   Change of Values Which Undergird Business System

PROTESTANT ETHIC . . . has shifted to . . .	PLURALISM AND SELF-FULFILLMENT
1. Hard work	1. Salary and status
2. Self-control and sobriety	2. Self-fulfillment
3. Self-reliance	3. Entitlement
4. Perseverance	4. Short-term view: if not successful here, move on
5. Saving and planning ahead	5. Immediate satisfaction: buy on time, little savings
6. Honesty and observing the "rules of the game"	6. Obey the law; in any case, don't get caught

a broader perspective, to what extent do the current values of business contribute to the common welfare, and to what extent do values that businesspeople espouse make attaining the common good more difficult? Let us turn our attention to these basic issues.

SHORT TERM
AND SHORTSIGHTED

Americans now value consumption over saving. Inflation, advertising, and materialistic values encourage us to buy on time. We purchase a car or television and pay for it over its lifetime. A better life is measured in greater consumption: bigger house, more travel, and more club memberships. Moreover, in inflationary times, a financial analyst would not advise an individual to save her or his earnings in a savings account, bonds, or even most common stocks. Rather, the best inflation hedge is investing in property, gold, rare coins, and the like—hardly a productive use of capital. Since so little is saved, we are short of the necessary capital for investment in critically needed new plant, equipment, and research. We are far behind other countries in our rate of saving. The Germans and the English save 14 percent of their income, the French save 16 percent, and the Japanese save 18 percent; we in the United States save only 5.2 percent of our income.[1]

At the same time, self-discipline and self-control have yielded to self-fulfillment. What is important is *my* life, *my* career, *my* leisure. Self-reliance has given way to a sense of entitlement. Rather than working hard for success, we now feel that jobs, housing, medical care are owed to us (see Table 6-1).

[1]*International Economic Indicators* (Washington, D.C.: U.S. Department of Commerce, 1981), p. 12.

Lack of Planning and Research
Bespeak Values

Industrial productivity in the United States has fallen dramatically in the last decade.[2] Japanese and Western European firms are not only becoming more competitive but have taken entire markets away from American firms—cameras, watches, television sets, autos, stereos.

Executives and managers generally are convinced that the lessening in productivity increases is due to unmotivated workers, labor unions, and intrusive government. On the other hand, many other observers point to American management itself, its practices and values, as the principal culprit.[3] Some of the current failures of American managers are the following:

1. They prefer measurable, and hence visible, short-term returns over long-term growth through research and new investment in more productive plant and equipment.
2. What is called "long-range" planning within the firm is more concerned with planning prospective acquisitions and mergers than with devising strategies to create new products or enter new markets.
3. Managers often focus their attention on their own personal career, knowing that they will be at this particular job only a short time, and thus they do not look to the long-term benefit of the firm as a whole.
4. They have institutionalized the time-consuming and expensive "confrontation mode" of management: management versus labor or business versus government.
5. Chief executives coming from accounting and finance, often without experience in a particular firm or industry, have little direct knowledge of engineering, product, or markets and so tend to manage "by the numbers" alone.

Productivity gains stem from effort at the workplace, innovation, and investment. Focusing on quarterly or year-end return on investment does not provide a long enough time horizon to generate gains in productivity. Moreover, as concern for self-fulfillment has increased, productivity gains have decreased.

Let us examine some data that will illustrate our lack of emphasis on research and development and our overemphasis on expensive control mechanisms. In the decade preceding 1978, the percentage of the American work force who were scientists and engineers engaged in research and development declined 13 percent. This decline took place while the percentage of scientists and engineers in the work force rose in competitor countries: the USSR, 55 percent; West Ger-

[2]"Our Aging Production Base," *Fortune*, March 9, 1981, p. 82. For a fuller statement of these issues, see Gerald F. Cavanagh, "Free Enterprise Values: Delayed Gratification or Immediate Fulfillment," *Journal of Social Economy*, 40, no. 3 (December 1982), 330-39.

[3]See Robert Hayes and William Abernathy, "Managing Our Way to Economic Decline," *Harvard Business Review* (July-August 1980), 67-77; also Robert Jackall, "Moral Mazes: Bureaucracy and Managerial Work," *Harvard Business Review*. (September-October, 1983), 118-130; Alfred Rappaport, "A Fatal Fascination with the Short Run," *Business Week*, May 4, 1981, pp. 20-22; and Nina Hatvany and Vladimir Pucik, "Japanese Management Practices and Productivity," *Organizational Dynamics*, Spring 1981, pp. 5-21.

many, 59 percent, Japan, 62 percent.[4] Another way of looking at this relative emphasis would be to examine the proportion of scientists and engineers in the population for both the United States and Japan. For every 10,000 citizens, the United States has seventy scientists and engineers, while Japan has four hundred. On the other hand, for every 10,000 citizens the United States has twenty lawyers, while Japan has one, and forty accountants, while Japan has but three.[5]

Rather than develop new and better products and engage in basic research and development, we have encouraged and supported "paper entrepreneurs." Lawyers and accountants do not devise better products or production processes; they do not provide new goods. Rather, they provide for information gathering and less risky use of already existing resources. And they add dramatically to the payroll, thus adding significantly to overhead costs and dragging down industrial productivity.

Managing Information or People

The use of excessive numbers of lawyers and accountants, and the decline of research and development, are results of management decisions. American management in recent years has done less long-range planning, is more risk avoiding, and has become more concerned with short-term returns.

Management by information and focusing on numbers encourage looking backward. These are the records of transactions that have already taken place. Many executives blame excessive contemporary record keeping on government. Surely some additional information is required by government, but more information than is either necessary or desirable is sent up the line to top management. It is expensive to gather this information, and even more so to attend to it. We are indiscrete in the amount of information that we collect. Moreover, it is a costly indiscretion.[6]

When we in management speak of the attitude of immediate fulfillment in the workplace, we often blame the blue-collar worker for absenteeism, tardiness, a lack of willingness to work overtime, and a lack of pride in work. Nevertheless, an excessive focus on immediate and personal goals is also a problem with management. Often management's criteria for success are this year's or this quarter's return on investment and increase in market share.

Bonus plans are generally geared to last year's performance. We expect to be in our current job just a few years and then to move up either in this organiza-

---

[4]National Science Board, 1979, *Business Week*, November 24, 1980, p. 138.

[5]James Fallows, "American Industry—What Ails It, How to Save It," *Atlantic*, September 1980, pp. 35-50.

[6]See Thomas H. Naylor, "Management Is Drowning in Numbers," *Business Week*, April 6, 1981, pp. 14-16. Larry L. Cummings, in his presidential address to the Academy of Management, August 4, 1981, points out how management is shifting from "management by information" to "management by ideology," largely because information tends to be distorted, poor in quality, obsolete, and costly.

tion or to move to a better opportunity elsewhere. If one's performance is judged on the recent past, and that person is on a "fast track," there is little incentive to plan for the long term. Someone who later takes one's place will reap the reward of better performance. Thus there is little incentive to show returns over a longer period, say five or ten years. Nevertheless, substantial growth is only accomplished when a firm and its managers plan for the long term.

The larger and more diversified a firm is, the less able is top management to have a knowledge of specific products, markets, or employees. With this distance from production, new product ideas, consumers, and the public, management turns to what it *can* understand—the only control mechanism that is then available: "the numbers." Management then relies on return on investment, market share, and other quantitative indices of success. This, too, tends to focus attention more on short-term results. Moreover, not only does this focus on the short term tend to reduce productivity, research, and risk taking but it also undermines the effort to look to the ethics of management decisions. That is, the same pressure to achieve short-term results in the "numbers game" also short-circuits attempts to examine broader ethical criteria.

We have all watched current merger activity. Mergers are not new. Of the Fortune 500 firms listed twenty-five years ago, fully 166 are no longer among the 500 because they have been acquired by *other* firms. The current Fortune 500 firms have acquired roughly 4,500 other firms over the past twenty five years. Employment of the Fortune 500 firms has increased 105 percent in twenty five years, while the employment of U.S. manufacturing in general has increased only 30 percent.[7] This increased employment and concentration of power have come about because of mergers. Today there are fewer entrepreneurs and fewer "family firms" because of mergers. Often a firm is acquired by a larger corporation mainly because it will diversify operations and increase gross sales and thus look good to the financial analysts. The larger corporation is thus forced to employ more management control mechanisms. Numerical targets and indices of successful performance are issued. Remote top management is therefore less likely to take a chance on a new idea and is less concerned about the local community of a distant facility. Sometimes the newly acquired firm is closed, its assets liquidated, and its employees thrown out of work, simply because the parent company judged it had better use for the assets acquired.

In sum, the principal underlying cause of lessened productivity is shortsightedness in management. Managers too often take the easy way out; they prefer measurable, short-term results, so that they appear to be superior managers. Note that this is the same sort of underlying motivation that often leads to unethical behavior. So it is fair to conclude that the values that lead to lower productivity are the same values that undermine ethics in the workplace. The argument is

---

[7]Linda Snyder Hayes, "Twenty-five Years of Change in the Fortune 500," *Fortune*, May 5, 1980, pp. 88-96.

not that ensuring long-run return on investment will automatically bring about better ethics. This is not the case. However, it will carry us some considerable distance along that road.

not much Public Confidence in the Corporation and Executives

Americans currently do not have much confidence in either business executives or the firms they lead. This is not surprising, given the short-term perspective of many managers and their concern with their own careers. For these reasons, and others that will be noted later in this chapter, confidence in the business system has fallen dramatically in the last two decades.

Attitudes toward our economic and business system have been examined in a series of opinion surveys. Some of the items pertinent to our inquiry are shown in Table 6-2. There is currently less dissatisfaction with the distribution of income and wealth than was true ten years ago. On the other hand, more than one-half of all young people over the last ten years, even including graduate business students, have felt that "business is overly concerned with profits and not concerned enough with public responsibilities." A majority also continued to maintain that U.S. foreign policy "is based on narrow economic and power interests." In accordance with this, about 87 percent feel that the real power in the United States rests with the "giant corporations and financial institutions." That is, the public perception is that there is a locus of power, but that it is being exercised by corporations for their own interests. This is a significant change from ten years ago, when there appeared to be no center of power and Americans did not feel that corporations had such great influence on public policy.

Confidence in society and its institutions is essential for the health and survival of these institutions. Americans now have dramatically less confidence in the leadership of our major institutions, least of all the leaders of business firms (Table 6-3). Over the last two decades, trust in all those institutions and their leaders has dropped precipitously. Some of this drop may be attributed to the poor performance of the economy, yet most of it seems to be much longer term. If only 18 percent of Americans have confidence in corporate executives, that is not good news. It means that the average American perceives these leaders not to be working for the best interests of the people as a whole.

Frank T. Cary, chairman of IBM, pointed to these attitudes some years ago as the most important problem facing the country. His assessments may be even more accurate today. He felt that "the nation's lack of belief in its own institutions and in the leadership of these institutions" is the major problem facing the United States.[8] Pointing to the Harris poll, Cary said, ". . . not one of our professional, social or governmental institutions commands a majority vote of confidence from the people queried." He was especially concerned that public confidence in busi-

[8]*New York Times*, January 7, 1973, sec. F, p. 37.

TABLE 6-2   Attitudes on Issues Underlying the Business System

| | PERCENTAGE OF GROUP AGREEING | | | | |
| | MANAGERS | YOUTH | GRADUATE BUSINESS STUDENTS | | |
	1969	1969	1974	1981	1983
Business is overly concerned with profits, and not concerned enough with public responsibilities	36	92	75	70	51
Our foreign policy is based on narrow economic and power interests	36	75	70	75	54
Economic well-being in this country is unjustly and unfairly distributed	46	76	80	34	34

| | NONCOLLEGE | COLLEGE | GRADUATE BUSINESS STUDENTS | | |
	1973	1973	1974	1981	1983
The real power in the United States rests with					
a. The Congress	30	24	52	61	69
b. The giant corporations and financial institutions	33	54	81	88	87
c. The public	12	11	43	45	56

Sources: The 1969 figures are taken from "What Business Thinks," *Fortune*, October 1969, pp. 139–40, 196; the 1973 attitudes are from Daniel Yankelovich, *The New Morality* (New York: McGraw-Hill, 1974), p. 122. Graduate business students' attitudes are from the author's classes at Wayne State (1974) and the University of Detroit (1981, 1983).

TABLE 6-3   Confidence in Leadership of Major Institutions

	1966	1971	1976	1979	1981	1982
Major companies	55%	27%	16%	18%	16%	18%
Major oil companies	X	X	X	X	11	X
Wall Street	X	X	X	X	12	X
U.S. Congress	42	19	9	18	16	13
The press	29	18	20	28	16	14
Television news	X	X	28	37	24	24
Higher education institutions	61	37	31	33	34	30
Medicine	73	61	42	30	37	32

Source: Louis Harris, "Public Confidence in Key Institutions Is Down," *The Harris Survey*, November 25, 1982, pp. 2–3.

ness, which was only a bare majority twenty years ago, had fallen to a fraction of that.

Henry Ford II tried to probe the roots of this malaise. He said that our most important national problem is "our failure to achieve the level of human relations and basic human satisfactions that we, as a society, are capable of achieving."[9] He continues: "Divisiveness and deep-seated antagonisms have weakened our will to listen to each other. The decay of inner cities is an alarming symptom of widespread denial of fundamental human values." Ford concludes, "If we do not pull ourselves together into a more humane, cohesive and tolerant society, we will have neither the will nor the strength to meet effectively the many other problems besetting us." Disenchantment of Americans and business leaders is clear, and conditions have not improved since these men expressed their concern. If anything, the situation is even less stable today.

Institutions here, as elsewhere, depend for their existence and successful operation on the trust of the people. There is serious question as to how long these institutions can last in their present form when that confidence and trust are lacking. Such a lack of confidence is destabilizing; it is an early warning that there undoubtedly will be attempts to rectify this, perhaps through legislation that would make the corporation more accountable to the needs of people and to the common good. But before speaking of new values and reform, it is essential to probe some of the underlying reasons for this disillusionment.

The Contemporary Corporation: Cornucopia or Citizen?

The manner in which many businesspeople view their own purpose has contributed to the decline in confidence in the business system. Business has traditionally assumed that by pursuing its own, rather narrowly construed ends, it contributed best to the welfare of the majority of the American people. This rationale also extends to the individual: An individual pursuing her or his own ends automatically benefits others. This rationalized self-interest stems from the conviction that the best that IBM can do for society is to provide quality computers at the lowest possible price, and in so doing provide a good return for shareholders. Assuredly, if IBM fails in this, it is a failure as a business firm. On the other hand, being successful within these narrowly conceived boundaries is no longer sufficient.

To narrow the purpose of the firm to that of making a profit for shareholders, as does Milton Friedman and some corporate managers, is especially myopic. Kenneth Mason, when president of Quaker Oats, said: "Making a profit is no more the purpose of a corporation than getting enough to eat is the purpose of life. Getting enough to eat is a requirement of life; life's purpose, one would hope, is somewhat broader and more challenging. Likewise with business and profit."[10]

[9]Ibid.

[10]Kenneth W. Mason, "Responsibility for What's on the Tube," *Business Week*, August 13, 1979, p. 14.

Earlier we examined the value system that held that when the firm and even the individual pursued her or his own self-interest, the play of market forces and Adam Smith's "invisible hand" brought about the most efficient use of resources and resulted in the satisfaction of everyone's needs. Clear challenges to this simplistic ideology arose early in the Industrial Revolution with sweatshops employing ten-year-olds for seventy-hour work weeks during the nineteenth century. Similar challenges continue on such diverse issues as safety of product and workplace, dumping of toxic wastes, energy use, and water, air, and other types of pollution. Pursuing narrow self-interest was a cause of these problems in the first instance, so we can hardly expect that same rationale to contribute to an effective solution.

Rationalized self-interest has for many decades worked rather well for both the firm and the individual. Furthermore, it was justified by economic theory and blessed by the Protestant ethic. The unrestrained right of individuals and businesses to pursue their own self-interest has taken us fast and far in economic growth. Enlightened self-interest builds upon the recognition that people tend to be selfish. Capitalism or free enterprise takes into account this human quality and tries to direct it to work for the benefit of the entire society. When it does work in this fashion, it is one of the system's strengths. Yet these atitudes can also breed an arrogance in pursuing narrowly construed goals, a self-righteousness that results in indifference to consequences. The attitudes thus engendered in those directing the corporation have been described flippantly as "creative greed": Acquisitiveness coupled with creativity makes our economic system successful. Critics point out that the system thus lionizes those who are most innovative in their selfishness, provides them with material and psychological rewards, and thus reinforces and institutionalizes self-centeredness and narrowness of vision.

These personal values are judged effective and worthwhile, since it can be readily shown that they contribute to achieving our national economic goals. Moreover, these economic goals—continually increasing gross national product and average personal income, greater productivity, and the availability of more and better goods—are even said to be the most important goals of our society. These material and measurable ends of American society were graphically paraphrased by President Calvin Coolidge in an adage we all heard in grade school, "The business of America is business."

Rationalized Self-Interest

Focusing narrowly on the ends of profits and productivity provides both theoretical and psychological support to those businesspeople who "look out for number one first." Colonial Pipeline, jointly owned by nine of the largest American oil companies and itself the largest oil pipeline firm in the country, was finishing the construction of its line into New Jersey in 1962.[11] A site for a storage

---

[11]Morton Mintz, "A Colonial Heritage," in *In the Name of Profit,* Robert Heilbroner and others (New York: Warner Books, 1973), pp. 59-96.

area was needed, and tank farms were not popular with the people of Wood-bridge, New Jersey, the area selected. Although public hearings were required by law, both the mayor and the president of the town council said they would see to it that Colonial received its building permit if the firm would give a $50,000 "campaign contribution." To look for another site would delay the project, and laying additional pipeline to the spot could cost the firm millions, so Colonial paid the $50,000 (and later an additional $100,000). It is illegal for a firm to contribute to political campaigns. In addition, the firm and the local leadership conspired to deprive citizens of their right to be heard on the issue. Nevertheless, it was a far less expensive alternative for management. Management had counted on not being caught, having decided it was better for the firm to break the law than to expose itself to additional costs. In spite of cleverly hidden accounts and transfers of funds, however, the scheme was accidentally exposed. Ensuing events showed that similar campaign contributions by large firms are common practice. Rationalized self-interest thus leads firms to seek the lower cost alternative—not surprising in the context of an "everyone for himself" ethic.

When a firm emphasizes profitability exclusively, it will then attempt to push some of its own costs of production off on others. Pollution is a classic example, whether that be from production facilities or moving vehicles. Others who may or may not be benefiting from the product pay the cost by ingesting disease-causing pollutants. There are numerous examples. A large-scale dump for toxic chemicals was established by Hooker Chemical (now a division of Occidental Chemical) in the old Love Canal near Niagara Falls, New York. Homes and a school were built over the dump, and various physical ailments began appearing among the residents: miscarriages, birth defects, and mental retardation. Hundreds of people were forced to leave their homes. In another case, the pesticide Kepone was manufactured by a firm under license from Allied Chemical (now Allied Corporation) in Hopewell, Virginia. The highly toxic chemical was handled casually, and waste was flushed into the river. Serious illnesses among employees and the contamination of the entire James River resulted.[12]

The National Cancer Institute and the World Health Organization estimate that between 60 and 90 percent of the cancer in men and women is caused by substances introduced into the environment by human beings. Some pollutants affect especially workers in certain industries and the population of certain geographic areas. Leukemia was found to be three times higher than the national average among Firestone and Goodrich synthetic rubber plant workers.[13] Certain areas of the United States suffer a higher incidence of cancer: New Jersey, because of the chemical firms in the vicinity, and Los Angeles, because of the smog from motor vehicles. In most of these instances, efforts have been made to clean up the pollution, but with spotty success.

---

[12]For an account of the Love Canal, Kepone, and other cases, see "The Chemicals Around Us," *Newsweek*, August 21, 1978, pp. 25–28. Also "Who Pays? Cleaning Up the Love Canals," *New York Times*, June 8, 1980, sec. F, pp. 1–5.

[13]"The Leukemia Link to Synthetic Rubber," *Business Week*, May 17, 1976, p. 40.

The central point here is that rationalized self-interest leads a firm to dump its toxic materials on innocent third parties; it is cheaper to do so. Users of pesticides, rubber, autos, and various plastic products are thus not paying the full cost. Those who ingest the toxic substances pay by suffering ill health and having months or even years taken off their lives. An evenhanded and just system would require that manufacturers "internalize" these real costs of production and thus pass them on to those who actually use the products. The Environmental Protection Agency was set up to accomplish this. Whether or not we feel the EPA is efficient, it is clear that the unconstrained free market has no good mechanism for controlling pollution. In fact, it encourages firms to pollute as long as they are not penalized in some fashion. When it comes to pollution, the challenge to government is to regulate in as efficient and effective a manner as possible.

Executives and Firms Pursue Their Own Self-Interest

Most executives take their social responsibilities seriously; some of these business statesmen will be discussed in the next section. On the other hand, there are still too many executives who focus exclusively on dollar return—and that to the detriment of the larger society and ultimately to the efficient operation of the firm. Some conglomerates, such as Litton Industries, Gulf + Western, and ITT, have long had a reputation for self-interested behavior. Whether customer, employee, or supplier of these firms, it is wise to check one's contract closely and leave little to a handshake.

Charles G. Bluhdorn, who died in early 1983 at fifty-six years of age, was chairman of Gulf + Western Industries; he left behind a poor example of executive responsibility. He has been charged by the federal government with using company assets to enhance his own personal wealth. The Gulf + Western pension fund purchased 32,000 shares at a loss in a company in which Bluhdorn had a substantial personal interest. Bluhdorn received personal loans from banks that sought company business. The company and Bluhdorn have also been charged by the Securities and Exchange Commission with "improper" financial reporting to shareholders and other "fraudulent courses of conduct."[14] The atmosphere established by Bluhdorn spread the me-first thinking to others: An executive vice president and a close adviser to Bluhdorn were convicted of financial wrongdoing. One embezzled $2.5 million; the other falsely charged the company with $78,000 of his personal expenses.

ITT, Gulf + Western, and Phillips Petroleum, all of which have been involved in serious unethical dealings in the past decade, have tried to clean up their images by means of advertising. ITT and Phillips tell us what fine products they are providing for humanity. Gulf + Western took out full-page ads in ma-

---

[14]"G&W and Bluhdorn Are Sued by the S.E.C.," *New York Times,* November 27, 1979, sec. A, p. 1.

jor newspapers to announce that it had made a major breakthrough in batteries, so that they were light enough to make electric automobiles practical. Electric autos would, of course, be a great benefit because of lessened dependence on petroleum, negligible pollution, and quiet operation. The major block to electric autos has been batteries, as lead batteries are too heavy to power efficiently an auto any significant distance. It has been several years since Gulf + Western publically touted its "major breakthrough," yet nothing has been heard from it since. Its announcement was at best premature and at worst outright deception.

ITT is the firm that offered $1 million to the U.S. Central Intelligence Agency to finance disruption of the presidential elections in Chile so that the eventual winner, the late Salvadore Allende, would not be elected. Political "contributions" by corporations are illegal in the United States. Would not the same ethical norms apply to clandestine interference in the internal political affairs of a foreign country? How would Americans react on hearing that a German corporation secretly offered $1 million to overthrow an American president?

Moreover, once Allende was democratically elected president, ITT worked to disrupt his presidency and to overthrow him.[15] He was killed in a military coup in 1973. The military had ITT and Nixon administration support in its revolution. There has not been a democratic election in Chile since. Chile, with a sixty-year history of democratically elected governments, is today ruled by a military dictator trained in the United States and supported by the United States.

If ITT admits to tampering with the internal affairs of Chile, what are we to judge of the multitude of other charges leveled against it? Recall the $400,000 pledged to the Republican administration's campaign just when ITT was seeking U.S. antitrust division approval of its acquisition of Hartford Life. The Securities and Exchange Commission accused ITT of making numerous "illegal, improper, corrupt and questionable payments" to government officials and businesspeople in Algeria, Chile, Indonesia, Iran, Italy, Mexico, Nigeria, the Philippines, and Turkey, which amounted to no less than $8,700,000. The SEC complained that the climate at ITT was so unethical that there should be appointed a "special master" to supervise ITT's in-house investigation, and new independent directors should be appointed.[16]

These examples of corporate unethical conduct unfortunately reflect a climate that not only tolerates such actions but that pressures middle managers to generate profit at all costs. Such pressure, combined with a lack of ethical standards, is likely to result in unethical and illegal activities. However, not all corporations are so shortsighted and unethical. On the contrary, many corporate leaders are true statesmen, and the firms they guide are models of corporate responsibility.

---

[15]For a chronicle of these and many other cases of ITT wrongdoings, see "Harold Geneen's Tribulations," *Business Week*, August 11, 1973, pp. 102-7; see also the fuller account by Anthony Sampson, *Sovereign State of ITT* (Greenwich, Conn.: Fawcett, 1973).

[16]"ITT, Exxon on the Spot," *Newsweek*, November 13, 1978, p. 101. For a detailed view of concentration of corporate power, not always acting responsibly, see Edward S. Herman, *Corporate Control, Corporate Power* (Cambridge: Cambridge University, 1981).

Executives as Statesmen

William C. Norris is founder, chairman, and chief executive officer of Control Data Corporation (CDC). Norris fears that the United States, including the business community, is becoming "a risk-avoiding, selfish society."[17] Norris and his Minneapolis-based firm are surely not that. In addition to being highly successful in manufacturing and selling electronic equipment, they have also launched a number of projects aimed at meeting some of society's pressing needs.

Norris maintains that such programs are more important in a Reagan-style presidency, when there is less federal help available for disadvantaged youth, rural poor, and other social needs. "The only possible hope is for business to step in and begin to view major unmet social needs as profitable business opportunities."[18] Norris urges government to provide incentives for business to hire and train poor and disadvantaged youths. Even without major tax incentives Control Data has long been doing just that. CDC has set up several plants to provide jobs for the poor in the inner cities of Minneapolis and Washington, D.C., and in the second poorest county in the United States, in Kentucky. CDC has adapted its computer hardware to educational programs for prisoners and the poor. It is also involved in urban revitalization projects in Miami and Toledo, Ohio. Norris and CDC have deliberately used their products and plants to provide jobs and tools for those who need them.

Harold M. Williams has been president of Hunt-Wesson Foods, chairman of the board of Norton Simon, dean of the Graduate School of Management of the University of California at Los Angeles, and chairperson of the Securities and Exchange Commission. Such broad experience would lead one to expect that Williams would have more than the usual breadth of vision.

Williams was successful as a business executive and as a dean, but perhaps his most significant contribution was in urging greater corporate accountability during his tenure as chairperson of the SEC. He insisted that corporations must become more responsible to their various constituencies, including society as a whole, in order to avoid further government regulation, which he, too, wished to avoid. Williams wrote many articles and gave many speeches in an attempt to alert his business manager colleagues to greater accountability.[19] Specifically, Williams pointed out how directors, who are either full-time employees or who

---

[17]William C. Norris, "A Risk-Avoiding, Selfish Society," *Business Week,* January 28, 1980, p. 20.

[18]*U.S. News & World Report,* September 21, 1981, p. 74. See also William C. Norris, "Responding to Society's Needs," in *Corporations and Their Critics,* ed. Thornton Bradshaw and David Vogel (New York: McGraw-Hill, 1981), pp. 103–13.

[19]For example, Harold M. Williams, "The Role of the Director in Corporate Accountability," address to the Economic Club of Detroit, May 1, 1978; "Audit Committees—The Public Sector's View," *Journal of Accountancy,* September 1977, pp. 71–74; "When Profits Are Illusions," *Across the Board,* June 1978, pp. 71–75; "Inflation, Corporate Financial Reporting and Economic Reality," *Journal of Accountancy,* March 1978, pp. 79–85.

have some business dealings with the company in question, often have a conflict of interest when major policy issues are discussed. A vice president can hardly be free to raise objections to a proposal, when the president, who is also his boss, is making the proposal. So Williams urged that the president be the only "insider" on the board. He especially counseled that the nominating and the audit committees be made up entirely of outsiders. Because of the board chairperson's role in setting the agenda and leading the meetings, Williams also urged that the chairperson not be a full-time employee of the company.

American firms are moving in this direction. Most have nominating, audit, and social responsibility committees made up of outside directors. About 90 percent have a majority of outside directors on the board. However, very few have all outside directors or an independent chair of the board.

Williams received criticism for his views. Some accused him of wishing to extend government regulation and control, which was precisely what he was trying to avoid. Williams was convinced that greater corporate accountability is in the long-term best interests of both the individual firm and society as a whole. Hence, he crisscrossed the country speaking to business and other groups, and he wrote many articles in order to present these views—and all of this at considerable cost to himself.

Donald Melville is president of Norton Company of Worcester, Massachusetts. In his mid-fifties, Melville will undoubtedly have his position for at least ten years. Norton is an old-time manufacturer of grinding wheels and sanding belts; it has recently, and profitably, gotten into drilling bits and other industrial products. Norton has plants in twenty-eight countries, and it is known as a leader in social responsibility and business ethics. Melville and his predecessor, Robert Cushman, developed a realistic code of ethics and a committee to oversee the ethics of the firm.

Donald Melville himself will not argue for government actions simply because they would be good for business. In fact, he judges many government initiatives of the early 1980s, which were for the benefit of business, as not in the best interests of the people. Melville is quick to point out that "getting the government off the back of business" is not always the best for the environment, for equal employment opportunity and for a host of other public policy issues. He maintains that such actions are often a net loss to American society. Thus if business becomes single-minded in the pursuit of its own interests, the American people will be poorer because of it. Melville has the courage to speak out on these issues, even though many of his fellow chief executives are more conservative.[20]

Norton, under Melville's leadership, publishes a social report which spells

---

[20]Donald Melville, "Business Responsibilities in the Eighties: Opportunities and Risks," address to University of Santa Clara Executive Conference, May 20, 1980; "See Spot Run," *Forbes,* May 10, 1982, pp. 140-1; Theodore Purcell and James Weber, *Institutionalizing Corporate Ethics* (New York: AMACOM, 1979); *Investing in People Worldwide* (Worcester: Norton, 1981).

out not only accomplishments, as do many firms, but also targets that were not reached. Norton is a leader in institutionalizing ethics in the firm: a code, a committee to oversee its enforcement, and a candid social report.

Michael Blumenthal, chairman of Burroughs Corporation, former secretary of the U.S. Treasury, and chair of Bendix Corporation, was born in Germany. He spent World War II in Shanghai, China, and speaks six languages. After coming to the United States as a penniless immigrant in 1947, Blumenthal worked first at menial jobs. Later, he studied for and received a Ph.D in economics at Princeton.

As chair of Bendix, he demanded honest and ethical behavior of all: behavior well above what the law requires. Even before the overseas bribery scandals of the 1970s, Blumenthal instructed Bendix managers not to offer bribes or to engage in any illegal or immoral transactions abroad. He also spoke out against selling arms to governments in the Middle East, even though Bendix itself would benefit from those sales.

Blumenthal went farther by proposing that a code of ethics be established for American business. He detailed his ideas in writing and then devoted himself to discussing the proposal with other chief executive officers and influential people.[21] Thus the proposal received a great deal of attention. Executives supported the general idea of an ethical code, but when an element of the proposed code restricted an executive or an executive's firm, they were not so enthusiastic. So, while executives acknowledged the need for a code of business ethics, the idea foundered because they could come to no agreement on the specifics of the code. Blumenthal at present is successfully leading Burroughs, and we can be sure that soon we will once more hear Michael Blumenthal's new ideas and proposals that look to the common good.

Kenneth Mason, as president of Quaker Oats, was successful by every criteria. He rose in the firm through marketing and advertising and is considered a marketing expert. Nevertheless, Mason feels that the "invisible hand" will not protect businesspeople from themselves. He is convinced that too often executives merely look to the short term.

Before coming to Quaker Oats, Mason had his own advertising firm. As president of Quaker Oats, he worked to better the quality of its products and its advertising. As early as 1979 he agreed with a group of mothers from Boston who were worried about the growing influence of television on the attitudes and values of young children, especially with regard to sweets in ads and the general quality of programming. Mason publicly lamented the fact that ". . . not one major broadcaster or advertiser offered to help this group of concerned mothers in their attempt to seek improvements in children's television."[22]

---

[21]W. Michael Blumenthal, "New Business Watchdog Needed," *New York Times,* May 25, 1975, sec. 3, p. 1; also "Business Morality Has Not Deteriorated—Society Has Changed," *New York Times,* p. Fl, January 9, 1977; Bro Uttal, "The Blumenthal Revival at Burroughs," *Fortune,* October 5, 1981, pp. 128-36.

[22]Mason, "Responsibility for What's on the Tube."

Mason finds some of his fellow corporate executives lacking in vision and responsibility. He thinks that by means of television and advertising they are subverting free enterprise values, those values that they themselves lament as passing.[23] Although Mason was successful in bringing about more nutritious products and more constructive advertising at Quaker Oats, he had less impact on the food industry, ad agencies, or TV broadcasters. Perhaps partially because he was discouraged, he resigned his presidency in 1979, even though he was in good health and destined to be chief executive officer of the firm.

MEDIA AND MULTINATIONALS SHAPE VALUES

Advertising and television have a profound impact on American values. While forty years ago the family and the church were the most important influences on the values of children, there is mounting evidence that today television and peers have taken their place. Advertising and television also heavily influence our perception of business and of individual firms. Printed and television advertising not only sells goods but also presents a carefully crafted picture of products and firms. It provides thousands of windows through which we are able to view managers and firms.

Since advertising costs us about $60 billion each year,[24] it is appropriate to ask if businesspeople and consumers are getting their money's worth. Is advertising selling products well? And, more importantly, does advertising present an accurate and balanced picture of business? The answer is not simple. Some advertising is informative and tasteful and supports the values of a humane and democratic society. Other advertising is deceptive, crude, and demeaning.

If we were to list the information we receive on most products through advertising, that list would not be long. Industrial advertising spells out a product's qualities. Retail advertising lists prices. Print advertising for autos and large appliances often does a better job of informing. Television ads are more concerned with building an image. Some ads, especially on television, are crafted in ways that can be detrimental to health; laxatives, aspirin, and other pill ads can lead one to use these products and perhaps give less attention to good diet and exercise. Ads for soft drinks and candy aimed at small children can lead to tooth decay and excess sugar in the system.

Rather than provide information on products, advertisers often concentrate on how the product will make one happier, sexier, and more enviable. Leo Burnett, past president of the advertising agency that bears his name, gives this advice: "Don't tell people how good you make goods; tell them how good your goods make them."[25]

---

[23]Myron Magnet, "Chucking It," *Fortune*, July 27, 1981, pp. 82-88.

[24]*United States Statistical Abstracts, 1981*, p. 572.

[25]Leo Burnett, *Communications of an Advertising Man* (Chicago: Leo Burnett, 1961), p. 242.

⎧To make an intelligent purchase decision, the consumer needs information.⎤ What new information do the following successful advertising strategies provide: "Coke, the Real Thing," "Fly the Friendly Skies of United," "Come to Marlboro Country," "You've Come a Long Way, Baby" (Virginia Slims cigarettes)? Or cosmetics or automobile ads that appeal to our insecurities or desire for status? What is communicated is often irrelevant, trivial, and not useful to intelligent decision making.

Recently, designer jeans marketers have taken the lead in using sex-ploitation ads to sell their wares. There is little product information that would lead an intelligent purchaser to buy their high-priced jeans. Hence they, plus marketers of perfume, Noxzema shaving cream, and even Citibank traveler's checks, have turned to sex in their ads to get the attention of tired and jaded consumers. The *Wall Street Journal* says that such ads are "turning prime time into a sea of undulating posteriors." What, then, are we to say of the traditional American values of privacy, modesty, and the family?

⎧By any measure, we find that American people are distrustful of advertising.⎤In a national poll, more than two-thirds of Americans thought that "advertising causes people to buy things they don't need."[26] More than half feel that advertising does not present a true picture of the product advertised and insults the intelligence of the average citizen.[27] Even more troubling is the conviction of more than two-thirds that government intervention is necessary in order to get essential information.[28]

Hence it is clear that Americans are suspicious and cynical about what is presented in advertising. We have always felt that deliberate deception was unethical and was not "playing by the rules of the game." Yet here we have examples of deliberate exaggeration, distortion, and deception, and they are clearly recognized as such by Americans.

Children's Television: Sugar and Violence

The one group that is not suspicious of advertising and what they see on television is young children. Children have not yet had the experience to build their critical judgment. Up to age seven they tend to take at face value what they see on television. Often it is even difficult for them to distinguish the ad from the program.

⎡The Federal Trade Commission has basic supervision over advertising. The Federal Trade Commission Act (Section 5) forbids the use of "unfair or decep-

---

[26]William J. Wilson, "Consumer Reality and Corporate Image," in *The Unstable Ground: Corporate Social Policy in a Dynamic Society,* ed. S. Prakash Sethi (Los Angeles: Melville, 1974), pp. 490-91.

[27]Clarence Eldridge, "The Role of Advertising," in *Advertising's Role in Society,* ed. John S. Wright and John E. Mertes (St. Paul, Minn.: West, 1974), p. 183.

[28]Wilson, "Consumer Reality and Corporate Image."

tive advertising.*]* Recently the FTC considered controls on advertising directed to children. The FTC staff found that the average two- to eleven-year-old watched television more than twenty-five hours per week. At 1,300 hours per year, that is more time than school-age children spend in the classroom. These children annually saw an average of 20,000 television commercials, and about 60 percent of these were for sugar-coated cereals, candy, and other sweets and eating establishments. In addition, they reported that children are much more influenced by what they see on television than are adults.

Attempts to control advertising of sugar-coated products to young children or to require nutritional and health messages funded by advertisers were vehemently opposed by the television networks, advertising agencies, and food manufacturers. At no time during the hearings on the proposal did any of these firms acknowledge that children's television or advertising to children could be improved.[29] Quaker Oats was an exception. At that time, its president Kenneth Mason, of whom we spoke earlier, lamented the quality of children's programming and advertising and urged voluntary efforts by the industry to improve both. As Mason put it:

> We at Quaker Oats Co. believe that the key to corporate responsibility is for the business community to encourage, not evade, discussion of those problems that arise when activities of business conflict with the needs and concerns of society.[30]

Violence on television is another cause of concern. The National Institute of Mental Health now maintains that studies show that violence on television leads directly and indirectly to violence in real life.*]* The National Coalition on Television Violence has monitored network television and it maintains that violence is increasing. "The amount of violence on television is 200 times higher than in real life."[32] The group found NBC the most violent network and ABC the most violent in children's programming. CBS has a considerably better record. The organization lists the heaviest sponsors of prime-time violence as Mazda, Sterling Drug, Esmark, Seven-Eleven, and Johnson & Johnson. The heaviest sponsors on children's programs that carried excessive violence were Nestle, Wrigley, Mattel, Quaker (Mason was gone!), and McDonald's. The National Coalition on Television Violence advocates a consumer boycott of these sponsors.

Effect of Advertising on Values

The effect that advertising has on our values is a vital question for all citizens and consumers. However, it is also an issue on which it is difficult to show

---

[29]Mason, "Responsibility for What's on the Tube." See also Charles Atkin, "Observation of Parent-Child Interaction in Supermarket Decision-Making," *Journal of Marketing,*October 1978, pp. 41–45.

[30]Mason, "Responsibility for What's on the Tube."

[31]*U.S. News & World Report,* May 17, 1982, p. 17.

[32]"NCTV Says Violence on TV Up 16%," *Broadcasting,* June 22, 1981, p. 63.

a clear causal connection. We do know, however, that[advertising very often intentionally appeals to social status, fear of ridicule, and materialism.]Advertisers seek to convince us that if we feel unattractive, ill, or unhappy, they have just the right product for us. Something we can purchase (provided it is the right brand) can solve our problems.

Advertisers have commonly been accused of being "creators of dissatisfaction." The image they present of the beautiful, immaculately groomed and dressed, plastic men and women is a false picture of the world—both as it is and as it should be. This image can create unnecessary and unattainable expectations and hence frustration, especially for the young and the less affluent. To judge a person largely by his or her perfume and clothes is shallow and dehumanizing.

Misleading advertising and marketing practices by Nestle in poor countries has led to its being labeled a "baby killer." Those who make the accusation are aware that some mothers are unable to nurse their infants, and so there are sound medical reasons for infant formula. The problem arises when Nestle advertises its infant formula and thus conveys the impression that infant formula is the more modern, more nutritious, and more healthful way to feed an infant. This is false and deceptive and has resulted in malnutrition and death of infants in third world countries.[33]

[Advertising encourages consumption, and this in a time of diminishing resources.[Advertising, and the life style it promotes, also present an image of Americans as being materialistic, shallow, and self-centered.]On the other hand, advertisers tell us that they do not create values, they merely build on the values that they find already present. Nevertheless, it is fair to say that advertising reinforces and solidifies those embryonic self-centered and materialistic values that we find in all people, especially in the young and less mature. Advertising thus values brand-name junk foods over fruits and vegetables, sports cars over people, tooth paste and deodorants over theater and art, soap operas and police stories over reading and self-entertainment. It promotes the more self-centered and acquisitive values.

Advertising firms are even being hired to provide an image for and to "sell" political candidates.[34] In the last two decades we have been subjected to thirty-second television ads in place of in-depth discussion of complex issues. We are presented with a few words and an attractive face—and then are expected to elect that person to an important office. A thirty-second ad hardly provides the time or atmosphere to discuss difficult issues. Even worse, if the ad is successful, it often communicates that the issues are really quite simple and easy to resolve.

[33]James E. Post and Edward Baer, "Analyzing Complex Policy Problems: The Social Performance of the International Infant Formula Industry," in *Research in Corporate Social Performance and Policy,* ed. Lee E. Preston, vol. 2 (Greenwich, Conn.: JAI Press, 1980), pp. 157-96.

[34] S. W. Dunn and A. M. Barban, *Advertising: Its Role in Modern Marketing* (Hinsdale, Ill.: Dryden Press, 1978), pp. 92-3. See also Joe McGinnis, *The Selling of the President 1968* (New York: Trident, 1969).

Being an actor becomes a considerable asset in running for political office in this age of the media.

Advertisers sometimes tell us that, like engineers and accountants, they are value-free. They are professionals, and they offer their skills and knowledge without regard to the merits of a particular firm or product. Nevertheless, it is quite clear that products and advertising strategies differ widely. Some products are more worthwhile than others. Some advertising campaigns are informative and uplifting, while others are manipulative, trivial, and even deceptive.

Advertising and Television Present Business to the Community

For most Americans their most immediate contact with business, and hence much of their impression of business, is obtained through advertising. If much of the advertising we experience is more manipulative than informative, more trivial than substantive, more rude than tasteful, then we Americans begin to think less of business and businesspeople.

Unfortunately, the level of confidence that Americans have in business leaders seems to support such a conclusion (see Table 6.3). While confidence in major companies is at an all-time low of 16 percent, confidence in advertising is even lower, at 11 percent.[35] Americans have less confidence in advertising and its leaders than in any other major American institution. Advertisers are at the bottom when it comes to Americans' feeling that they can be trusted. This severely negative attitude affects public confidence toward business in general. Advertisers, who are hired to provide the link to consumers, to communicate the benefits of the product and the firm, often are not doing this well.

Given the fact that advertising touches the citizen and the consumer so intimately, and that citizens judge business as a whole on the basis of the advertising that comes their way, one would think that advertisers would take special care to be truthful, substantive, tasteful, and ethical. Moreover, one might expect that firms would demand this of their advertisers, and that advertising firms on their own would try to be leaders in ethics. This does not seem to be the case.

Advertising can have a destructive impact on our values. It can undermine our personal securities by insisting that we need deodorant or the correct clothes; it can lead us to greater acquisitiveness and self-centeredness, since it constantly bombards us with goods and services that we *must* possess. From the standpoint of the business sector, advertising presents the image of firms and managers being smooth, clever, and articulate, but nonetheless not to be taken at face value and engaging in exaggeration at best and outright deception at worse.

Advertising and television come to mind when we hear the words of Jerry

[35]Louis Harris Survey, 1978.

Brown of California: "The principles of covetousness, gluttony and greed are far more predominant than those of sacrifice, humility, poverty." Brown goes on to say that he is convinced that the world today needs

> . . . an awakening that an ethic of throwaway planned obsolescence, accumulation and military definitions of what are essentially human problems must be replaced by an ethic of stewardship, conservation, caring and frugality.[36]

Multinational Corporations and Third World Countries

The business firm with operations and sales in many foreign countries has long been recognized as a generator of jobs and wealth and an instrument of technology transfer. The multinational firm also brings many of the values of the home country to poorer peoples and puts the firm and its managers in contact with multiple sets of national values, thus challenging the firm to understand and internalize these values. In short, by its very operations, the multinational firm espouses and explicitly promotes many values.

The multinational corporation is much discussed; it is both praised and blamed. Critics charge that the multinational firm exploits poorer nations and peoples.[37] More specifically, they maintain that the multinational corporation (1) sends profits from operations in poorer countries back to richer home nations; (2) supports right-wing dictatorships over democracies because they are stable, predictable, pro-business regimes; (3) widens the gap between the rich and the masses of the poor in the host country; (4) intrudes on and threatens the sovereignty of host countries; (5) closes plants abruptly when wage rates rise or regulations become burdensome; (6) uses local capital for its own purposes; (7) undermines local business initiative and leadership; (8) encourages urbanization; (9) encourages the use of expensive, unnecessary, and sometimes dangerous consumer goods (perfumes, cigarettes); (10) promotes inappropriate technology transfer and capital-intensive operations.

Let us examine the first two charges in more detail. ITT ran advertisements to defend itself against the charge that it was exporting jobs, which hurts American labor and the American economy. ITT boasted that it had a net return from foreign investments of $332 million in just one year. These are the returns that come back to the United States after deducting any outflow of funds for new investments. The company went on to say that of the $180 million newly invested in the same year, "half of these dollars were reinvested in the countries in which

---

[36]*Los Angeles Times*, March 1, 1980, p. 30.

[37]See, for example, Richard J. Barnet and Ronald E. Muller, *Global Reach: The Power of the Multinational Corporations* (New York: Simon & Schuster, 1974); and Richard J. Barnet, *The Lean Years: Politics in the Age of Scarcity* (New York: Simon & Schuster, 1980).

they were developed. The other half were fresh funds borrowed abroad."[38] ITT's ad seems to confirm the accusation that American multinational firms exploit developing countries in that these firms take more dollars out of a developing country in profits than they bring in via investments.

Even though per capita income in the United States is many times that of developing countries, there is still a net flow of capital from the poorer countries to the United States. This is true even when the relatively small and declining dollars of American foreign aid are taken into account. John F. Kennedy pointed out how in one year, 1960, the capital inflow from underdeveloped countries to the United States was $1,300 million, while the capital outflow from the United States to these same countries was $200 million.[39] At a GM Conference on Areas of Public Concern, Chairman of the Board Thomas A. Murphy cited similar figures, showing that GM's foreign operations, rather than being a drain on the American economy, had in eighteen years resulted in a net inflow of $15 billion.[40] In a discussion after his presentation, Murphy acknowledged to the author that this inflow from poorer nations was a "two-edged sword." Although it improves the U.S. economy and is a stimulus to business, Murphy recognized that it is a drain of needed capital from poorer peoples.

The private investors and the multinational corporations that seek to begin operations in another country look for political stability, local banks willing to lend, and a potential work force that is willing and trainable. They prefer a society in which the government can guarantee law and order and a sympathetic environment. Brazil, for example, has received billions in foreign investments in recent years, and its per capita income is going up rapidly. But that increased income is going largely to a small minority of the already wealthy, and the very poor benefit hardly at all. In the period during which the Brazilian GNP has increased by 25 percent, the wealthiest 20 percent of the people received 50 percent of that increase, while the poorest 20 percent received but 5 percent.[41] Even Brazilians who have jobs work at wages a fraction of what they would receive in the United States, and Brazilian law forbids them to strike. Brazil is ruled by a right-wing military dictatorship that has an expressed goal of bringing in more foreign investment and of keeping the country stable, even if that be at the expense of citizens' rights.

[38]*Newsweek*, November 26, 1973, pp. 12-13. Peter Gabriel, "MNCs in the Third World: Is Conflict Inevitable?" *Harvard Business Review*, 50 (July-August 1972), urges multinational management to be more aware of local needs.

[39]Andrew Gunder Frank, "On the Mechanisms of Imperialism: The Case of Brazil," in *The Radical Attack on Business*, ed. Charles Perrow (New York: Harcourt Brace Jovanovich, 1972), p. 99.

[40]Thomas A. Murphy, "The Worldwide Corporation: An Economic Catalyst," in *General Motors Corporation 1974 Report on Progress in Areas of Public Concern* (Warren, Mich.: GM Technical Center, 1974), p. 8.

[41]Lecture of World Bank officer, Wayne State University, Detroit, November, 1973.

For years, Litton Industries had been unable to negotiate a contract with Greece to aid national development. Then came a military coup, and the rightist military dictators *invited* the company in.[42] Litton could help the new government gain legitimacy in Washington, and also worked well with a government much like its primary customer, the Pentagon. The military government of Greece had a clear chain of command; there were no conflicting and uncertain interests to be considered. In a military dictatorship, it is obvious where the power lies. It is not surprising that a corporation prefers to operate in a stable, law and order, rightist, dictatorial type of society—precisely the kind of society American citizens would find intolerable. Working cooperatively with private business interests, the American government itself has for decades been helping to "stabilize" most of the Latin American countries by means of the aid, loans, and support it has given rightist military regimes that deny individual freedoms. Chile, when it had a freely elected leftist government, was denied American aid and loans. After the military dictatorship took over, aid flowed freely. Chile, Brazil, Uruguay, and a number of other Latin American countries not long ago had free, elected governments. With encouragement from the American government and from American business interests, these countries now have rightist military dictatorships.

Latin American police and military officers were brought to the United States and given the latest in weapons, hardware, and training in "antisubversion and interrogation techniques." When these military people went back home, they had established ties with influential Americans in our State and Defense departments. When there came either a perceived or a real leftist threat to their governments, they could contact their American friends for a reading on whether the United States would support a new government. They then moved in with tanks and guns and formed a military government. There are two interpretations of the help the United States gave. The first is that the United States inadvertently provided the means whereby democracy fell in each of these Latin American countries; it was an accident. Another view, and the one more commonly held in Latin America itself, is that the United States supported the right-wing coup so as to make the country a more cooperative setting for U.S. firms to do business.

On the other hand, supporters of the multinational corporation point to the many positive contributions that it makes. The multinational corporation (1) brings technology, management, and capital to poorer countries; (2) develops leadership and provides training for local peoples; (3) reinvests at least some of the profits in the local economy; (4) provides orders, and hence business and jobs for local firms, both for suppliers and through workers' purchases; (5) provides mechanization, fertilizers, and other aids to local agriculture; (6) produces foreign exchange by exporting goods; (7) aids the host nation's development plans; (8) encourages the development of engineering and other professional skills among local people; (9) works with local and shared ownership projects.

---

[42]David Harowitz and Reese Erlich, "Litton Industries: Proving Poverty Pays," in *The Radical Attack on Business*, ed. Charles Perrow (New York: Harcourt Brace Jovanovich, 1972), pp. 48-54.

The multinational firm is on the frontier of communication among peoples. In an era when political regimes and even the United Nations are often caught up in nationalism and bureaucracy, the multinational corporation is able to cross boundaries and deal with local peoples on an individual basis[The person-to-person contact that it brings, and the necessity to understand and work with another set of values, are principal advantages of the multinational firm.]

Of the problems listed above, many can be controlled by legislation and pressure in the host country.[43] And, as on all the other issues discussed in this volume, the firm itself has the power and the responsibility to monitor its overseas operations. Whether the issue be working conditions, salaries, pollution, product safety, or cooperation with an oppressive dictatorship, management has the responsibility to address the issues and to make conscientious decisions that are in the long-run interests of both the firm and the local peoples. Some multinational firms do this far better than others.

WORKPLACE, SHOP FLOOR, AND STRATEGIC PLANNING

[People look to their roles and work within a society for satisfaction and fulfillment.]Satisfaction generally comes from raising a family, from doing a job well, from contributing to the success, growth, and happiness of people. This fulfillment, this feeling that one's life is worthwhile, gives a person not only satisfaction but also renewed motivation to direct his or her energies to the unfinished work. Industrial society demands specialization of task and interchangeability of personnel. As work becomes segmented and depersonalized, much of the joy of success is taken away from the individual. Workers rarely produce the finished good themselves; they perform but one small portion of the process because of the lower cost of specialization of labor. The large corporation and automation further this segmenting of the job and the resulting distance between the individual worker and the finished product.

As a result, in contemporary industrial society something that "is vital and essential for human life is left out, neglected, suppressed and repressed."[44] Sociologists and Marxists call this vacuum "alienation"; theologians call it "estrangement." The purposes of industrial society—production and growth—take precedence over the goals of the person. Whenever nonhuman objectives are valued over persons, isolation, loneliness, and alienation result. Even though we have more science, technology, and affluence, life seems even less fulfilling. Our expectations have been raised by politicians and advertising only to be dashed by reality. In

---

[43]See Tim Smith, "The Ethical Responsibilities of Multi-National Companies," in *Corporations and Their Critics*, ed. Thornton Bradshaw and David Vogel (New York: McGraw-Hill, 1981), pp. 77–86.

[44]Walter A. Weisskopf, *Alienation and Economics* (New York: Dutton, 1971), p. 16.

the very act of accumulating wealth and developing a sophisticated technology, we have lost a basic sense of achieving and contributing to something worthwhile. We have emphasized material goods and wealth more than we have the person. This tension is one of the causes of the "career crises" we hear about so often (see Chapter 4). People who are by all external standards successful drop out of highly paid managerial jobs in order to retire to a farm or work at some craft.[45] Dissatisfaction and alienation seem to be as common among successful executives as they are on the assembly line. Meaningful work is important for all those who work whether with their hands or their minds. It is ironic that as our personal incomes and the number of material goods we possess increase, our work and our very lives seem to offer less and less satisfaction and fulfillment.

Job Satisfaction

A principal reason for this lack of satisfaction is that our work ethic no longer has any foundation. When the Protestant ethic was the basic value system of Americans, personal values supported work values. As Daniel Bell sees it, this is not the case today:

> What this abandonment of Puritanism and the Protestant Ethic does, of course, is to leave capitalism with no moral or transcendental ethic. It also emphasized . . . an extraordinary contradiction within the social structure itself. On the one hand, the business corporation wants an individual to work hard, pursue a career, accept delayed gratification—to be, in the crude sense, an organization man. And yet, in its products and its advertisements, the corporation promotes pleasure, instant joy, relaxing and letting go. One is to be "straight" by day and a "swinger" by night.[46]

However, within the firm today there are major efforts to make work more "participative," and hence more satisfying, and to recognize the rights of individual workers to privacy and individual conscience. The much discussed "quality of work life" programs at General Motors and other firms are an attempt to encourage worker participation and to tap the best interests, energies, and talents of all employees. Some old and new forms of workers' participation in U.S. corporations are

1. Suggestion box
2. General opinion-climate survey and survey feedback
3. Open door policy by management
4. Management by objectives
5. Worker representation on boards of directors
6. Flexible schedules ("flextime")
7. Team building

[45]For example, "The Failure of the Successful," *New York Times*, June 3, 1973, sec. E, p. 11.

[46]Daniel Bell, *The Cultural Contradictions of Capitalism* (New York: Basic Books, 1976), pp. 71-72.

David Ewing— bring civil liberties into workforce

8. Job enrichment
9. Joint labor-management committees
10. Semiautonomous or "self-managed" work teams
11. Quality control circles
12. Quality of work life programs

Our purposes here do not permit us to discuss each of these forms of worker participation. However, the mere listing reminds us of the vast array of programs that are being used to enlist greater worker involvement in the production process. American management has come to realize that without grass-roots support and concern for quality and efficiency, there is no way that American industry can increase its quality and productivity. Ironically, it is declining productivity rates that have encouraged the use of each of these techniques; nevertheless, the resulting work environment is also more satisfying.

A second major current effort is to build and protect the personal rights of individual workers. This movement runs all the way from ensuring privacy to determining the conditions under which an employee may blow the whistle. David W. Ewing has been a leader in the examination of employee rights, or, as he puts it, "bringing civil liberties into the workplace."[47] "Whistleblowing," or the conflict between the actions of the organization and the individual has also received attention. The discussion has focused on those difficult cases where an individual has information that, for example, a product or process is dangerous to the public, and this situation is not recognized by those with authority within the organization.[48] These embryonic movements are again examples of recognizing the abilities and integrity of the individual who spends forty hours per week or more within the organization. Surely the organization deserves loyalty and hard work from its employees. It is also true that the organization must recognize the personal rights, the good judgment, and the informed conscience of its workers.

Loss of Personal Initiative and Sense of Community

A decline in personal initiative in American society is lamented by many. Businesspeople point to a lack of entrepreneurial spirit. Control Data Chairman William Norris calls us a "risk-avoiding, selfish society." He says that our emphasis on immediate payoffs has led to a bureaucratic spirit:

[47]David W. Ewing, *Freedom Inside the Organization* (New York: McGraw-Hill, 1977), and " 'Constitutionalizing' the Corporation," in *Corporations and Their Critics*, ed. Thornton Bradshaw and David Vogel (New York: McGraw-Hill, 1981), pp. 253–68; also David F. Linowes, "Employee Rights to Privacy and Access to Personal Records: A New Look," in *Private Enterprise and Public Purpose*, ed. S. Prakash Sethi and Carl L. Swanson (New York: Wiley, 1981), pp. 277–82.

[48]Kenneth D. Walters, "Your Employees' Right to Blow the Whistle," *Harvard Business Review* (July–August 1975), 26–34; Alan F. Westin, ed., *Whistle Blowing: Loyalty and Dissent in the Corporation* (New York: McGraw-Hill, 1981); Sissela Bok, "Whistleblowing and Professional Responsibilities," in *Ethics Teaching in Higher Education*, ed. Daniel Callahan and Sissela Bok (New York: Plenum Press, 1980), pp. 277–95.

Votaw - equal opportunity has shifted to equal results

> But big business is not alone [in this]. It shares its apathetic, risk-avoiding, selfish, and reactionary profile with other sectors, including academia, organized labor, private foundations, the churches, and government.[49]

The intrusion of big government and the growth of the sense of entitlement are blamed by many for this new attitude of doing the least amount of work for the best possible pay. Dow Votaw has pointed out how the ideal of equality of opportunity has gradually shifted to the ideal of equality of result (that is, job, income, wealth)—and this under the heavy influence of a basically uncaring government bureaucracy.[50] If all are equal or should be equal, what is there to strive for?   *Novak - democratic capitalism encourages individuals as main source socio-economic energy*

Michael Novak has examined the roots of the entrepreneurial spirit.[51] According to him, the distinguishing feature of democratic capitalism is that it encourages the individual as the main source of social and economic energy. In fact, its past success in the United States puts it in a vulnerable position: Democratic capitalism is envied by poorer peoples and nations and thus criticized by them and others as exploitative; and parents who grew up in poverty do not know how to bring up their children under affluence. Both of these factors blunt the spirit of innovation and the attitudes that encourage the entrepreneur.

At the same time, many Americans feel a loss in the sense of cooperation and community. One of the most basic human needs is to share one's joys, problems, and aspirations with others. Our deep-rooted attitudes of individualism and enlightened self-interest, although supportive of and perhaps even necessary for a free enterprise economic system, nevertheless run contrary to the need for community. Our social system, responding to people's material wants and the resulting needs of the economic system, has valued the person who is mobile, energetic, creative, and ambitious. This mobile, ambitious sort of person was attracted to the New World and has thrived here in succeeding generations. We as a society, however, have rarely acknowledged the negative qualities of that same sort of person. Granted, the New World gained and encouraged the energetic and the daring; it also gained more than its share of "the rootless, the unscrupulous, those who value money over relationships, and those who put self-aggrandizement ahead of love and loyalty." It is even more critical that we gained many people who, "when faced with a difficult situation, tended to chuck the whole thing and flee to a new environment."[52] The same qualities that we value so highly—mobility and willingness to risk—encourage us to flee the difficult situation, in the hope

---

[49]Norris, "A Risk-Avoiding, Selfish Society."

[50]Dow Votaw, "The New Equality: Bureaucracy's Trojan Horse," *California Management Review,* 20 (Summer 1978), 5-17.

[51]Michael Novak, *The Spirit of Democratic Capitalism* (New York: Simon & Schuster, 1982); see also Novak's *Toward a Theology of the Corporation* (Washington, D.C.: American Enterprise Institute, 1981).

[52]Philip Slater, *The Pursuit of Loneliness: American Culture at the Breaking Point* (Boston: Beacon Press, 1970), p. 14. On the need for community, see also Weisskopf, *Alienation and Economics,* pp. 16, 52-55, 190.

of leaving our problems behind when we begin again. We have all seen the lives and careers that have been shattered when some person walks out—whether it be on a firm, a group of friends, or a marriage. It is *easy* to escape long-term responsibility in the tolerant, freedom-loving United States, if one has a mind to do so.

⌈Two current trends in our political life accelerate the loss of community in the United States: narrow special interests are now stronger and more vocal, and there is a paralyzing lack of consensus as to national priorities and direction⌉ The confrontation mode of dealing with others has long been a part of the American way. Modeled after the adversary system of the law courts, we have institutionalized conflict, for example, labor versus management, business versus government. The rhetoric is one of "battle" and "struggle," "win or lose," as if a loss for one group is a win for another. Special interest groups have gathered in the political arena to push for their narrow objectives, whether these are the American Medical Association (physicians), National Educational Association (public school teachers), auto dealers, antiabortionists, or the New Right, who target members of Congress who are not to their liking. A lack of communication and trust grows at a time when cooperation is badly needed.

In line with the above, it is becoming clear that the only issues upon which Americans can agree are those that they are against. National elections are often decided by voting against the most disliked candidate. When asked what we are for, or what kind of society we desire, we fall strangely silent.⌈We Americans have neither been encouraged nor aided in sorting out our priorities and the resulting tradeoffs, in order to decide what sort of society we want. These two factors tend to encourage Americans to be unlistening and to be distrustful of one another. Finding a common bond and developing a sense of community become even more difficult.⌉

Limits of a Finite World Affect Corporate Planning

In the past decade it has become increasingly apparent that economic growth is not an unqualified good.[53] Indeed, growth can devour precious finite resources; it can pollute, crowd, and even bring on famine. Such growth cannot be described as "development"; it is cancerous. Nations now face an anguishing dilemma: Peoples aim for better standards of living, yet the cost of resources and energy has made development very expensive. Most developing nations are already heavily in debt to wealthier nations.

We were given an early warning of these difficulties in the seminal work

---

[53]Hazel Henderson, "The Entropy State," *The Planning Review*, 2 (April-May 1974); also Henderson's *Creating Alternative Futures* (New York: Putnam's, 1978). See *Wall Street Journal* editorial, "Growth and Social Progress," for a call to distinguish between "those components of the Gross National Product that indicate progress and those that simply record increased output" (March 27, 1974, p. 12).

Limits to Growth—probably the most influential and controversial book of the decade.[54] In the early 1970s, a team of MIT systems analysts set out to investigate how present rates of development projected into the future would affect the world. The team studied global development in five areas—population increase, agricultural production, depletion of nonrenewable resources, industrial output, and pollution of the environment—and concluded that present rates of exponential growth cannot continue. Within a few generations the system (the world, in this case) will break down because of starvation due to lack of food for an increasing population; exhaustion of basic and essential resources such as petroleum, iron ore, and copper due to accelerating industrialization; or fatal deterioration of the environment due to increasing industrialization in all countries. It is clear that these projections are interdependent. For example, if population and industrialization continue to increase at present rates, malnutrition and exhaustion of resources and the environment will come rather quickly. If pollution and population are controlled but industrialization continues, we still face chaos when resources are prohibitively expensive, although it will take a bit longer.

The United States, with but 6 percent of the world's population, consumes 30 to 40 percent of most of the earth's nonrenewable resources. At this rate, we strain the world's resources; moreover, if the developing nations were at our stage of development, there would not be enough resources to go around. Food production and diets are an example. With present world population, there is approximately one acre of arable land for each person in the world. A meat- and milk-based diet such as we have in the United States takes roughly three acres per person. Nevertheless a diet based on vegetable protein (soybeans, legumes) takes roughly one-fourth of an acre of land.[55] Clearly the peoples of the world cannot obtain a diet such as we have in the wealthier nations. On the other hand, the world could support a much larger population than exists at present if we used our land more efficiently. Such efficiency is measured in terms of the number of people who can be fed per acre.

Use of land is but one example. The same sort of case can be made for the use of petroleum, iron ore, copper, and many other resources. Are we now to tell the peoples of Asia and Africa that there are not enough resources for all, that they must remain at their present stage of development? Will these peoples not look to the developed countries and charge that we are using far more of the earth's goods than we have a right to?

Although the details of these studies have been heatedly debated, policymakers and others now agree that they have contributed three new elements to

---

[54]Donella H. Meadows, Dennis L. Meadows, Jorgen Randers, and William W. Behrens III, _The Limits to Growth_ (New York: Signet Books, 1972).

[55]This is the sort of data that form the core of the now classic work of Francis Moore Lappe, _Diet for a Small Planet_ (New York: Ballantine, 1973). See also Lester R. Brown, _By Bread Alone_ (New York: Praeger, 1974).

planning: [A simplistic national goal of growth is not only unwise but is also self-defeating in the long run; the present generation has a responsibility to pass on to future generations a world that is essentially healthy, without grossly depleted resources, arable land eroded, being polluted; and when planning, it is essential to take a long-range and large-scale view.]

The last point runs counter to the analytical training of corporate managers: to focus their view on this firm and "hard" data. It is also contrary to advice given to doctoral candidates to "seek specific projects where they can 'carve out' a manageable piece of work." As a father of systems analysis and quantified models puts it: It is "foolish advice to a mind bent on understanding the world and people's place in it."[56]

Corporate planners and executives have benefited from *The Limits to Growth* and the additional reports that the Club of Rome have published.[57] Indeed, executives give this viewpoint a prominent place in corporate policy. Chief executive officer of General Electric, Reginald H. Jones, in a talk entitled "Managing in the 1980s,"points to the new constraints: "In retrospect, it appears that the booming expansion of the world economy in the 1950s and the 1960s was an oil boom."[58] Expanding on the same theme Richard J. Bennett, CEO of Schering-Plough speaks of

> . . . an era of "heroic materialism." That era is obviously over. Although now in the Age of Limits, we still don't like the idea of cutting back or being told that there is no return to the easier times and greater expectations of the past.[59]

These were decades of overconsumption and under investment. Moreover, during that period economists overstated productivity gains. They did not figure in the real overhead that was pushed off onto the larger society in the way of "social costs." We were not paying the full price for our products: We were using subsidized energy; we were polluting the air and water and not counting the costs of the resulting disease, injuries, and deaths as part of the cost of production. Both executives then go on to chart a course for their firms that takes into account this "age of limits."

---

[56]C. West Churchman, "The New Rationalism and Its Implications for Understanding Corporations," in *Rationality, Legitimacy, Responsibility: Search for New Directions in Business and Society,* ed. Edwin M. Epstein and Dow Votaw (Santa Monica, Calif.: Goodyear Publishing Co., 1978), p. 60.

[57]See also Mihajlo Mesarovic and Eduard Pestel, *Mankind at the Turning Point: The Second Report of the Club of Rome* (New York: Dutton, 1975); Jan Tinbergen, coordinator, *Reshaping the International Order* (New York: Dutton, 1976); and Ervin Laszlo and others, *Goals for Mankind,* (New York: Dutton, 1977).

[58]Reginald H. Jones, "Managing in the 1980's," address at Wharton School, February 4, 1980, p. 3.

[59]Richard J. Bennett, "A New Compact in the Age of Limits," address at Fordham University, November 5, 1981, p. 3.

Obsolete Values

One of the major themes of this book has been the erosion of accepted values that undergird our free enterprise system: individualism, the Protestant ethic, and delayed gratification. The lack of goals in business schools is an example of this erosion. When a society's basic values dissolve, its members are left without purpose and guidelines for their lives. As we have seen, these values have not always been very clearly articulated, but they have been the foundation for marketplace activities and even for an entire way of life. A large part of this difficulty stems from the inability or unwillingness of the American people to adjust and adapt their values, in spite of their vaunted flexibility and pragmatism. For example, many elements of 1920s capitalism were resurrected during the Reagan presidency: the "cowboy economy," the downplaying of the need for government direction, the "America first" mentality. For whatever reasons, Americans find it difficult to cast aside obsolete values and to eliminate or restructure institutions that no longer serve good purposes.

To a large extent, the current business ideology is firmly held because it has developed as a legitimation of personally held wealth and social class. It therefore has firm roots in social institutions and the social system; and such institutions are notoriously inflexible. Maynard Seider examined business values and ideology by means of a content analysis of executives' speeches.[60] He then looked for the origins of these values and argued that ideology develops in the individual through a socialization process. Business ideology is largely derived from the values of the upper class, and these in turn are handed down through "prep schools, Ivy League colleges, fraternities, and social clubs." There thus exists "one metropolitan upper class with a common cultural tradition, consciousness of kind, and 'we' feeling of solidarity." It is a nationally held set of values, developed largely to legitimate the position of the wealthy and powerful.

In a democracy we hold that the judgment of the needs and values of a society must be made by the people themselves. Even if there were a way to circumvent the disproportionate influence that powerful individuals, money, the media, and advertising have on us, in our society it is still difficult to carry out reforms directed toward the poor: "A society mainly motivated by financial self-interest has great difficulty carrying out altruistic measures; funds destined for the poor and disadvantaged seem to stick too easily to the fingers of those who are supposed to administer such funds."[61] Moreover, democracy based on majority rule finds itself particularly inept when faced with trying to help minorities. In the United States for the first time in history, the poor, the disadvantaged, and the segregated are in the minority. As such, they are often unseen and unheard. Americans thus tend to cling to the easy, familiar values and even engage

Seider values develop via socialization

---

[60]Maynard S. Seider, "American Big Business Ideology: A Content Analysis of Executive Speeches," *American Sociological Review,* 39 (December 1974), 802-15.

[61]Weisskopf, *Alienation and Economics,* p. 15.

in nostalgia. Looking to the future with a willingness to amend values requires self-confidence and a sense of direction.

No Self-Confidence

[Both personal and national self-confidence stem from a sense of purpose.][62] However, the inherited goals of American society are no longer clear. Change has come so rapidly that it is impossible for any one of us to know what sort of lives our children will have. We don't know where or how they will live or what sort of careers they will have. In more stable societies, a child's future was pretty well determined by the role of the parents in that society. This sort of continuity gives individuals and society equilibrium, security, and self-esteem.

Most of the larger problems facing American society (unemployment, lessened productivity, pollution, dwindling resources, unequal distribution of goods) are problems that affect the entire world [When society is stable, it is far easier to understand "the common good."] When the larger society is changing rapidly, coupled with the fact that individuals and nations are increasingly interdependent, it is far more difficult to cast a steady look at society in order to probe basic problems and make policy changes. Working and sacrificing for the "common good" and for future generations is far more difficult when I have only a vague idea of the type of society that will exist twenty-five years from now.

To delay gratification, to deny myself now for the sake of my children or others is what some would call an "old folks" virtue. Eyes on the future, they would save for their children or for a rainy day. Our ancestors knew that if they saved and invested today, they would reap much greater benefits tomorrow. This is the postponed life: the tendency not to look for present satisfaction, but to plan for it in the future. Being future-centered is a mark of the older generation. Given the rapid change and the fact that it seems increasingly difficult to anticipate or plan for the future, young people are more concerned with the immediate. They look to present job and life satisfactions. They are impatient with those who tell them to work hard now for the sake of a cloudy and uncertain future.

The malaise and pessimism of present-day America is well articulated in Robert Heilbroner's *The Human Prospect*.[63] Heilbroner describes himself as a liberal and an optimist by nature, yet he has serious doubts about the ability of humanity to survive, for most of the reasons we have discussed—urban decay and distrust, world food shortages, pollution, dwindling resources, nuclear holocaust. In his view, present attitudes and trends indicate that civilization is rapidly heading for chaos and its own destruction. He also sees that [neither of the two major socioeconomic systems, capitalism and socialism, is capable of addressing

[62]For a strong and clear statement on this, see Steven Muller, president of Johns Hopkins University, "Universities Are Turning Out Highly Skilled Barbarians," *U.S. News & World Report,* November 10, 1980, pp. 57-58.

[63]Robert Heilbroner, *The Human Prospect* (New York: Norton, 1974).

the problems and altering the direction toward suicide⌋ He suggests that the road ahead calls for stronger leadership and thus more authoritarian governments. In the future, he sees the prospect of convulsive change: wars, starvation, and environmental disasters, all coming because of people's inability to cope with their own world⌈Heilbroner feels that if there is any possibility for people to survive, it will be by living a very different kind of life based on new values and goals⌋

The possibility of a collapse of the world system or a nuclear holocaust casts a cloud over planning for an affluent, happy, and satisfied personal life. The immense problems facing individuals and society could lead us to despair. Self-confidence is surely shaken. We will return to these issues and try to view the values of the future in Chapter 7. But let us now turn to the more immediate problems that face the firm and the ways in which firms and society are coping with those problems.

PATCHWORK AND COMPROMISE: *NADER*
THE MODERATE REFORMERS

In the wake of criticisms of business activities over the last two decades (for example, product quality and safety, equal employment opportunity, "shareholder democracy"), there have been numerous efforts to make the firm more responsible. These efforts have ranged from government legislation and regulation to voluntary responses of individual firms. To many defenders of free enterprise, the efforts are ill-informed tampering, thus at best making the system less efficient and at worst selling out to Marxists. On the other hand, to the few ideological purists, who see the system as intrinsically exploitative, these efforts are halfhearted and token. However, pragmatism has been the "American way"; progress comes in short, compromising steps. Following some of these steps tells us much about the values of the people involved. It also instructs us on the emerging values of the business system.

A hero to consumer advocates and an ogre to some businesspeople, Ralph Nader epitomizes this movement. Nader was born in 1934, nine years after his parents emigrated to the United States from Lebanon. The Nader family lived in Winsted, Connecticut, where they made it a habit to discuss values and public issues at the dinner table, and as a boy Ralph was considered peculiar because he enjoyed reading the *Congressional Record*.[64] He graduated Phi Beta Kappa from Princeton and then went on to obtain a Harvard law degree. He is highly critical of the latter institution, and maintains that it is designed to produce cogs for the corporate legal machinery.

Nader was a lone Don Quixote in the late 1960s⌊his main attack was

[64]Richard Armstrong, "The Passion That Rules Ralph Nader," *Fortune*, May 1971, p. 144.

centered on the auto industry. His impressively documented challenge to the safety of the American automobile, *Unsafe at Any Speed*,[65] had a profound influence on the auto industry and the auto-buying public and thrust its author into national prominence. In this book Nader accused the auto industry of "over-emphasis on style, disregard for the safety of the driver and passengers, and engineering stagnation."[66] His indictment, which seemed exaggerated and severe then, is being widely repeated today by financial and management analysts of the auto industry.

Nader lives a devoted and frugal life. He lives in a small and poorly furnished apartment and operates out of a cramped office. His sources of income from books, speaking fees, and contributions are all used to support his work and not himself. This famous corporate gadfly loves his work and finds tremendous energy for it; he often works sixteen or eighteen hours a day. He sees his job as that of transferring power from the managerial suites to consumers, employees, and stockholders. This rather democratic intent is sometimes misunderstood by those who hear him when he puts it more graphically as trying "to smash corporate power."

Much of Nader's vehemence comes from his conviction that he is pressing the case of the defenseless consumer or employee. He is convinced that the crimes committed in boardrooms or managerial offices are far more serious than petty theft. Bribery, changing test data, and financial manipulation are far more serious crimes in a society that is so totally dependent on large institutions. Even though these crimes undermine the very credibility of the institutions, they most often go unpunished and even unnoticed by many of the public. Nader, like many others, feels that stiff prison sentences in place of token fines would be a more effective deterrent to unethical business practices.

Ralph Nader worked essentially alone from 1965 to 1968. In that summer he was joined by a group of law students, and this pattern has continued and expanded to the present. The first summer group did a study of the Federal Trade Commission, and in 1969 a larger group expanded their efforts. From their Center for the Study of Responsive Law later sprang Campaign GM, Public Interest Research Group, the Center of Science in the Public Interest, and a number of other parallel organizations. The model is the same: Do your homework carefully, write up the results clearly and convincingly, and get the message out to those who can do something about it. Nader's Raiders appear before congressional committees and/or release their findings to the press. While their work does not always generate full agreement, it is generally respected because it is thorough and well documented.[67]

[65]Ralph Nader, *Unsafe at Any Speed* (New York: Pocket Books, 1966).

[66]See S. Prakash Sethi, "General Motors' Nadir, Ralph Nader," in his *Up Against the Corporate Wall*, 2nd ed. (Englewood Cliffs, N.J.: Prentice-Hall, 1974), p. 374.

[67]For a collection of the work of many Nader-inspired individuals and organizations, see Mark Green and Robert Massie, Jr., eds., *The Big Business Reader: Essays on Corporate America* (New York: Pilgrim, 1980). An earlier collection on nutrition and the food industry is Catherine Lerza and Michael Jacobson, *Food for People, Not for Profit* (New York: Ballantine, 1975).

Chief Executive Officer and Board

⎾Those who bear the ultimate responsibility in a firm are top management, especially the chief executive officer and the board of directors. The CEO can have immense influence on the attitudes, values, and ethics of the workplace and the firm as a whole⏋CEOs today are better educated than their forebears and they are less autocratic.[68] They spend more time informing subordinates and seeking consensus. Moreover, they themselves deal much more with public policy issues and with government. Pressures of the office have brought about greater turnover among chief executives, and the average age of the CEO has risen because of the need for more experience.[69] Today's CEO must be far more sensitive to attitudes and abilities of coworkers and to emerging public attitudes and community values.

As pointed out at the end of Chapter 1⎾the board of directors is really an autonomous unit; it is responsible to itself⏋This fact has triggered renewed discussion on the need for greater accountability for the board.[70] Some suggestions to achieve this are at least a majority of outside directors (that is, not in the employ of the firm); nominating, audit, and social responsibility committees of the board made up exclusively of outside members; and an outside chairperson of the board. The values undergirding these changes are that the corporation can no longer afford to act in a narrow, proprietary, and secretive fashion. Its actions impinge upon thousands of people, so in addition to the interests of management and shareholders, it must also take into account the concerns of consumers, employees, and the larger community.

Ethical Investors
and Shareholder Democracy

Institutional investors (university endowments, pension funds, foundations, trust funds, and banks) began voting their shares of common stock on various social responsibility issues during the 1970s.[71] Among the many issues that have

---

[68]David Rockefeller, Irving Shapiro, and Reginald Jones, "Life at the Top—What It Takes to Run a Big Business," *U.S. News & World Report,* June 15, 1981, pp. 38-40; also Isadore Barmash, *The Chief Executives* (Philadelphia: Lippincott, 1978).

[69]Douglas Bauer, "Why Big Business Is Firing the Boss," *New York Times Magazine,* March 8, 1981, pp. 22-25, 79-87; also Barmash, *Chief Executives.* On this and other related issues, see Mark Mizruchi, "Who Controls Whom? An examination of the Relation Between Management and Boards of Directors in Large American Corporations," *Academy of Management Review* 8 (July, 1983), pp. 426-35.

[70]Harold M. Williams, "The Role of the Director in Corporate Accountability," address to Economic Club of Detroit, May 1, 1978; Business Roundtable, *The Role and Composition of the Board of Directors of the Large Publicly Held Corporation* (New York: Business Roundtable, 1978); William R. Dill, ed., *Running the American Corporation* (Englewood Cliffs, N.J.: Prentice-Hall, 1978); "Outsider-Dominated Boards Grow, Spurred by Calls for Independence," *Wall Street Journal,* November 3, 1980, p. 26; also "Outside Directors Multiply," *Wall Street Journal,* March 9, 1982, p. 1.

[71]John G. Simon, Charles W. Powers, and Jon P. Gunnemann, *The Ethical Investor* (New Haven, Conn.: Yale University Press, 1972); and Bevis Longstreth and H. David Rosebloom, *Corporate Social Responsibility and the Institutional Investor* (New York: Praeger, 1973).

been presented to shareholders for vote in recent years are nuclear power, operations in South Africa, disposal of toxic wastes, equal employment opportunity, and sales of infant formula. By placing these issues on the ballot for shareholder vote, the initiating group is able to focus top management's attention on the issue, inform the general public, and sometimes negotiate to achieve its ends with management.

The Project on Corporate Responsibility, a Nader-inspired group, pressed General Motors for reform through the shareholders resolution mechanism throughout the 1970s. While no shareholder resolution which opposed management has obtained anything near the 51 percent vote which would compel management to comply, even a few percent of shareholders often represent hundreds of thousands of shares and many prestigious institutional investors who are questioning management policy. The embarrassment of having these shareholders vote against management is often pressure enough. For example, while the proposals of the Project on Corporate Responsibility did not receive even 3 percent of the shareholder vote, they did help to produce some significant results at General Motors: publication of an annual social report; establishment of a public policy committee of the board; increased minority numbers in management positions; appointment of black activist Reverend Leon Sullivan to GM's board; increased purchases from minority suppliers; and use of minority banks.

The Interfaith Center for Corporate Responsibility (ICCR) is now the principal agent for placing social issues on the shareholders' ballot. The ICCR is a division of the National Council of Churches. It represents 14 Protestant denominations and about 170 Roman Catholic orders and dioceses.[72] In 1983, 156 resolutions were presented to more than 100 firms. Of these, 45 were successfully negotiated with management and withdrawn. Hence 111 were voted upon. Of that number 54 received a sufficient number of votes to be eligible to be resubmitted the following year.[73] To help institutional investors reach a judgment on the merit of the various proposals, the Investor Responsibility Research Center (IRRC) was set up "at the instigation of President Derek Bok at Harvard and with the assistance of the Ford, Carnegie and Rockefeller Foundations."[74] The IRRC (not to be confused with the ICCR) presents the position of both management and the activist group which has introduced the proposal. The IRRC then analyzes the proposal and poses the critical questions, as it sees them. The IRRC does not recommend how to vote; that is the investor's decision. At the end of the proxy season the IRRC publishes a summary of the season's voting. It lists the firms, the issues, and the percentage of shareholders supporting the proposal, and it often indicates which institutional investors supported or opposed individual proposals and why.

The shareholder resolution as an instrument of raising social policy issues

[72]Theodore V. Purcell, "Management and the 'Ethical' Investors," *Harvard Business Review* (September–October 1979), 24–44.

[73]*The 1983 Proxy Season: How Institutions Voted on Shareholder Resolutions and Management Proposals* (Washington, D.C.: Investor Responsibility Research Center, 1983).

[74]Purcell, "Management and the 'Ethical' Investors," p. 26.

is now accepted by most institutional investors. The "Wall Street rule" of blindly supporting management or selling your shares is largely gone. This change reflects the reality that ownership carries with it at least minimal responsibilities to express one's opinions on major policy issues. The shareholders resolution can also be an aid to management. It brings to the attention of management many questions that could easily be overlooked. Moreover, it provides an early warning system to management that these issues may well become more important, in which case they deserve more careful attention. The ethical investor movement is a mechanism in which the larger community can catch the attention of management. It reduces the chances that management will be locked into a narrow and bureaucratic mindset.

Sunlight as Disinfectant: Voluntary Disclosure

Unethical behavior thrives in secrecy. This is no less true of business activities. Firms which are communicative about their operations tend to be more socially responsible. The opposite is also true: Firms that are excessively secretive are rightly treated with suspicion.

Thomas Clausen is now chairman of the World Bank. When chairperson of the Bank of America, he made a strong plea for voluntary disclosure among large American firms. He began by quoting John deButts, chairman of American Telephone & Telegraph. Business can best demonstrate its accountability "by adopting a sufficient openness to public inquiry . . . to make clear that we recognize that what once we might have been disposed to call 'our' business is in fact the public's business and that the public, having a stake in our decisions, should have a voice in them as well."[75]

⌊The case for disclosure is based precisely on the fact that information is required for the free market to be effective. Without accurate information, inevitably there are misallocations and inefficiencies.⌋As Clausen put it, " . . . a company's actions simply cannot be judged 'efficient,' 'responsive,' 'accountable,' or 'consistent with the public interest,' unless sufficient information about its activities is available." Clausen maintains that if ever government regulation or even socialism becomes the "American way," it will be because business leaders were not sensitive to the needs of their constituencies.

Among the more important strategies for implementing adequate disclosure and socially responsible behavior are oversight by the board of directors, perhaps with the help of an ethics or social policy staff or committee of the board; and a corporate social report on public interest issues. More than 100 large firms now have ethics, social policy, or public policy committees of their boards.[76] Among

---

[75]Thomas Clausen, "Voluntary Disclosure: An Idea Whose Time Has Come," in *Corporations and Their Critics*, ed. Thornton Bradshaw and David Vogel (New York: McGraw-Hill, 1981), pp. 61-70.

[76]"Business Strategies for the 1980's," in *Business and Society: Strategies for the 1980's* (Washington, D.C.: U.S. Department of Commerce, 1980), pp. 33-34.

the firms with active ethics or social policy committees are General Electric, Levi Strauss, Mead Corporation, Norton Company, and Bank of America. These board committees are charged with overseeing the implementation of the corporate code of ethics. In addition to a board committee, many firms have a public policy staff along with a social issues planning group. These departments are charged with following government activities, being alert to changes in community attitudes and values, doing political and social planning, and preparing corporate policy on these issues.

A number of firms also publish an annual or periodic social report on corporate activities. These reports contain a list of all corporate activities that have a social impact (for example, waste disposal, energy saving, equal employment opportunity, South African operations) and a systematic assessment of the successes of those activities. Equal employment opportunity and pollution control activities can be accurately measured and reported. Firms have been measuring their activities in these areas for years, as in both areas clear targets and measurable results are easy to obtain.

Clearly, no social report can be attempted until the business firm sets forth clear policy as to what sort of social response it intends to make. Social reporting requires, first, a series of decisions that are heavily influenced by value judgments. Social reporting demands that the goals of the firm and its impact on society be rethought and publicly restated. About 90 percent of Fortune 500 firms report on social performance in some fashion, most often briefly in their annual financial report. Thirty-two publish separate reports on social performance.

Among the firms doing a detailed report on their social activities are General Motors, Control Data, Aetna Life and Casualty Company, Norton Company, and Atlantic-Richfield. The reports of the first three are prepared internally and go into some details on what the firm is doing on socially important issues. For example, General Motors Public Interest Report-1983 covered clean air, electric car, small car safety, acid rain, plant closings, and quality of work life. These social reports tell shareholders and the community about the activities of the firm in each of these areas.

While also prepared by in-house staff, the Norton Company report goes a step further by acknowledging some social targets that have not yet been reached. Atlantic-Richfield is the only American firm to this author's knowledge that asks an outside expert to assess the corporation's performance.[77] Migros of Switzerland, a large food retailer, publishes what is probably the most candid social

[77]Kirk Hanson of Stanford Graduate School of Business is the author of this section of *Participation III* (Los Angeles: Atlantic-Richfield, 1980), pp. 77-82. Additional references to this important issue of social reporting are *Corporate Social Reporting in the United States and Western Europe* (Washington, D.C.: U.S. Department of Commerce, 1979); *The Measurement of Corporate Social Performance* (New York: American Institute of Certified Public Accountants, 1977); David H. Blake, William C. Frederick, and Mildred S. Myers, *Social Auditing: Evaluating the Impact of Corporate Programs* (New York: Praeger, 1976); and Raymond A. Bauer and Dan H. Fenn, Jr., *The Corporate Social Audit* (New York: Russell Sage Foundation, 1972).

report.[78]It, too, is done by an outside management consulting group. When a firm acknowledges its own failures and publishes assessments that are not totally flattering to its own activities, it lends credibility. One is much more likely to believe what is said in such a report, especially the firm's claims of significant progress in other areas.

As noted above, the social impact of a firm's activities and successes is stated also in annual financial reports (Ford, IBM, Xerox, CDC), as well as in executive speeches and advertisements (Exxon, W. R. Grace).

Blocks to Reform:
Apathy and Cynicism

In spite of evidence of sensitivity and responsiveness on the part of most business executives, there is concurrent evidence of public apathy and even cynicism. Unemployment and sagging productivity, the ineffectiveness of government and other large institutions and lessened confidence in their leaders, the danger of a final nuclear holocaust, and other more immediate dangers of urban decay, alienated children in suburbia, alcoholism and drug addiction, street crime and assassinations—all have cast a pall over what was an optimistic spirit in the United States. There is a growing feeling that the problems are too big to be solved. For many, the best "solution" seems to be to move to a location where they can isolate themselves from as many of these threats as possible. Although historically there has always been a great deal of apathy in the United States toward public issues, the present uncertainty has worsened the problem. The supposed landslide by which Ronald Reagan was elected in 1980 represented only about one-third of the electorate, because so many did not bother to vote. Participation rates in U.S. elections are now the lowest they have been in recent years.

Rationalized self-interest, when faced by seemingly insurmountable challenges, can result in retreat and protecting what one already has. Special interest groups abound and have been remarkably successful in achieving their purpose in Washington—even when it is opposed to the wishes of the majority. Special interest groups have fractured us into competing factions. Various candidates are "targeted" for defeat in elections. Witness, for example, the interests of rifle owners, used car dealers, or the New Right. By comparison organizations such as Common Cause and the League of Women Voters, which are designed to represent the interests of the person in the street, do not command the support of large numbers. Although the United States is the oldest modern democracy, in many ways it is also quite backward: "In America the nonparticipation of the

---

[78]For the substance of the audit, see "Migros of Switzerland Prepares a Social Audit," *Responsive Capitalism,* ed. Earl A. Molander (New York: McGraw-Hill, 1980). For a view of the process by the director of that audit, see Meinolf Dierkes, "Corporate Social Reporting and Performance in Germany," in *Research in Corporate Social Performance and Policy,* ed. Lee E. Preston, vol. 2 (Greenwich, Conn.: JAI Press, 1980).

masses is an inherited and persistent trait. Americans find that natural and, therefore, do not inquire why it is so, how it has come to be so, or how it could be changed."[79]

Perhaps this apathy, and now cynicism, are unfortunate by-products of an old and weary democracy. Rather than try to solve problems ourselves, we search for a strong leader who will tell us everything is all right. It makes us feel better when we hear: "We are still the strongest nation in the world." "We have no energy shortage." "No one in the world is going to push us around." Leaders thus fail to address the real issues with honesty and humility; they are more concerned with their own reelection. And we fall farther behind in being able to understand what besets us. Then, when a leader fails to produce, we throw that person out and try someone else.

It is thus impossible to achieve a consensus on what sort of a society we want. About the only time we can muster a majority for anything is on what we do not like. However, people have very different reasons for disliking a proposal or a candidate. So no consensus emerges and we still have no sense of what kind of society we want and what tradeoffs we are willing to make.

Most of the necessary changes in American society (for example, dealing with energy shortages, unemployment, hostile labor-management relations, and crumbling cities and transportation systems) require honesty and humility in assessing the situation and in suggesting solutions. Moreover, most models for renewal are to a large extent people-centered and focus on the local community. Nevertheless, even in the face of this general apathy, there is a willingness to try new ideas. Some encouraging new attitudes and movements are emerging. These will be considered in the next chapter.

When Free Market and When Regulation?

This issue is one of the most central and yet most controversial in this book. The argument for the free market or for government regulation can easily be overstated and can become emotional. The issues have been discussed implicitly throughout the previous chapters. Hence this section will summarize the major arguments and issues surrounding the strengths and limitations of the free market and government regulation.

All who examine Western socioeconomic systems agree that their strength lies in the free market. The free market has provided the multitude of goods and services that we have available, along with the tens of millions of jobs. The system has tapped the immense energy and imagination of millions of people and has directed that work and energy in constructive ways. All will agree that the free market has been the strength of our system. Most will also agree that government regulation ought to be kept to a minimum. Regulation adds to the cost of

[79]Gunnar Myrdal, "Mass Passivity in America," *Center Magazine*, March-April 1974, p. 74.

things: more forms, paper-pushers, bureaucracy, and thus additional overhead. A critical issue, then, is: Is the cost of regulation offset by the benefits in, for example, cleaner air and safer products?[80]

In addition, we Americans have overburdened our legal system, expecting it to solve all the problems of society.[81] Whether the problem is one of job discrimination against the elderly or a safe working environment, we enact legislation as a solution. Moreover, an exaggerated sense of entitlement urges individuals to sue when they feel aggrieved. Because "it is owed to me" a frustrated few can clog the legal system and demand untold hours of managers and other corporate personnel.

On the other hand, within the firm, when a difficult social or public policy issue arises at a business meeting, businesspeople will call on corporate counsel for an opinion on the legality of the move. For many, the opinion of the lawyer settles the question—if it is not illegal, it is all right. Ironically, often these businesspeople are the same ones who are most insistent on getting the government out of business operations. Yet they will not go beyond what the law demands in determining corporate policy and actions. If management thus waits until an action is demanded by law before complying, that stance encourages new legislation. If management wants the government to refrain from enacting restraining legislation, they must take some initiative in addressing the problem themselves—either as an individual firm or in conjunction with others through a trade association.

There are some basic, long-standing, and essential interventions of the government in business operations—for example, method of incorporation, social security, unemployment and antitrust. Much of the early federal regulation was an attempt to regularize the market, especially in transportation: trucking, railroad freight, and airline passengers. In these cases, it now seems wise to allow competition to discipline the market. Hence we have witnessed efforts at deregulation.

⌐Regulation is also called for in cases where a firm, pursuing its own self-interest, jeopardizes the health and safety of the public.⌐For example, if dumping toxic wastes in the nearest landfill is cheaper than safe disposal, attempts to reduce operating costs will lead a firm to do so. The same argument can be made for air and water pollution legislation, and also for basic regulations on product and workplace safety⌐When efforts to cut the cost of production would lead a business to neglect basic health and safety issues, regulation is appropriate⌐ If, for example, one automobile manufacturer offers an automobile which generates far

---

[80]See Ira M. Millstein and Salem M. Katsh, *The Limits of Corporate Power* (New York: Macmillan, 1981); and Paul H. Weaver, "Regulation, Social Policy, and Class Conflict," in *Regulating Business: The Search for an Optimum* (San Francisco: Institute for Contemporary Studies, 1978), pp. 193–216.

[81]Christopher D. Stone, *Where the Law Ends: The Social Control of Corporate Behavior* (New York: Harper & Row, 1975); Edwin M. Epstein, "Societal, Managerial, and Legal Perspectives on Corporate Social Responsibility—Product and Process," *Hastings Law Journal*, 30 (May 1979), 1297.

less pollution, but the catalytic converter adds $300 to the cost of the car, that firm will be at competitive disadvantage with other firms in selling its products. With regulation, all firms must comply with the same clean air standards, so no one firm would be severely penalized simply because it was attentive to the health of the public.

⌈Hence given democracy and the free market, it is up to the people to decide what sort of society they want, and how they want to spend their resources.⌉ One nation may opt for faster industrial growth at the expense of polluted air and water. Another will decide that the health and safety of its people are more important than the lower cost of the products produced; that is, it decides that the producers must pay those costs fully and not expect third parties to bear the burden of the secondary effects of cheaper manufacturing processes.

⌊We can thus conclude that the free market is in general preferable, to the extent that it can handle the problems through the long-term "invisible hand" of Adam Smith and through voluntary actions of firms. Regulation adds costs: costs of people to administer the law, costs of gathering the necessary information, costs to the regulated in dealing with the regulator.[82]⌉

Still, there are now many cases where regulation is the only fair and effective method of achieving a certain purpose decided upon by the people. Moreover, as society becomes more complex, the number of these cases will grow, as the actions of one party infringe on the rights of another. The challenge, then, is to make the regulation simple, direct, effective and less intrusive and less expensive.

SUMMARY AND CONCLUSIONS

Contemporary business activities and policies evidence an underlying, often unspoken, set of values and goals. This chapter describes a cross section of such business operations. Short-term thinking has caused the economic system to falter. While short-term thinking builds on classical economic self-interest and the contemporary "me-oriented" pop psychology, it is causing a serious decline in research, new product planning, and the long-term health of the firm. This in turn has even further eroded the confidence of society in the corporation and its managers. Values and ethics are communicated by the chief executive officer. While there are some executives who are notorious in their self-seeking behavior, there are others who are statesmen. Humane, open, and ethical values can create over time a more participative, attractive, and wholesome climate. Members of that organization will use the best of their abilities to seek the goals of the firm.

Television and advertising are businesses, but they are far more influential on values than the average firm. Americans' values are heavily influenced by what

---

[82]Charles L. Schultze, *The Public Use of Private Interest* (Washington, D.C.: Brookings Institution, 1977).

is beamed to them via television and advertising. Violence, sex-ploitation, and materialism characterize much of television and advertising. Small wonder that people in other countries get a narrow and warped picture of Americans when they see what U.S. television provides them. And it should come as no surprise that these values are becoming more prominent in the younger generation.

While American firms operating overseas bring jobs, new investment, and technology, some also bring the values of self-interest, narrowness, lack of interest, and understanding of local culture. Paradoxically, many American managers support right-wing dictators in third world countries, not because it is the best government for the local people, but because it is the easiest government for business to deal with.

The American promise of jobs, equality, peace, and basic comfort and happiness for all remains an unfulfilled, perhaps an unattainable, dream. The resulting disappointment and malaise that have settled over American society have also profoundly affected business and business leadership. Expectations may be too great, but business, especially television and advertising, has encouraged them. The gap between expectations and reality causes frustration and then despair and apathy. This frustration and distrust are even more apparent when the large corporation is viewed from the perspective of the poor and disadvantaged, whether within the United States or in Asian, African, or Latin American countries.

Large organizations, division of labor, and impersonal relationships leave people feeling alienated, powerless, and apathetic. Under such circumstances, the organization does not get the best effort and most creative thinking from its workers. In an effort to tap these abilities, a large variety of worker participation programs have been developed, among them quality of work life programs. Meanwhile, Americans use five to eight times their share of the world's resources. Individualism and the Protestant ethic carried Americans fast and far in development, but now delayed gratification has given way to the consumer ethic of "buy now; pay later." Individualism encourages various legitimate and illegitimate "get rich quick" schemes, not always to the benefit of society.

In the traditional American pragmatic fashion of incremental change, there are signs of hope. Various public interest groups have been successful in urging firms, for example, to give greater attention to product safety, to hire and promote minorities, and to communicate corporate public interest activities to shareholders and the community. Many endowments, pension funds, and foundations now exercise their ownership responsibilities and vote their shares in a socially responsive fashion. Although they are as yet only a small minority of all shareholders, they do represent a form of industrial democracy. Moreover, the additional disclosure that we witness in many firms allows the public and shareholders to obtain more information, and thus to make more informed and intelligent purchase and public policy decisions. The intervention of the government into the free market is appropriate when there is no other way to achieve an important end and when the cost of the new regulation will be more than offset by the benefits to the larger society.

DISCUSSION QUESTIONS

1. Why do Americans choose to consume more and save less than other peoples? How does this affect (a) productivity and (b) values?
2. Outline the reasons why management bears prime responsibility for poor productivity in the United States.
3. What is the evidence for a loss of confidence in American business?
4. What analogy does Kenneth Mason, former president of Quaker Oats, use in rejecting Milton Friedman's position that the purpose of a corporation is to maximize returns to shareholders?
5. What are the strengths and weaknesses of self-interest as a motive for corporate managers?
6. Does rationalized self-interest as a goal of businesspeople necessarily cast the government into the role of a regulator? How so?
7. What causes most of the cases of cancer in men and women? What are the implications of this for private sector planning? For public policy?
8. How would you characterize the differences in values between the less ethical executives and firms and the "statesmen executives"?
9. In what way do the media and advertising influence values? Does advertising present a false and deceptive image of business to citizens?
10. You are president of a firm about to set up operations in a Latin American country. For plant location you have a choice of two countries which are relatively equal in wage rates, resources, and marketing opportunities. The first is a democracy much like the United States with elections, labor unions, and permits required of national and local officials. The second country is a stable dictatorship which outlaws unions and labor disruptions, has but one strong central authority to deal with and which is very friendly to American business. Which country would you recommend to your board of directors for the plant site? Why?
11. Outline some of the problems that face the contemporary manager with regard to worker attitudes, shareholder relations, future planning, and values.
12. Who are the "moderate reformers"? What are some of the changes that have come about because of their efforts? Do they make business more democratic? More efficient? More responsible? Have any of these changes been institutionalized? How so?

CHAPTER SEVEN
BUSINESS VALUES
FOR THE FUTURE

We do not see (the poor of the world's) faces, we do not know their names, we cannot count their number. But they are there. And their lives have been touched by us. And ours by them. . . . George Bernard Shaw put it perfectly: "You see things, and say why? But I see things that never were, and I say why not?"

—Robert S. McNamara, conclusion of his last address
as president of the World Bank

Strategic planning is essential to business success. Planning in turn is based on projections of what to expect in the coming decades. New product possibilities and the attitudes of potential customers and people in the future work force are among the most important elements in corporate planning. These in turn are heavily dependent on changing values of people. Being alert to these changing values also enables a firm to formulate better public policy and to be a better citizen. This chapter summarizes present values, examines the importance of possessing a coherent business ideology, presents material on future scanning for business, and attempts to chart the direction of changing values over the coming decades.

TODAY'S BUSINESS VALUES

Past and present values of the business system have been examined in the previous chapters: how these values developed and how they influence current corporate policies. Business is not an isolated institution. It operates in society and is influenced by both government and social values (culture). Business, as well as government and culture, exist within society. Within that society, business has relationships with both government and with the local culture; they influence each other across a broad range of issues. For a schematic view of these relationships see Figure 7-1. The most visible, and perhaps the most critical, relationship is that of business and government: the extent of government regulation of business and the degree of business lobbying of government to obtain its own desires. Government regulation here is understood as that which is directed to achieving better the public interest, so as to obtain a social good that the free market most likely would not have brought about.

The extent of government regulation, and indeed the extent to which the individual firm should accede to the public good, is hotly disputed. However, the heat of this debate has obscured the fact that corporate managers and their public advocacy critics (Nader-inspired activists and others) share much common ground. Let us outline those issues on which these two groups agree and disagree.

FIGURE 7-1   Business, government, society, and culture relationships

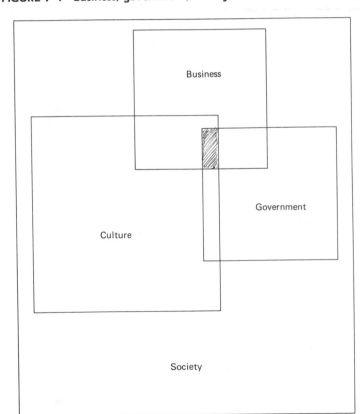

Source: Adapted from the interpenetrating systems model of Lee E. Preston and James E. Post, *Private Management and Public Policy* (Englewood Cliffs, N.J.: Prentice-Hall, 1975). See also Preston and Post's "Private Management and Public Policy: Ideas for the Eighties" (Baltimore: Center for Business and Public Policy. University of Maryland, December 1980).

Managers and Critics Agree

Almost all corporate managers and business activists agree:

1. Free enterprise is the most efficient, productive, flexible, and innovative socio-economic system yet devised.
2. Free market mechanisms are not sufficient in themselves to provide for social goods that are costly to firms, for example, clean air, safe drugs, accurate advertising.
3. Business operates today in a new, changing sociopolitical environment:
   a. The federal government regulates many aspects of business, for example, safety of product and workplace, employment of minorities and women, air pollution from stationary sources and automobiles.
   b. Firms have institutionalized many aspects of corporate social responsibility, for example, new company officers, codes, board committees (see Chapters 5 and 6).
   c. Voluntary, not legislated, corporate social responsiveness is acknowledged as essential for several reasons: It prevents further government regulation; it improves the image of the firm and of business as a whole; and it is the good thing to do, regardless of law or image.
4. Additional cooperation is needed among business, government, working people, and community groups.
5. While the United States may be facing these problems earlier than other countries, they eventually will be common to all industrialized countries.
6. Among business managers and government officials, there is a need for sensitivity to ethical issues and for the ability to solve ethical problems (see Chapter 5).

Before examining in greater detail these areas of agreement, let us indicate the one major area in which managers and critics have a substantial level of disagreement: Under what circumstances should free enterprise be unleashed and when should government regulation be used to help achieve the most just policy and the best outcome for society?

Intelligent Dialogue Between Business Managers and Critics

Free enterprise is clearly the most efficient and flexible socioeconomic system yet designed. Although productivity and innovation have fallen in the last few years, bolstering them is a top priority among executives today. John W. Gardner, public advocate and founder of Common Cause, put it clearly: "Virtually every far-reaching social change in our history has come from the private sector; we must find ways to preserve that kind of independence." Gardner acknowledges that there have been abuses, "But they have been trivial compared to the great and lasting benefits in preserving our free society."[1]

---

[1] John W. Gardner, *Corporate Ethics Digest*, 1 (September–October 1980), 2. For a superb survey of the characteristics of the best performing U.S. firms, see Thomas J. Peters and Robert H. Waterman, *In Search of Excellence* (New York: Harper & Row, 1982).

Free markets, competition, and potentially large financial rewards, personally and for the firm, have encouraged innovation and dedication to the task on the part of some of the most talented people of our society. Many of the most intelligent, energetic, and capable people have devoted themselves to supplying our goods and services. Compared with the status given the businessperson in other cultures, the manager in the United States has been accorded high prestige. Undoubtedly this prestige has been one of the factors that draw these people into business. Completing the supporting cycle, this prestige has rested at least in part on the incomparable success of business.

In regard to the second agreement, there is no inherent incentive for individual firms to produce social goods (that is, goods that cannot be sold or will not enable the producer to ask a higher price for the product), even though these goods may be of great benefit to society. Moreover, economic incentives reward the unscrupulous manager for making a quick buck through unethical practices, so long as that manager doesn't get caught. Fletcher L. Byrom, chairman of Koppers Company, notes the ineffectiveness of the free market:

> There may be countering arguments, but I am willing to assume that, in terms of the needs of generations to come, many of the resources we now use and for which we have found no substitutes, are in short supply and should be allocated to avoid waste. . . . We cannot continue to misuse our resources for life styles that are self-indulgent at their best and frivolous at their worst.[2]

Byrom says that natural resources are cheap today and hence we use them for trivial purposes. Yet these same resources will be precious to future generations. In the same fashion, pure free market incentives encourage polluted water and fire-prone buildings, since clean water and fire-resistant buildings are costly.

Third, business operations today have many more impacts on society, from methods of solid waste disposal to the money provided to political candidates by its political action committees. This is a much more interdependent business-social-political environment than twenty years ago.[3] Various government agencies (federal, state, and local) seek to extend their brand of social control over the quality and safety of product, workplace, and environment. Meanwhile, to address these same problems on their own, many firms have set up new company officers and departments, quality of work life programs, and two-way communication at shareholder meetings. Moreover, in the future, business,

---

[2]Fletcher L. Byrom, "Corporate Policy Applied to a Finite World," speech, October 21, 1975, pp. 7, 15, quoted in Neil W. Chamberlain, *Remaking American Values: Challenge to a Business Society* (New York: Basic Books, 1977), p. 88. For a carefully reasoned statement, see Robert B. Ashmore, "The Public Interest and Business Decisions," *Proceedings of the American Catholic Philosophical Association—1981* (Washington, D.C.: American Catholic Philosophical Association, 1981), pp. 278-87.

[3]Francis W. Steckmest, with a resource and review committee for the Business Roundtable, *Corporate Performance: The Key to Public Trust* (New York: McGraw-Hill, 1982).

government, and other agencies will have even more interrelationships because of the increasing complexity of business operations.[4]

Fourth, current management observers are not only calling for additional cooperation but have put the burden on management to initiate this cooperation and trust (see Chapter 6). Business is in a position of strength when dealing with both government and labor. The fifth and sixth areas of agreement are self-explanatory.

The principal disagreement is on the practical question of on what issues and at what point the free market ought to be constrained by legislation or regulation in order to achieve the common good. Some have put the problem as: At what point do we effect the tradeoff between efficiency and justice? However, it is not always a tradeoff. As noted in Chapter 6, productivity has declined for the same underlying reason that makes firms less socially responsible: a short-term time perspective. Management has failed to take a long-range view of its operations. A more basic reason for this disagreement is the absence of a public policy consensus. Rampant pluralism in values makes it difficult to gain agreement on public policy questions. We Americans find it far easier to agree on which political candidates and legislation we dislike (our reasons are diverse, of course); but we find it far more difficult to reach agreement on which candidates or issues we support.

Basic Beliefs Support an Ethic

The disagreements over policy questions can generally be traced to quite different basic beliefs. An individual's fundamental ideology can be charted from one's answers to such questions as

1. What do I see as my fundamental purpose in life?
2. Are men and women basically self-seeking, or are they basically good and generous?
3. Do men and women have a transcendental and spiritual end, or is this present life, with its pleasures and material satisfactions, all there is?
4. Is there any such thing as a moral absolute, or is everything relative?
5. Does society exist for persons, or do people exist for society? Or is the relationship more complex?
6. What is the purpose of the state? What is the purpose of the business firm?
7. Are the forces of history determined, and if so, are these forces moving toward the inevitable long-term progress of humanity?

Energizing the Human Spirit

An individual's answers to the above questions give some indication as to what motivates that person and what energizes that person's spirit. The responses

---

[4]For an outline of the changes and a projection of future movement in corporate social responsibility, see William C. Frederick, "From CSR₁ to CSR₂: The Maturing of Business-and-Society Thought," Working Paper, Graduate School of Business, University of Pittsburgh, WP-279, 1978.

provide information on my own perceptions of life and its purpose, and how I perceive how the majority of others look on their own lives. A more detailed method of examining our own values and life goals was proposed in Chapter 4, in planning our own lives and career.

The answers to these questions may show that I am centered on my own interests and pleasures and that other people are largely secondary or instrumental for me. Or, on the other hand, my responses may show that I have a stronger concern for others and perhaps am often willing to sacrifice myself for others. To gain yet another perspective, I might imagine myself in the position of hiring new people to work for me. From a potential employee, toward what responses to these questions would I be most positive? Talent and experience being equal, who would I choose to hire? Or closer to home: What profile of responses would I prefer from a future business partner or even a possible spouse?

As a general question, I might ask myself what sort of firm I would choose to work for, or kind of country I would like to live in—one made up of individuals who are concerned with their own interests and pleasures or one made up of people who are concerned for others? In which sort of firm would I be likely to do better work and enjoy that work more? Given either kind of firm, would it make any difference whether my own personal motivations were centered on my own life and career or whether I was more concerned for others? In which would I be more successful? In which more satisfied? In any case, in planning and adjusting a socioeconomic system, in proposing either regulation or voluntary actions, my perceptions of how others act and are motivated are most important.

Chances are that in any random group of citizens there will be a wide variety of responses to these basic belief questions. It is partly because of this wide diversity on such basic ideals that we find it so difficult to achieve consensus on basic questions. In general we have lost much of what our religious heritage provided for us. James Kuhn of the Columbia Graduate School of Business says that ethics must stem from an ethic of a lived community. It thus draws on the moral consensus of the larger society. Ethics here is understood as both the norms whereby one distinguishes right from wrong and also the basic value scheme of the individual. The younger generation in the United States is a generation cut off from its roots. We have lost many of the basic convictions that Christianity had brought to us. For example, we have lost the Christian notions of serving, calling, community, and sinfulness.[5] Each of these notions provided the foundation for an ethic and were also pillars upon which a civilization was built. They thus profoundly affected laws and personal relationships. They brought attention to the need of the other person, the fact that God calls me to my life and work, that we are together in one body, and that we are all sinners and thus need forgiveness. Selfishness and arrogance were recognized for what they were: not

[5]These ideas were presented informally by James Kuhn at the Workshop on Business Ethics, American College and Stanford Graduate School of Business, October 8-10, 1981.

just an individual's personal peculiarities, which are as acceptable as any others, but as values which either evidenced a less mature individual or in a mature person were considered wrong and sinful.

A VIABLE BUSINESS CREED

As has been pointed out consistently by those who have examined business values, the most salient and precious of these is freedom: free markets, free competition, free movement of people and capital, and most especially freedom of the individual. Current efforts to deregulate are geared to obtaining the values of the free market. Antitrust legislation, however effective it may be, is an attempt to preserve the free market.

Important as personal freedom is in our society, it is not unlimited. An individualism that is not conscious of other people leads only to mistrust, frustration, and ultimately chaos. Using a familiar example, one does not have the freedom to shout "Fire!" in a crowded theater. Traffic lights introduce coercion that was undoubtedly objected to by early libertarians. A business firm does not have the freedom to mislead in its product advertising or to dump its waste in a lake. As people live closer together and become more dependent on one another, freedom must be constrained by both internal and external checks. In fact, some argue that real freedom emerges only when a people have formed internal constraints: ". . . freedom is endangered if a free society's shared values are no longer sufficiently vigorous to preserve the moral cohesion on which the discipline of free men rests."[6] Although it may seem a paradox to the individualist, activities limited by a consideration of others, such as the traffic lights or truth in advertising, introduce an even greater freedom for all.

One of the strengths of American business ideology has been its pragmatism: how to get the job done without much concern for inconsistencies. Simply put, pragmatism says that which works is by that fact good and true. Daniel Bell puts it bluntly:

> . . . the ideology of American business in the postwar years became its ability to perform. The justification of the corporation no longer lay primarily in the natural right of private property, but in its role as an instrument for providing more and more goods to the people.[7]

Pragmatism thus led us to accept values and goals simply because they work, and often regardless of inequities and undesirable by-products. Now that free enterprise is not working so well, its fragile ideology is crumbling and there is a frantic scurrying about to build a new creed.[8]

---

[6]Peter Viereck, *Shame and Glory of the Intellectuals* (Boston: Beacon, 1953), p. 196.

[7]Daniel Bell, *The Coming of the Post-Industrial Society* (New York: Basic Books, 1973), p. 272.

[8]See, for example, the wide attention given to Michael Novak, *The Spirit of Democratic Capitalism* (New York: Simon & Schuster, 1982). *Time, Fortune, Business Week,* and many other journals gave it extensive review.

Any substantive defense of the values of the business and economic system cannot rest merely on the values of efficiency and freedom, for the obvious questions arise: Productivity for what? Freedom for what? These values and the business system they support are therefore not ultimate ends in their own right but are good insofar as they allow a person to pursue other more valuable goals in life. Higher productivity allows a society to produce the goods and services it needs with less effort and thus allows its citizens to pursue these other goals. This is no small benefit.

Aristocratic Economics

The American political system is democratic; the economic system is aristocratic. Politically, every person has but one vote, but because some people earn more than fifty times the average annual income, they possess fifty times the economic "voting power" of others. They may spend their personal income on expensive clothes, second and third homes, lavish vacations, or even political influence, while others, who work just as hard or harder, find it difficult to pay the rent and grocery bills. While we say that wealth is the reward for hard work, we also know that good fortune—especially in the way of birth and resulting opportunities—is even more important. Those who inherit wealth have a most comfortable life; there is little relationship between the work they do and the income they receive. Inheritance and progressive income taxes have attempted to reduce this inequity, but recent tax reductions have disproportionately benefited the wealthy.

A more profound and far-reaching weakness of free enterprise values is the encouragement of what are ultimately selfish activities. Free markets, competition, and flexibility—all guided by Adam Smith's "invisible hand"—supposedly result in the most economic use of resources. Or, as the seventeenth-century British pamphleteer Bernard Mandeville put it, "Private vices make public benefit." He showed how blind and greedy profit seeking contributes to the public good. In fact, capitalism does reward the selfish. Furthermore, it provides a rationalization that promotes and blesses self-seeking, ego-centered behavior.

Making consumer sovereignty a central value is convenient because it distributes responsibility. Who is responsible for the many problems that we have drifted into the past generation—use of scarce resources, the quality of the air over Los Angeles or Denver, toxic waste disposal? Consumer sovereignty implies undirected, promiscuous economic growth. Coupled with the free market, it is also a convenient principle for economists who proclaim a "value-free" economics. This principle presumably enables them to dodge value questions. But such an approach in fact values the individual over the community, encourages self-seeking behavior, and leads to other personal and national impasses. Seen in this way consumer sovereignty and free enterprise thus enable their proponents

---

⁹Bernard Mandeville, quoted in Peter Drucker, *Management: Tasks, Responsibilities, Practices* (New York: Harper & Row, 1973), p. 809.

to avoid the vital question of what kind of society we want as a people—until flexibility is gone, options have been narrowed, and crises are upon us.

Nineteenth-century capitalism in the United States was built on rugged individualism and enlightened self-interest. Huge fortunes were amassed before much social legislation was enacted. The little person, whether worker or producer, was often hurt by the robber barons. Nevertheless, these wealthy individuals eventually used much of their fortunes to benefit the public. Indeed, Andrew Carnegie's defense of wealth was based on the ability of the rich person to better use those funds for public purposes (see Chapter 2). John Rockefeller funded and built the University of Chicago, Carnegie built libraries across the United States, and Collis Potter Huntington built a superb rapid transit system for Los Angeles (which was dismantled in the 1950s by a combine of GM, Firestone, and Standard Oil of California). Various foundations—Carnegie, Rockefeller, Ford, Mellon—are all set up to serve the public purpose, and they have been instrumental in funding valuable new planning and programs. Are fortunes made in this decade used similarly for public purposes?

Democracy and Special Interests

There has been a lack of planning in the past two decades: There have been few new libraries, museums, or parks; and suburbs have sprawled haphazardly, paving over areas that would have been set aside as parkland or rapid transit right-of-way a generation ago. Vision and planning make a city livable, and we seem to have less of both today. Our attention has been focused on new homes, new plants, new expressways. Meanwhile our cities are deteriorating because so many of our parks, libraries, roads, and public transit facilities were built fifty or sixty years ago. This realization of the deterioration of our infrastructure comes as a shock. Each individual pursuing his or her own self-interest does not always work to the best interests of the entire community.

This discussion of the strengths and weaknesses of the American business system brings us to the core question: How does that system go about adapting to change? How are inefficiencies and inequities repaired? What does the economic and business system have at its disposal that will enable it to meet the future with confidence?

Change in the past has been accomplished primarily through the political process: voting and legislatures. On public interest issues Americans are generally committed to an open system and to consensus. This process works slowly, but it does bring about changes in law and thus in life. When it comes to the inadequacies of the business system, we often need a good swat from a baseball bat to alert us. It took the urban race riots to force us to realize the extent and injustice of job discrimination. Lake Erie died before we began to realize the dangers of pollution. It took the Three Mile Island nuclear plant disaster to alert us to the dangers and the expense of nuclear energy. Bank of America executives acknowledge that it took the bombing and burning of a branch in Isle Vista, California, to force them to be more responsive to the needs of the larger society.[10]

A democratic people act when they personally feel a need. Hence, a democracy works slowly and generally requires a crisis to awaken its citizens to new public needs. This may be a fatal flaw of democracy. It makes planning extremely difficult. The pressure is on legislators to make an immediate impact on problems of home constituents. There is no incentive to trade off present goods for future goods, and any investment policy is just that. On the contrary, special interests, short elective terms, and felt needs back home militate against any sort of long-term investment of time or capital in research or planning that will pay off a generation from now. Moreover, many of the needs now facing us are serious and long term (pollution, urban decay, dwindling resources, lower productivity). If a crisis must affect us before we understand the seriousness of each of these problems, there will be no time or flexibility left to find solutions.

Lack of Clear Values

The director of a research institute reported a few years ago that young people were quite critical of the beliefs of their parents and other adults. They were not critical of *what* they believed, but of what seemed to be a lack of beliefs and convictions. Their elders' values seemed to be largely inherited and absorbed passively from the surrounding culture; they had very little in the way of thought-out, internalized goals and values of their own.

Young people, as well as their elders, are often victims of mass, homogenized education and passive entertainment. Mass education has an influence not only directly on thinking but also indirectly through clothes, food, and TV programs that are currently "acceptable."[11] Mass education thus has as much influence outside the classroom as inside. It substitutes tastes and fads for critical thinking and the development of personal goals and values. Often young people and adults escape thinking by turning on the television set. Thus the moral and intellectual fiber of our country has been softened "by being pounded by passive entertainment all these years."[12]

Young people's cynicism, apathy, and confusion with regard to goals and values put an even greater burden on their elders to articulate their own values. If adults in a society, who have traditionally been thought of as experienced and wise, do not have some considered notion of their own life goals and aspirations, there would seem to be little hope for young people. It is especially important that individuals have fairly clearly articulated values in a time of rapid change. Otherwise, these persons are left with no rudder, pushed by events from one job or neighborhood to another. Without values and goals, they are not in con-

---

[10]See Louis B. Lundborg, *Future Without Shock* (New York: Norton, 1974). Lundborg was chairman of the board of the bank.

[11]"The Nation's Real Values—Still Alive," *U.S. News & World Report,* July 5, 1982, pp. 47-50.

[12]Ibid., p. 48.

trol of their own careers, lives, or destinies. Opportunities, challenges, and crises now come rapidly, and individuals who have never reflected on what they do and why they do it are unable to deal with these events, so that they, their families, and others may profit and grow. Rather, such people will be less fulfilled, their families confused and frustrated, and others hurt.

One of the functions of education is to enable and encourage students to reflect on their own values and make them explicit, so that they may then be able to grow and make clear life choices. Alvin Toffler, in analyzing precisely this problem, has harsh words for the schools:

> . . . students are seldom encouraged to analyze their own values and those of their teachers and peers. Millions pass through the education system without once having been forced to search out the contradictions in their own value systems, to probe their own life goals deeply, or even to discuss these matters candidly with adults and peers. . . .
>
> Nothing could be better calculated to produce people uncertain of their goals, people incapable of effective decision-making under conditions of overchoice.[13]

The need for individuals to search out and make explicit their own values and goals is underscored in a period of rapid change, and a primary vehicle for this sort of examination and evaluation is the school—yet the school, from kindergarten to university, has failed in this respect. Educators maintain that education should be "objective," and that values are too controversial a field for a public institution. What they fail to recognize is that such a position is itself a value position. A generation growing up without internalized goals and values has contributed to national cynicism, apathy, and confusion. The resulting individualism and inability to gain a consensus on public policy questions have created severe strains in our democratic society.[14]

Economic Planning

In the early 1980s some politicians on the national scene said that national planning was not necessary; competition in the private sector would provide new income, jobs, and growth. Ironically, these policies did not achieve new jobs and income. On the contrary, firms themselves know the importance of planning. It is essential as industrial activities become more complex and interdependent. Because of the delicate balance of demands for technology, capital, and markets, large firms have long since engaged in planning. However, such private sector planning focuses on the growth and health of the individual firm and is not directly concerned with the public welfare. For example, in deciding standards, there is a clear tradeoff as to how clean a society wants its air and water to be and how

[13]Alvin Toffler, *Future Shock* (New York: Random House, 1970), p. 370.

[14]Alvin Toffler, "The Political System Cannot Cope with Today's Diversity," *U.S. News & World Report,* June 9, 1980, p. 80.

much they are willing to pay for it. The more basic question is: What sort of a society do the citizens want?

Economic planning for the public welfare thus becomes even more essential. A major goal of public economic planning is to bring the goals and operations of private enterprise into better alignment with the overall goals of society. Adam Smith's "invisible hand" does not provide assurance that the pursuit of private gain will automatically work to the benefit of society.[15] Americans long ago decided that the free market was not a good indicator of what should be spent on such public goods as national security, fire protection, and parks. In the last two chapters of this book, we have specified many other areas, such as the environment, the use of scarce resources, and overseas bribery, in which the free market has not only *not* solved the problem but has contributed to it.

The U.S. Congress, too, has recognized the necessity for economic planning and the anticipation of unforeseen and undesirable consequences of gross industrial growth. Beneath every tax, subsidy, and government regulation lie value judgments as to what sort of economic activities should be encouraged. Sometimes, unfortunately, these judgments are more influenced by special interests than the public welfare. To look at these problems, Congress has established its Office of Technology Assessment, through which to review recent and proposed technological and industrial activities and innovations in order to examine all side effects—especially the otherwise unforeseen "downstream" effects.

However, free markets and competition generally do provide greater economic efficiencies and encourage self-reliance. Perhaps more important, it has long been an American principle to encourage local autonomy, to support local and small activities rather than usurp them at the federal level. Sociologist Peter Berger has called for the support of "mediating structures." His point is that, wherever possible, public policy should support institutions closer to people— family, church, school, and corporation—as opposed to larger institutions such as the federal government. Berger maintains that only then will people feel responsible and be willing to take on even greater responsibility for their own lives. When unseen government assumes authority over too many aspects of people's lives, those people tend to become withdrawn and apathetic. Hence Berger formulates these two principles:

1. Public policy should protect and foster mediating structures (family, church, school, corporation).

2. Whenever possible, public policy should utilize mediating structures as its agents.[16]

---

[15]See the detailed study, Edward S. Herman, *Corporate Control, Corporate Power* (Cambridge: Cambridge University Press, 1981); also George F. Rohrlich, "The Challenge of Social Economics," in *Social Economics for the 1970s*, ed. George F. Rohrlick (New York: Dunellen, 1970), pp. 3-5.

[16]Peter Berger, *Facing Up to Modernity: Excursions in Society, Politics and Religion* (New York: Basic Books, 1977), p. 138ff.

These principles thus encourage the support of intermediate institutions, or "mediating structures." These institutions are vital to any society, and to the extent they are weakened by federal government intervention, the weaker our society becomes. Moreover, when they are undermined, it touches individuals closely, so is felt more immediately, and thus more readily brings feelings of lack of control, apathy, and finally cynicism.

To focus on these principles and their use with business: How can the individual business firm be channeled, without undermining or seriously weakening it, so as to achieve the goals of society? Putting the question differently: How can individual private sector decisions be more effective in contributing to the benefit of society as a whole? Surely longer term issues, such as research and development, job satisfaction, the use of finite resources, job discrimination, and even hunger are already entering into some corporate decisions. These considerations have become part of corporate decision making either because of the social responsiveness of the firms acting on their own, or because of government constraints (tax incentives, regulations, subsidies). Tax credits for investment in research, for recycling scarce materials, and for new, small enterprises or additional taxes on excessive energy use are examples.

Economic planning for the public welfare will therefore be carried out in two ways. First, those public goods that can best be provided by government directly (parks, police, urban public transportation) will continue to be so provided. Moreover, this segment of the economy will probably grow. Second, on the basis of its long-term policies, government will encourage the private sector to serve also the public good through such incentives as new regulations and changes in the tax laws.[17] For these initiatives to be successful, the reexamination and restatement of economic and public policy will be required.

Government Aids Business

⌈European and Asian governments cooperate much more with the private sector than does the U.S. government⌋ Policies to encourage research and development, stimulate overseas markets, aid small and medium-sized business, and loans to new high-risk entrepreneurs are common overseas and have been suggested here.[18] Urban free enterprise zones would be a subsidy to firms to bring jobs back to the cities.

Executives acknowledge the need for government regulation of business. However, they do ask that these regulations be reasonable, feasible, and meet cost-benefit criteria. Some simple guides have been suggested that would make government rule making more effective and less burdensome:

[17]Ira C. Magaziner and Robert B. Reich, *Minding America's Business,* pt. VI, "Toward a Rational Industrial Policy" (New York: Harcourt Brace Jovanovich, 1982), pp. 329–80. See also the classic and still valuable study of John Maurice Clark, *Social Control of Business* (Chicago: University of Chicago Press, 1926).

[18]Ira C. Magaziner and Robert B. Reich, *Minding America's Business,* "The Substance of a Rational Industrial Policy," (New York: Harcourt Brace Jovanovich, 1982), pp. 343–63.

FIGURE 7-2   The corporation and its stakeholders

1. Set rules that are clear and consistent.
2. Keep the rules technically feasible.
3. Make sure the rules are economically feasible.
4 Make the rules prospective, not retroactive.
5. Make the rules goal setting, not procedure prescribing.[19]

The legal and traditional model of the corporation is that of management being responsible to the board of directors and the directors in turn responsible to the shareholders. Twenty years ago, if one were to ask an executive to whom he or she was responsible, the answer would be to the stockholders. The answer to the same question today brings a quite different response. Customers, in fact, are mentioned most often as being the party to whom management feels most responsible. Thus the executive perceives herself to be responsible to a wide variety of stakeholders: customers, employees, suppliers, government, members of the local community, as well as shareholders. To gain a better understanding of these relationships, see their graphical representation in Figure 7-2.[20]

[19]Jerry McAfee, "How Society Can Help Business," *Newsweek*, July 3, 1978, p. 15.

[20]Thanks to Kirk O. Hanson, of Stanford Graduate School of Business, for this diagram. More sophisticated models of the business and society relationship have been developed. See, for example, Archie B. Carroll, "A Three-Dimensional Conceptual Model of Corporate Performance," *Academy of Management Review*, 4 (October 1979), 497–505; and S. Prakash Sethi, "A Conceptual Framework for Environmental Analysis of Social Issues and Evaluation of Business Response Patterns," *Academy of Management Review*, 4 (January 1979), 63–74.

MANAGING
SOCIOPOLITICAL
FORECASTING

Business planning cannot be done without some idea of what to expect in the future. Some information is available from public sources: demography, availability and price of resources, employment skills, and economic forecasts. Also needed are forecasts of what public policy issues will emerge in the future. Most of the issues discussed in Chapter 6 are public policy questions.

Organizing for the Future

More than 200 of the Fortune 500 corporations have formally established senior positions and staff to aid in the development of public issues.[21] These corporate offices are designed to obtain, analyze, and report information on the social and political environment. The advantages of having such information and using it within the firm are that it lessens managerial surprises, reduces the cost of regulatory compliance, permits "smooth changes," and enables a firm to focus on opportunities and to get ahead of the issues.[22]

A number of sources of information and information-gathering techniques are available to aid the corporation in this effort. Considerable information can be gathered from social indicators, for example, population characteristics, changes in family compensation, and perceptions with regard to what constitutes quality of life.[23] A number of private services are available to firms that, for a substantial fee, will provide some of this information. Among such organizations are Institute for the Future, Center for Futures Research at the University of Southern California's Business School, and the consulting firm Yankelovich, Skelly and White, Inc.

Capital-intensive firms in stable industries have more need of advance warning of future developments because their investment is so large and they are less flexible.[24] Firms that are more flexible in resource deployment can more afford to wait for events to take place. There are a number of techniques that can be utilized to obtain "best guesses" on forthcoming sociopolitical issues. The Delphi technique is a structured method for obtaining a consensus of opinions from a group of experts. The Center for Futures Research used this technique with a

---

[21]William L. Renfro, "Managing the Issues of the 1980's," *The Futurist,* 16 (August 1982), 61.

[22]John E. Fleming, "Public Issues Scanning," paper presented at Social Issues Division, Academy of Management, August 1979, p. 12. For an excellent presentation of corporate planning in an ethical context, see LaRue T. Hosmer, *Strategic Management* (Englewood Cliffs, N.J.: Prentice-Hall, 1982).

[23]Fremont Kast, "Scanning the Future Environment: Social Indicators," *California Management Review,* 23 (Fall 1980), 22–32.

[24]John E. Fleming, "Public Issues Scanning," in *Research in Corporate Social Performance: A Research Annual,* ed. Lee E. Preston, vol. 3 (Greenwich, Conn: JAI Press, 1981), pp. 155–173.

panel of business and academic leaders for its twenty-year forecast of "The Future of Business-Government Relations."[25]

Public Issues Scanning

A major technique used by a large number of firms is called public issues scanning—a process whereby certain critical issues are followed in an effort to determine the direction and speed of their future development. Firms use a number of methods to specify initially these issues. Sometimes the chief executive officer or a group of top managers chooses the issues. At other times staff units scan media sources to determine which issues are becoming paramount, or they might do a structured polling of managers.[26]

Printed media can often provide early indications of emerging trends. Firms can obtain the results of periodic surveys of selected "opinion leader" media— for example, the *Wall Street Journal,* the *New York Times,* or the *Washington Post.* Either corporate staff or an outside consultant can do a brief summary of articles on the specified public policy issues. Over a period of time, it will become clear that interest in a certain issue is increasing, such that there may be new markets, new pressures on the firm, or new legislation forthcoming. Public issues scanning provides an early warning system of these potential developments.

General Electric Company has been the corporate leader in sociopolitical forecasting for almost two decades. The importance given to this function is illustrated by the themes and content of a series of presentations by the chief executive officer of General Electric.[27] Ian Wilson set up the office at GE and developed it as a model for corporate social and political forecasting. Wilson did a series of studies in the late 1960s and 1970s to alert GE's top management to the major social, political, and economic trends in the GE environment. In this fashion, General Electric was able to anticipate many of these movements and save itself much time, money, and embarrassment.[28]

Careers with a Future

Based on the aging of the population, the need for increased productivity in the workplace, the increased cost of energy, and a multitude of other projected changes in the coming decades, there will be new career needs. An under-

[25]For the results, see James O'Toole, "What's Ahead for the Business-Government Relationship?" *Harvard Business Review,* 57 (March-April 1979), 94-105.

[26]Robert H. Moore, "Planning for Emerging Issues," in *Private Enterprise and Public Purpose,* eds. S. Prakash Sethi and Carl L. Swanson, (New York: Wiley, 1981), pp. 373-78.

[27]See, for example, Reginald H. Jones, "Managing in the 1980's," speech presented at Wharton School, February 4, 1980, as an example of the premium Jones and GE put on being able to predict future sociopolitical attitudes and events.

[28]For an account culled from Ian Wilson's own articles and speeches, see "Sociopolitical Forecasting at General Electric," in *Responsive Capitalism: Case Studies in Corporate Social Conduct,* by Earl Molander (New York: McGraw-Hill, 1980), pp. 239-49.

standing of computers is going to become increasingly important in many more occupations: communications, office management, as well as manufacturing, banking, and information management. There will be need for people to set up and operate these new systems.

With manufacturing shifting more to robots, there will be increasing need for people who can design, manufacture, and maintain robots. Cable TV will bring many new jobs, as will laser technology. Energy conservation, alternate energy sources (including solar energy), and the disposal of hazardous wastes are also needs that will demand new technical and managerial skills.[29]

The aging of the population means that health care will demand an increasing share of national resources and energies. There will be new careers in technical fields, such as physical therapy, as well as in the management of hospitals, medical offices, and clinics. Genetic engineering is an area of great current research effort. When there are research breakthroughs, there promises to be considerable future in such fields as microbiology, molecular biology, chemistry, and biophysics. Engineering and business skills will continue to be important as society becomes even more complex.

It is also important to examine the organizational and work environment of a prospective employer. James O'Toole has separated work environments into four major types: meritocratic workplace, behaviorist workplace, entitlementarian workplace, and humanistic workplace. Each is quite different, and it is important that the individual be aware of and seek out the type of work setting in which he or she can work most fruitfully.[30]

FUTURE BUSINESS VALUES

American business and its values have shifted dramatically over the last decade. The earlier sections of this book have attempted to chart these shifts. Because changes continue at a rapid rate, both for the sake of individuals and for the sake of corporate planning it is imperative that we have some sense of the direction and the substance of those changes.

In this final section we will review the changes that are taking place and make some predictions of the future business environment. We will then try to assess their impact on American business values. We will try to identify emerging values that will have a significant impact on the people, firms, and the American business ideology of the future. Note that these emerging values are actually extensions of traditional American values; there are few sharp breaks (Table 7-1). We

[29]*Occupational Outlook for College Graduates, 1980-81* (Washington, D.C.: U.S. Bureau of Labor Statistics, 1980); also Marvin Cetron and Thomas O'Toole, "Careers with a Future: Where the Jobs Will be in the 1990s," *The Futurist,* 16 (June 1982), 11-19.

[30]James O'Toole, "How to Forecast Your Own Working Future," *The Futurist,* 16 (February 1982), 5-11.

TABLE 7-1   Future Values as Extensions of Traditional Values

FUTURE BUSINESS VALUES . . . stem from . . .	TRADITIONAL AMERICAN VALUES
1. Lessened expectations	1. Empirical realism
2. Central role of the person	2. Dignity of the individual
3. Participation in management decisions	3. Entrepreneurship and democratic spirit
4. Business as a servant of society	4. Business as a provider of goods and jobs
5. Efficiency, flexibility, and innovation	5. Growth and productivity
6. Interdependence of people, institutions, and nations	6. Builders of railroads, radio, telephone, television, canals, etc.
7. Harmony with the environment and decentralization	7. Respect for the land; self-reliance
8. Religious roots of new business creed; Theology for the future	8. Influence of religion and churches on American life
9. Concern for others	9. Help neighbor: building barns, labor unions, charitable organizations
10. New measure of success	10. Centrality of person, family, and local community
11. Vision and hope	11. Optimistic and open people

will try to avoid the charge of wishful thinking by adhering to what seem to be valid projections.

Lessened Expectations

It does not take a futurist to note that citizens of the United States now have lower expectations than they did a decade ago. The economy will probably never reach the rate of growth of the 1950s and 1960s, and people know that. Resources are more expensive; Japan and some developing countries are producing quality goods cheaper, and our firms have become less competitive. This phenomenon has been widely discussed and has already been treated in Chapter 6. The economy of the future, methods of organizing work, government policy, and personal values will all be heavily influenced by the coming era of declinging rates of growth.[31]

Central Role of the Person

A constant theme running through American life and thought is the importance of the individual person. Individualism, democracy, the free market, and

[31]James O'Toole, *Making America Work: Productivity and Responsibility* (New York: Continuum, 1981); Carter Henderson, "The Darkening Outlook for the U.S. Economy," *The Futurist*, 16 (February 1982), 23–27; and Hazel Henderson, *Creating Alternative Futures: The End of Economics* (New York: Perigee, 1977).

the courts have that principle as their foundation. As the average level of education rises and standards of living also rise, people become less willing to suffer uninteresting work and being treated, along with capital, as merely one of the inputs into the production process. To emphasize organizational efficiency, we often use the model of the machine to express how we work together—"a well-oiled machine." Yet being a replaceable part in a machine is not a role that emphasizes the importance of the person. A better description, one that stems from our religious roots, and one that acknowledges the centrality of the person is to compare an efficient firm to an organism, a body, in which the parts work intimately together and are dependent on each other. Each part is thus vitally important to each other and to the whole and is not easily replaceable.[32]

Future demands for increasing productivity, coupled with the acknowledgement of the central role of the person, will bring about a resurgence of skills upgrading and management development programs and more flexibility in planning an individual's workday, workweek, and work lifetime. Planned periods of work interspersed with extended periods for education, outside volunteer activities, and leisure will become more common.[33]

In this "postaffluent" era there is a continuing need to achieve personal esteem and personal growth. This will require restructuring of work and providing greater flexibility than was the case previously. Pension plans sometimes lock individuals into uninteresting jobs or dead-end careers. Requiring but a five-year period for vesting would enable employees to rotate among firms and into government when needed without losing pension rights.[34]

The era of egoism, the exclusive "me first" mentality, may be over. "It failed both psychologically and practically—that's why people are giving it up."[35] People are willing to go back to some of the old-fashioned commitments, like that of reinvesting emotion and energy in work—provided they are engaged in that work—and having a family—provided there is flexibility in defining responsibilities. The family will remain the bedrock of America's social structure.[36]

Social commentator Ivan Illich maintains that every tool (in the broad sense) should be designed and used to bring people closer together so as to live fuller

---

[32]Otto Bremer, "Religious Insights for Ethical Managerial Decision Making," paper presented at Western Academy of Management, April 10, 1981, p. 6. Thanks to Otto Bremer for suggesting the model Table 7-1, also. See also Peter K. Mills, "Self-Management: Its Control and Relationship to Other Organizational Variables," *Academy of Management Review*, 8 (July, 1983), pp. 444-53.

[33]"Next 20 Years: New Products, New Careers, New Ways to Work," *U.S. News & World Report*, December 1, 1980, p. 54; also *An Environmental Scan Report: What Lies Ahead* (Alexandria, Va.: United Way of America, 1980), pp. 16, 18.

[34]John Oliver Wilson, "After the Fall," *New York Times*, September 24, 1980, p. A31.

[35]Daniel Yankelovich, "Demise of Egoism: Why the 'Me' Decade Didn't Work," *U.S. News & World Report*, August 24, 1981, pp. 65-66.

[36]"Trends to Watch in This Decade," *U.S. News & World Report*, June 22, 1981, p. 60.

and happier lives. Yet he finds many tools divisive and disruptive, no matter who uses them:

> Networks of multilane highways, long-range, wide-band-width transmitters, strip mines, or compulsory school systems are such tools. Destructive tools must inevitably increase regimentation, dependence, exploitation, or impotence, and rob not only the rich but also the poor of conviviality which is the primary treasure in many so-called underdeveloped countries.[37]

He challenges the notion that progress means more elaborate tools in the hands of a highly trained elite, thus making each individual more and more dependent and helpless. The advent of microprocessors and robotics could make people more dependent. On the other hand, they are powerful tools that can relieve men and women of dreary and demeaning work and give them more responsibility and thus more challenging jobs.

The business firm will find that, in order to compete for talent, it must see that the development of its people is as important an objective as providing goods and services. High-technology firms in California's Silicon Valley, such as Hewlett Packard and Tandem Computers, provide a wide variety of such services. Highly educated workers demand such an environment. Without a work setting in which the individual is challenged, able to grow, and be fulfilled, the firm is at a severe disadvantage. This is, of course, especially true of the more talented, creative, and achievement-oriented white- and blue-collar workers.

A work environment that provides flexibility, that challenges the multitude of talents a person possesses, one in which co-workers and supervisors communicate and provide each other feedback on their work, is one in which an individual may grow as a person. Numerous programs of job enlargement and organization development have been tried. For example, Volvo assembles its automobiles in teams, rather than using the assembly line. Japan uses robots. General Motors and Ford are committed to quality of work life programs and more robotics. For a business firm that produces a worthwhile product or service, it is essential to structure its work in such a fashion that men and women can be engaged in and satisfied with what they are doing. The traditional notion that *any* work had value could be used to make people a means, a mere input for the production process. People were urged to work hard and to forget the fact that their work might be repetitive, unchallenging, and sometimes demeaning. This sort of attitude places more importance on the short-term value of a smooth running plant than it does on the growth, contribution, and satisfaction of the person. As many commentators rightly point out, modern American industry has been better at producing products and services than in providing challenging and

---

[37]Ivan Illich, *Tools for Conviviality* (New York: Harper & Row, 1973), p. 12.

satisfying work. Now, when failing in production, we are forced to examine the work setting.

Participation in Management Decisions *illusion of freedom*

In addition to restructuring the job, many workers are also asking for more influence on major decisions that are made at work.[38] Various schemes have been developed in the United States, Sweden, Japan, Yugoslavia, and elsewhere to obtain worker input and even to share in the responsibility for these decisions with workers. Decision making through consensus at the grass roots among workers (industrial democracy), as opposed to decisions being made exclusively at the top and handed down through the hierarchy, is a model now being used in many countries and in some plants in the United States. No doubt more American business firms will move in this direction in the coming decade. The encyclical letter of Pope Paul II, *On Human Labor,* asserts the primacy of persons. Labor has priority over capital, and persons have priority over production. It is essential, according to the pope, that work be structured so that the working person is able to develop and grow as a person. The worker should never be viewed as a mere means.[39]

Over a longer span, most people find that an essential element in a satisfying job is being able to enjoy the people with whom one works. If co-workers are unfriendly, insular, and uncooperative, it is difficult to enjoy a job. On the other hand, if co-workers are helpful and friendly and provide feedback—on job-related and other items—work can be satisfying and even something one looks forward to. Large national and international firms that formerly would transfer talented, high-potential managers every few years now recognize the need people have for establishing friendships and some stability, so as to be better able to contribute to job, neighborhood, and their children's development. Life on the job and in the suburbs has often been alienating, and what friendships there are, shallow and superficial. It is too great a risk to get to know people well, be transferred, and thus be forced to go through the pain of leaving real friends. It is simpler and less painful (risk averting) not to get involved.[40] Recognition of these human needs has caused major firms not to demand the same number of periodic moves of their achievement-oriented executives. They are now more

[38]Frank W. Schiff, *Looking Ahead: Identifying Key Economic Issues for Business and Society in the 1980s* (New York: Committee for Economic Development, 1980), p. 29; also O'Toole, *Making America Work,* chap. 6. For some notable successes in participation and its positive effect on productivity, see Thomas J. Peters and Robert H. Waterman, Jr., *In Search of Excellence* (New York: Harper & Row, 1982).

[39]John Paul II, *On Human Labor (Laborem Exercens),* in *Priority of Labor,* commentary by Gregory Baum (New York: Paulist Press), especially paragraphs 7, 12, 13.

[40]See the William H. Whyte, Jr., classic, *The Organization Man* (Garden City, N.Y.: Doubleday-Anchor, 1956), pp. 295–435; and George W. Pierson, *The Moving Americans* (New York: Knopf, 1973).

apt to recognize and respect the basic human need for friends, roots, and the resulting beneficial feedback. This, in turn, enables managers to increase their own self-esteem and confidence.

An individual without interest in work can readily become frustrated and alienated. Withdrawal from an active personal involvement then often follows, leading to the mass passivity that Gunnar Myrdal laments.[41] If only a fraction of a person is alive and operating at the workplace, it is clear that both the person and the firm are the losers—especially in the long run. Creativity, effort, innovation, and dedication to the task will decline and hence productivity and the health of the firm will suffer.

Many leading firms, General Electric and General Motors among them, have extensive programs designed to increase employee involvement and satisfaction. As an example, Ford Motor reduced the number of defects in its vehicles by 48 percent in a recent two-year period, and this largely by enlisting the efforts of workers. Where labor relations are not adversarial, management is able to ask employees to help improve quality by monitoring the product as it is made and by suggesting better manufacturing processes, so to lessen defects. Ford engineers took a prototype of the new Ranger mini pickup truck to line workers and asked for their suggestions. Larry Graham, an assembly-line worker, who had worked on a previous model pickup, suggested that the design be changed to allow assemblers to bolt the pickup cargo box from above rather than from below. When bolting from below, he had to lift a heavy pneumatic wrench over his head from a pit beneath the truck. Bolts were not firmly tightened, and customer complaints came in. The engineers used Graham's suggestions to redesign that assembly process, resulting in easier assembly and far fewer loose bolts and consumer complaints.[42]

Passivity may stem from our affluence. "Twenty-five good years can be bad for a largely secularized nation. . . . It has resulted in more bureaucracy, more inefficiency and more laziness—in both the public and the private sectors."[43] This lack of concern, if allowed to go unchecked, could lead to the rigidity and eventual decay of all our institutions, as well as to the frustration and alienation of people. On the other hand, mature, confident, generous people who are alert to opportunities, to life, and to what goes on around them are the major asset of any society. It is clearly to the long-term benefit of the firm and society if work activities are structured so that an individual is able to contribute, grow and develop as a person, and finally to enjoy work. Hence, a renewal of self-reliance, cooperation, and involvement will benefit all: individuals, families, neighborhoods, and firms.

[41]Gunnar Myrdal, "Mass Passivitiy in America," *Center Magazine*, March-April 1974, pp. 72-75.

[42]"A Better Idea: American Car Firms Stress Quality to Fend Off Imports," *Wall Street Journal*, August 26, 1982, pp. 1, 14.

[43]Herman Kahn, "Next Decade Will Be the 'Sobering '80s,' " *U.S. News & World Report*, August 20, 1979, p. 52.

Business as a Servant of Society

The unrestrained free market model of business viewed the corporation as individual, isolated and competing with other firms to survive and grow. As long as the firm showed a profit, financial analysts and *Barron's* called it a success. The firm was thus judged successful whether it made durable, high-quality, basic necessities, or whether it made trivial, dangerous luxuries—perhaps even at the cost of low-paid workers and pollution of neighborhoods. The models and ideology of these old school economists and businesspeople urged indiscriminate production and consumption. However, it is now apparent that these criteria of success are not specific enough. The business firm is a servant of society. It is chartered by the state to provide for the needs of citizens.[44] It is not an autonomous institution, intent merely on its *own* profits and growth. Corporate executives, especially of the larger and better firms, have acted on this notion of the firm for a decade. Chief executive offices have gone farther in actually structuring their firms, with new goals, officers, and departments, to ensure that these wider objectives are met.[45] New, growing industries that have been identified as having high growth potential for business graduates are geared to genuine human needs: robotics, solar power, office technology, energy conservation, cable TV, and genetic engineering.[46]

In contrast to the "cowboy economy" out of which we have recently moved, in which gross production and consumption are the measures of success, the newer "spaceship economy" has as a measure of economic success "the nature, extent, quality, and complexity of the total capital stock, including in this the state of human bodies and minds included in the system."[47] The notion of "more is better" is myopic and has many undesirable consequences: pollution, intrusive advertising, long hours of debilitating work to produce unnecessary and dangerous gadgets, disruption of urban and rural areas by ugly and unplanned asphalt, heart attacks and nervous strain stemming from obsessive competition and "keeping ahead of the Joneses", and families uprooted because of job transfer. If human needs and desires could be met with less production and consumption, heretical as it sounds, the economy would actually be performing in a superior fashion. In short, additional production and consumption are not only not goals in themselves but exclusive emphasis on them works to the detriment of people and the environment.

[44]Robert Hessen notwithstanding. For his position, see *In Defense of the Corporation* (Stanford, Calif.; Hoover Institution Press, 1979). For several case histories of this view, see "When Business Comes to Cities Rescue," *U.S. News & World Report,* August 9, 1982, pp. 42-43.

[45]See the excellent *Statement on Corporate Responsibility* by the Business Roundtable (New York: Business Roundtable, 1981), pp. 1, 8, 12-14.

[46]These six industries were selected for separate explanatory pamphlets for job-seeking graduates at Harvard Business School. See *Wall Street Journal,* April 1, 1982, p. 1.

[47]Kenneth E. Boulding, "The Economics of the Coming Spaceship Earth," in *The Futurists,* ed. Alvin Toffler (New York: Random House, 1972), p. 237; see also Kenneth J. Arrow, "Social Responsibility and Economic Efficiency," *Public Policy,* 23 (Summer 1973), 303-17.

There is a resistance to such a basic shift, since it requires reformulating goals and criteria of performance. Even more troublesome, it requires that we make judgments on the type of products, the type of growth we want, and what sort of tradeoffs we are willing to make.[48] Judgments require facts, discussion, and some consensus—a huge order for a troubled democracy. It is far easier to back off and allow the "free market" to make those allocations. However, the latter stance is wasteful of precious effort, land, and resources and is thus not a responsible policy.

Organizations tend to take on a life and purpose of their own. They are not likely to phase themselves out of existence once their initial purpose has been met. Organizations and institutions, whether government agencies, voluntary groups, schools, or business firms, seek to perpetuate themselves and to find or create new needs to which they can direct themselves. This is one of the characteristics of the bureaucratic organization.[49] Business firms are no different, and thus generally require more than a gentle shove in order to rethink their objectives and structures.

One of the major criteria of the worth of any work or handicraft up to the time of the Industrial Revolution was the relative value of the good or service to society. As we have seen, with the growth of industry, and especially the division of labor, an ideology developed that bestowed value on any work, regardless of its outcome. A growing number of men and women are questioning the value of some work, no matter how well paid it may be. For example, these individuals claim that they would not work for a strip-mining firm, a designer clothing manufacturer, a hard-line advertiser, or a nuclear missile manufacturer. They are thereby reintroducing criteria that had been pushed aside in the last few generations: The value of work is judged both by the contribution that the product or service makes to society and by the contribution of the individual to that product or service.[50] For example, some sort of individual transportation vehicles are necessary, and thus the work of the auto worker takes on an importance beyond the paycheck and benefits. Whether the two-ton, gas-guzzling, polluting, luxury sedan is able to win the same job satisfaction for its makers may be questioned, however.

Does it make any difference whether the manager or the worker is helping to produce canned foods, tractors, cigarettes, throw-away bottles, or nuclear weapons? All goods are not of equal value to society, and it is possible for individuals to make judgments on the relative value of these goods. In a small, primitive economy these questions do not arise, since there are only enough resources and effort available to provide the necessities. In a postaffluent society, luxuries are still possible, and this forces value questions. If resources are limited and people are not willing to work long hours, what goods are more valuable to society? The

[48]For some creative ideas on this, see Robert L. Heilbroner, "Does Capitalism Have a Future?" *New York Times Magazine*, August 15, 1982, pp. 20-22, 38-52.

[49]Warren Bennis, *Beyond Bureaucracy* (New York: McGraw-Hill, 1966).

[50]See the changes in the work ethic described earlier in Chapter 6.

values we present here should help us to provide these criteria. Perhaps goods and services could be judged insofar as they support life, build community, give freedom, and provide joy and happiness. These values are very general, but they may provide a basis for hammering out new criteria.

Efficiency, Flexibility, and Innovation

Efficiency, flexibility, and the ability to innovate will be sought-after qualities of both individuals and institutions over the next decade. The United States has a long tradition of pride in such abilities. Current declining rates of productivity have frightened Americans. The questions in the back of everyone's mind, often unarticulated, are: Has the United States already reached the peak of efficiency and world leadership? Are we already on the way down? The answers to those questions are not clear, but few are willing to surrender without our best national efforts to retain some leadership in such industries as steel, automobiles, rubber, and electronics. Efficiency, flexibility, and innovation are key to any attempt to remain productive.

With high wage rates and a high capital cost economy, increased efficiencies and innovation are our only alternatives. Efficiencies may be achieved in surprising ways. Railroads use far less fuel and cost far less to move a ton of freight a mile than do trucks. A given $100 million might be more effectively spent on upgrading our rail system than on patching the interstate highway system.[51] Decisions like this can only come from enlightened public policy; that is, public policy that is also designed to aid and support business efficiencies. Or, as Ken Walters has put it, "The major change that I believe is likely to occur is that the focus . . . will change from our past preoccupation with what public policy should do *to* business to an additional interest in what public policy can and should do *for* business."[52]

In Japan and in European countries, government aids the private sector in many ways. It is clear that government-business cooperation in the United States will be required to meet strong international competition. This does not mean government subsidy, nor does it mean that government neglects to oversee such issues as product safety, pollution, and equal employment opportunity. However, new efficiencies are required, and flexibility and innovation will be a part of these new efficiencies. They can best be achieved by alert individuals and firms and the selective, enlightened cooperation of government.

[51] This issue is raised by Frank W. Schiff, *Looking Ahead: Identifying Key Economic Issues for Business and Society in the 1980s* (New York: Committee for Economic Development, 1980), pp. 31, 52.

[52] Kenneth D. Walters, "New Directives for Research in Business and Public Policy," Research Workshop Keynote Address, Academy of Management, New York, August 15, 1982, p. 10.

Interdependence of People,
Institutions, and Nations

In a world of more people, more elaborate tools and life styles, and quicker transportation and communication, peoples and institutions are becoming more interdependent. A military coup or revolution in Latin America or Asia is in our living rooms in a matter of hours via television. Malnutrition and starvation in Africa are brought home to us quickly, along with the fact that our use of lawn fertilizer, dog food, and even meat may play a role in depriving those Africans of life-giving grain. When suburbanites try to flee the problems of the city, they find that their affluent sons and daughters, without parks, libraries, and corner stores within walking or bus distance, find little to do and become bored. Many then use drugs, drop out of school, and run away from home. Nationalistic policies that may have worked for England or France in the last century must be discarded today; the United States, powerful as it is, can no longer assume that what is good for the United States is therefore good for all the world.

The immense problems that face us also face all nations: unemployment, deteriorating environment, malnutrition, nuclear wastes and threat of nuclear warfare, imbalance of payments, dwindling resources, and inflation. No single nation can face these problems alone. Too often U.S. officials are insensitive to worldwide reaction to their actions. The U.S. lone vote against the WHO/UNICEF Infant Formula Code and the repudiation of the long-in-process Law of the Sea Treaty lost the United States much international respect.[53] Trying to thwart the European gas pipeline to Russia may seem to be good short-run policy for the United States, but it is not good for the Europeans. Corporate managers readily acknowledge that the narrow, nationalistic attitudes that might have served well a generation ago are now no longer sufficient.[54] Ultimately all peoples will depend more and more on each other. Looking on this extremely complicated interdependence tempts some social commentators to see the problems as immense and almost insolvable.[55] Since peoples and nations seem unwilling to limit their own individuality, sovereignty, and greed, they are convinced that there is no hope for humanity.

Sociologist of religion Robert Bellah sees America's failure in its emphasis on the atomistic self and rational self-interest and its break with the basic understandings of the Founding Fathers. In early American documents and times there was a strong social, collective emphasis: a consideration of citizens together as

[53]James E. Post, "Business, Society, and the Reagan Administration," chairperson's presentation, Social Issues Division, Academy of Management, New York, August 17, 1982, pp. 19-20.

[54]"Tomorrow's managers will be more world-minded than the present generation. . . . In the second half of this century, we are witnessing the emergence of an interdependent world economy." Jones, "Managing in the 1980's," p. 5. See also Schiff, *Looking Ahead*, pp. 2, 24-25.

[55]See, for example, Robert Heilbroner, *The Human Prospect* (New York: Norton, 1974).

responsible for the state. Bellah demonstrates how this comes from the biblical covenant between God and his people and from the gospel notion of a loving community based on charity and membership in one common body. Bellah is convinced that the economic system of contemporary industrial America has broken with and cannot be reconciled with the early American rationale of economic interdependence as the basis of political order.[56]

Perhaps these early ideals can be recaptured. In any case, the urgency and vital importance of the many problems that jointly face the nations of the world may force their leaders to work pragmatically to determine and carry out public policy together. The continued survival and well-being of all men and women may force nations to overcome nationalism, insularity, and greed in a way that ideals and altruism could not accomplish.

Harmony with the Environment and Decentralization

In addition to meeting citizens' real needs, the corporation will continue to operate with greater respect for the natural environment. Scarcity of resources, pollution, and undesirable by-products place constraints on the direction and pace of economic and business growth.[57] These physical constraints will become more obvious, and citizens' expectations of the firm living with and respecting those constraints will become more pronounced. Hazardous industrial wastes loom as an ever increasing problem during the coming decade. Their transportation and disposal, as well as determining liability, pose increasingly difficult problems for business in the future. The federal government has legislated a billion-dollar "super-fund" to clean up toxic dumps—the money coming from chemical firms—and safety requirements for the shipment of hazardous materials.

The physical and social environment in which we live and work also affects our values. Decentralization and simplification have traditionally been preferred to large size in the United States. Large size is unavoidable in some cases: where the interdependence considered above demands it, or when economies of scale require it in order to compete with equally large international firms (for example, steel, autos, computers). Nevertheless, encouraging entrepreneurship in the private sector and keeping the government's role as small as possible in the public sector are traditional American values. Even in providing human services, such as health, retirement, and education, the independent sector can generally deliver better services at a lower cost than the public sector. As long as these services are provided to the poor and handicapped, decentralization in both the public and private sectors has several advantages: (1) It eliminates layers of organizational bureaucracy; (2) it more clearly locates responsibility; (3) it gives people

---

[56]Robert N. Bellah, *The Broken Covenant: American Civil Religion in Time of Trial* (New York: Seabury, 1975).

[57]For an excellent overview of these and additional issues, see Lester R. Brown, *Building a Sustainable Society* (New York: Norton, 1981).

a sense of more control over their lives and work and thus provides increased personal motivation and involvement in neighborhood and work; (4) it is far less costly; and (5) it is in the American tradition of self-reliance.

Small businesses are already encouraged in the United States by lower tax rates. Except where it can be shown that large size is necessary, perhaps a graduated corporate tax rate could be devised with larger firms (measured by gross sales) paying a higher tax rate than smaller firms. When considering work and home life, many are opting for simplification. At present, for example, a great deal of time and energy are wasted in transportation. Much of the time that is saved in cutting down the hours of the work day is absorbed in getting to and from work, stores, schools, church, and so on. Whereas even little children could walk in older neighborhoods, in the more modern suburbs one is more dependent on driving or being driven. This is not only a waste of time and energy but also a waste of petroleum and other natural resources. It is a loss of freedom and is hardly progress. Similarly, time is wasted in filling out forms such as income tax returns, insurance applications, and questionnaires and in listening to advertisements. In speaking of these same issues in the concluding paragraph of his book *Alienation and Economics,* Walter Weisskopf urges, "Wherever there is a choice between making more money and simplifying life, the latter road should be taken." He goes on to spell out the details:

> . . . abandonment of the purely activistic way of life, of getting and doing more and more for the sake of power over and control of the external world including our fellow beings; taking seriously the Kantian maxim that men should never be used as means but always as "ends"; putting more stress on being than on doing by cultivating receptivity to nature, to others, to art, to feelings; more listening rather than talking, also in relation to one's inner life; taking seriously intuition and insight by trying to resurrect what is valid in mysticism and religion; recovering the art of faith by breaking through the value-relativism of technical reason and cultivating the inner powers on which faith rests.[58]

Most of these new attitudes are already observable among many segments of our society, and they seem to be spreading. These new human aspirations are going to have a significant impact on the firm and its activities. The successful firm will be alert to these changes in attitudes and will gear its own actions and policies to these shifting expectations.

Religious Roots of New Business Creed

Personal and societal goals in the United States have been heavily influenced by religion, especially by Christianity. We live on the foundation of a Judeo-Christian culture. Although the superstructure of values and attitudes is

---

[58]Walter A. Weisskopf, *Alienation and Economics* (New York: Dutton, 1971), p. 192; for another view, see John Naisbitt, *Megatrends* (New York: Warner Books, 1982), especially pp. 11-37.

now not well anchored, the older roots continue to provide sustenance and life. As our society becomes more pluralistic (each person's values are as good as every other person's) and atheistic (not acknowledging God as the source of life), our values become more free floating and hence without guy lines or foundation. The Protestant ethic stemmed from Christianity, and particularly Calvinist Christianity. Although it soon became rather secular, its religious roots are unmistakable. Since religious values have had such a profound influence on business and economic life in the past, it is appropriate to ask whether religious ideals will have a significant impact in the future. Even more important, if religion does have an impact on business and on our way of life, what will that impact be?

In spite of the current fashionable and tired cynicism, there has always been a strong streak of moralism in American culture. Our history is replete with idealistic public reaction to problems. In the last century the antislavery (abolition) and anti-big business (muckraking) movements were moral endeavors, and many involved received inspiration from the Gospels. Ralph Nader comes from a religious family with high ideals, and John Gardner's Common Cause appeals to the generosity and moral qualities of Americans. The shocked reaction of the public to congresspeople taking bribes and to corporate dumping of toxic wastes also showed high moral expectations.

The civil rights movement in the United States was led by Martin Luther King, Jr., a Baptist minister. He preached "love for the oppressor" and espoused a specific nonviolent technique to gain social justice for blacks. The record shows how effective the movement and his leadership were. Among those now protesting the dangers of nuclear weapons is a group of Catholic peace activists inspired by Dorothy Day and Daniel Berrigan, S.J. This group has picketed nuclear missile manufacturers and used a confronting, though nonviolent, strategy in presenting its case. Whether one agrees with the group's tactics or not, it is working for world peace here in the United States and in other nuclear nations around the world, including the USSR. More important here, most in the movement are prayerful people who are inspired by the Gospels and the life of Jesus. A man who is an inspiration to all these people is Mahatma Gandhi, who in turn was also inspired by the life of Christ. Moreover, as history testifies, his nonviolent approach to gaining independence for India from England was successful.

Many Catholic priests and sisters are being murdered in Guatemala, El Salvador, Bolivia, Chile, and other Latin American countries because they have taken up the cause of the poor and the peasants.[59] Their inspiration comes from Jesus and his emphasis on loving the poor and bringing justice to those at the bottom of the socioeconomic ladder (Matthew 5:3; Luke 6:20). In this role they have often come into opposition with local and multinational business firms and with local military governments. The vision motivating all these Gospel-inspired leaders and the movements themselves is liberation: freedom of the poor, or-

---

[59]For numerous examples, see Penny Lernoux, *Cry of the People* (New York: Penguin, 1980); and Martin Lange and Reinhold Iblacker, *Witnesses of Hope: The Persecution of Christians in Latin America* (Maryknoll, N.Y.: Orbis, 1981).

dinary citizen from the colonial or local oppressor; liberation of the black from white bigotry; freedom to work and thus earn a fair day's pay; freedom from the danger of nuclear holocaust; self-determination for people around the world.

Religion underscores the role of the manager or owner as a steward. Thus wealth and power are a trust that is held for others. Based on the understanding that the world and all its goods come from and ultimately belong to God, the individual businessperson holds all this in stewardship—in trust for others.[60]

From another font, fundamentalist Christianity has gained considerable attention in recent years. These Protestant preachers constantly cite the Gospels and tend to be conservative on such issues as racial equality, the environment, and the role and purpose of business. They insist that the United States is and must remain number one in the world. Fundamentalism has an advantage in being able to present its message to a television audience in clear, uncompromising and dramatic terms. On many critical issues, it tells its audience what it wants to hear; it reinforces existing biases. These preachers tell the individual exactly what he or she must do to be saved. This often means contributing large sums of money to the evangelist and his or her church. Fundamentalism defends the value of the family and the nation and is consistently conservative on social issues. The Moral Majority takes its inspiration from fundamentalist churches. Although many question whether their social positions are sufficiently rooted in the Gospels, there is no doubt that fundamentalists have had a profound impact on American life.

Creating some consensus on the role of business in our society, along with some agreement on what is right and what is wrong in business dealings, is a top priority among reflective businesspeople.[61] A foundation for this vision and the ethics that flow from it might be religion. Granted it would be difficult to achieve such a consensus, it would nevertheless provide a needed foundation for policy and decisions in both the private and public sectors.

Theology for the Future

Theology is almost a dirty word in American society. It connotes airy, idealistic speculation on one hand and coercion on the other. A theology, however, is merely an attempt to understand one's self, others, and God in the light of religious values, especially as experienced and presented in scripture. Speaking from the Christian perspective, business theologian Donald Kirby says that "theology aids the human person in staying human against a culture which constantly tries to shift people from the the human," and it "protects human beings

---

[60]William J. Byron, S.J., "Christianity and Capitalism: Three Concepts from the Tradition, Three Challenges to the System," paper presented at Marquette University Centennial Symposium, November 2, 1981. See also Oliver Williams and John Houck, eds. *The Judeo-Christian Vision and the Modern Corporation* (Notre Dame, Ind.: University of Notre Dame Press, 1982); also Michael Novak, *Toward a Theology of the Corporation* (Washington, D.C.: American Enterprise Institute, 1981).

[61]See, for example, Jones and his discussion of business ethics and responsibility, in "Managing in the 1980's."

from the distortion of the human by contemporary culture."[62]

One organized attempt at developing such a theology is underway in Latin America. Called "liberation theology," it began in Peru, Uruguay, Chile, and other Latin American countries, where the gap between the poverty-stricken average citizen and the few extremely wealthy landowners and industrialists is extremely wide.[63] Right-wing military dictatorships and their harsh police states have intensified the demand on the part of the people for liberation, for self-determination, and for individual control over jobs, cities, nations, and lives. In the same fashion as the people of Poland are oppressed by the Communist regime, so too are the peoples of Guatemala, Bolivia, Uruguay, Chile, Paraguay, and many other Latin American countries oppressed by United States-supported right-wing dictatorships. In Poland and in Latin America the Catholic church sides with the people, and a theology of liberation is developing. Liberation theology insists on beginning with an examination of people's actual condition in a given society. Thus one of the principal inputs is the experience of the struggle for liberation and self-determination for all. Such contemporary theology is built on the social conditions in which people find themselves.

In short, if religious values influenced economic life in the past, there is every reason to predict that they will do so in the future. These new theologies take as their starting point the individual person and her or his relation to God. They tend to side with the poor. The growth and success of the theology of liberation suggest that it and theologies like it will have a significant impact in future decades. If so, this will mean a continued demand for self-determination, whether at work, at home, or in the city. Such self-determination is not the old-fashioned individualistic sort, but one that is hammered out with others, in a community of men and women. It is important to note that proponents of liberation theology take a critical view of capitalism. Their own experience tells them that capitalism, profit maximization, and foreign ownership lead to the exploitation of the poor and the concentration of wealth in the hands of a very few. They thus opt for various forms of participation and, in the case of business, for worker control. No matter how the firm is structured, they would have some significant worker input into all decisions, both short- and long-range.

It is undoubtedly a healthy characteristic for American society to have streaks of utopianism, moralism, and even righteousness. The latter can be arrogant and unbending, but it can also provide the inspiration and motivation for a people to continue to have hope and demand the best from themselves, their society, and their institutions. Perhaps it is on the basis of this sort of idealistic desire for the best for ourselves and for all that a new sort of cultural superego could be built. One of the human necessities of the future will be, according to Daniel

---

[62]Donald J. Kirby, S.J., "Corporate Responsibility," paper presented at Workshop on Teaching Business Ethics, Fordham University, New York, August 9, 1982.

[63]See, for example, the fine work of Jon Sobrino, S.J., *Christology at the Crossroads,* tr. John Drury (Maryknoll, N.Y.: Orbis, 1978); also Gustavo Gutierrez, *A Theology of Liberation* (Maryknoll, N.Y.: Orbis, 1973).

Callahan,[64] a series of new cultural "thou shalt nots." He maintains that mankind will not be able to survive without a new set of accommodated appetites, a habitual willingness to conserve and preserve, and a general conscientious concern for others. Admitting that this is an almost impossible task, he concludes that it is nevertheless absolutely necessary if we are not to descend to starvation, war, and chaos. Taking the charge seriously himself, Callahan has set up the Hastings Center to encourage public and professional awareness of ethical issues. The center publishes a journal on ethics and bioethics and has recently completed a ground-breaking, large-scale project to aid the teaching of professional ethics.[65]

The alternatives presented by most social commentators who examine the future are stark: depression, decay, and chaos, or development of new spiritual and human values that become integrated into everyday personal life and institutional decision making. On this shrinking planet, economic and political planning must increasingly consider the larger issues. Paradoxically, it is "old-fashioned" religion that has traditionally urged the viewpoint of concern for *others,* especially the poor, people in other nations, and future generations.

Concern for Others

Self-centeredness and insularity are the vices of the child. As a person, loved and cared for, matures, that same person tends to be less defensive and turned in on the self. He or she begins to move out toward others and to love. Love is a basic human virtue. It is the act of a parent or a peer; it is an act of giving, often without hope of return. This sort of altruistic love is possible for any person, although it is more readily achieved by the person who has been loved. Self-giving love is essential for the growth of persons, families, and society, yet it is sometimes difficult. Speaking of this sort of love, economist Kenneth Boulding says:

> It always builds up, it never tears down, and it does not merely establish islands of order in a society at the cost of disorder elsewhere. It is hard for us, however, to learn to love, and the teaching of love is something at which we are still very inept.[66]

Much of the energy of the very poor is spent on obtaining the necessities of life. Once an individual's basic needs are reasonably satisfied, that person more readily has the time and the inclination to be concerned with the needs of the larger society. Affluence can put a person in a position where he or she is no longer totally dependent, with all energies consumed in obtaining the next meal.[67]

[64]Daniel Callahan, *The Tyranny of Survival* (New York: Macmillan, 1974).

[65]The journal is *The Hastings Center Report* (360 Broadway, Hastings-on-Hudson, N.Y. 10706), and the results of the project are in Callahan's book, *Ethics Teaching in Higher Education* (New York: Plenum Press, 1980).

[66]Kenneth E. Boulding, *The Meaning of the Twentieth Century* (New York: Harper & Row, 1964), p. 146.

[67]People's values can have a profound effect on their ethical judgments; culture affects values. For an excellent treatment of this issue, see William C. Frederick, "Embedded Values: Prelude to Ethical Analysis," Graduate School of Business, University of Pittsburgh, Working Paper no. 446, February 1981.

Greater availability of food and shelter provides a physical and psychological security that can enable people to reach out beyond themselves and their own concerns. A certain amount of material security can be the foundation for loving and self-giving. The problems of human life, development of the person, and interdependence of persons and institutions can be far more readily approached. There is evidence that such attitudes are growing, as has been indicated earlier in this chapter and in Chapter 6. Western society is uniquely ready for greater love and concern for others, and the problems we face together could be better solved given such an attitude.[68]

New Measures of Success

To survive and grow, the business firm must be efficient, innovative, and profitable. Until recent decades these were the exclusive objectives of the firm. However, corporate leaders now no longer claim that enlightened self-interest is the only goal of business, or that such a goal automatically benefits society. Earlier chapters, especially Chapter 6, have documented the many conflicts that exist between what is beneficial to the firm and what is good for society.

New measures of success for the firm arise from the realization that the business firm, along with all human institutions, operates to benefit people. The business firm is an instrument or a means to be of service to people—indeed *all* people. Those persons benefited by the firm's operations are not only customers and shareholders but also employees, suppliers, and the members of the local community. Moreover, it is not a zero-sum game. Benefits to one constituency are not always at the expense of another group. Indeed, often enough it is quite the opposite: Enlightened social policy is of benefit to all the corporate stakeholders.

Just as the financial audit sketches the firm's financial performance, the social report outlines the impact of the firm's operations on the firm's other constituencies. Criteria for judging social performance are critical if we are to judge accurately the success of a firm, as indicated in Chapter 6.

Business firms are well aware of the need for corporate social performance measures. The Business Roundtable, composed of the chief executive officers of the largest U.S. firms, has made clear its own position on the centrality of social goals for the firm and how to structure the firm so that these social goals are achieved.[69] Moreover, these CEOs also sponsored a handbook that aids firms in the achievement of their social goals.[70]

National and international government policy must also be based on the same sort of criteria: the betterment of people. In the 1980s, there seems to be

[68]CEO Richard J. Bennett of Schering-Plough makes many of these points in his "A New Compact in the Age of Limits," Sievers Lecture, Fordham University, November 5, 1981, especially pp. 6–8.

[69]*Statement on Corporate Responsibility* (New York: Business Roundtable, 1981); also the earlier Roundtable statement, *The Role and Composition of the Board of Directors of the Large Publically Held Corporation* (New York: Business Roundtable, 1978).

[70]Steckmest, *Corporate Performance.*

little positive national economic policy. A cogent and consistent national economic policy to lead us in this direction would be very desirable.[71]

These new measures of success are increasingly centered on the benefits that accrue to persons—all the stakeholders of the firm. This shift marks a fundamental change in perspective for the corporate manager. Because social goals are increasingly a part of the criteria for measuring the success of the corporate manager, they will continue to have a profound impact on the values and perspective of the corporate manager.

Vision and Hope

The problems that we face—unemployment, pollution, nuclear war, unjust governments, world food shortages—are so immense that some find them to be insolvable. These problems result either from a complicated tradeoff in order to achieve other goods or in some cases from a callous disregard for others' welfare. The question then becomes: Do we have the resources and the motivation to seek a solution and to change institutions that so much affect our lives and our values? Can we alter our business firms and our government so to make more intelligent tradeoffs on these issues? Can we build the values, structures, and institutions necessary for peace and justice throughout the world?

Vision and hope have always been characteristically American virtues. Ever since the days of the frontier, we have never had patience with defeatists or fatalists. Nevertheless, it would be foolish to be naive about the enormity of the tasks before us. Moreover, people today are more caught up in their own personal lives and careers. It is the rare individual who asks what he or she can do to solve these problems; women and men with that sort of vision have always been in a minority. Yet we also know that an individual or a small group of talented, generous people can have a profound impact on our lives and on our world.

SUMMARY
AND CONCLUSIONS

The American business system has achieved unprecedented efficiency, productivity, and growth. Nevertheless, it is now painfully clear that the free market itself is not able to provide such goods as clean air and water, safe products, and even fair competition. Too often, a firm that adds to the gross national product actually detracts from natural beauty, health, and personal happiness; its production processes may be dangerous or demeaning or may pollute or use up nonrenewable resources.

Understanding, cooperation, and looking to the common good are called

[71]Robert B. Reich, "Why the U.S. Needs an Industrial Policy," *Harvard Business Review*, 60 (January-February 1982), 74-81; and a fuller acount in Ira C. Magaziner and Robert B. Reich, *Minding America's Business: The Decline and Rise of the American Economy* (New York: Harcourt Brace Jovanovich, 1982).

for on the part of business, government, and other segments of American society. Special interest groups, coupled with general apathy and a lack of clear values and goals on the part of most of us, have led American society into many unfruitful, expensive, and frustrating traps. Some of these losing efforts are, for example, defective and dangerous products, collapsing railroads and urban public transportation, decaying cities, loss of farmlands, defective nuclear power plants, expensive and wasteful defense systems. Exacerbating the problem, traditional business ideology—individualism and self-interest—rewards selfishness and justifies self-seeking behavior. More humane personal values and some discussion of public goals would help to avoid these expensive and frustrating policy blunders. Many firms are now doing their own forecasting of future values, so that they can gear their product planning, employee participation programs, and advertising to these emerging new attitudes.

Future business values will ask efficient and innovative behavior of the firm; productivity and growth can no longer be taken for granted. Moreover, citizens will continue to demand that individual business decisions contribute to the overall goals of society. A business firm is no longer merely seen as a wholly private, self-interest-oriented enterprise; its role is to serve the needs of society. If such business firms are unable or do not choose to act responsibly, it will be necessary to enact prescriptive legislation or tax incentives to encourage social and discourage antisocial behavior.

Americans are seeking greater self-activity and self-reliance, even in the face of the dehumanizing factors of modern life. In spite of encompassing institutions, whether government or corporate, individuals still prefer autonomy, personal responsibility, and the ability to share decisions. Institutions and corporations can be better structured to encourage such self-reliance and responsibility.

Self-reliance, individual responsibility, and initiative give dignity and satisfaction to the individual, in addition to often bringing about a more efficient organization. We have found to our chagrin, however, that these motivations do not always automatically provide the best total society. Hence, it is necessary to clarify goals and to construct legislative and cultural inducements so that individual activities may better contribute to producing a more humane society.

Religion has in the past, and probably will in the future, provide a foundation for business ideology. True enough, traditional religious values generally run counter to self-interest and what has come to be known as the consumer ethic. The Protestant ethic demanded a moderated, planned, and self-sacrificing life. Unemployment, pollution, noise, anxiety, crime, and other current problems that accompany the operations of the impersonal, profit-maximizing bureaucratic corporation show the failure of the old ethic and the need for new values. Americans now seem ready for some sacrifice for the sake of a larger purpose. Most would gladly give up a Florida vacation or a third automobile if it meant a more satisfying job and life, better relationships, and the conviction that their own children and future generations would not inherit a nation ravaged by open-pit mines and cancer-causing chemicals—the fruits of this generation's selfishness. Western religions have traditionally directed peoples' attention out beyond themselves. With this sort of vision, Americans might share some of their expertise and resources with the poorer peoples of the world so that those less privileged can have some of the more important and humane fruits of industry. It is precisely religion that urges discipline of self and generosity toward one's neighbor based on a reverence for God and a loving concern for others.

Clarifying and internalizing values and goals is necessary for any person as he or she grows to maturity. Especially in a period of rapid change, these values provide a firm foundation upon which to build a stable, challenging, and satisfying life and career. These personal values are also the building blocks out of which, together with society's conditions and needs, can be fashioned the future goals and policies of the business firm. In this essential process of examining and articulating new values and goals, leadership is also needed. The problems are immense, pressing, and complex. Nevertheless, business, government, educational, and religious leaders may yet be able to point out directions and to inspire confidence.

DISCUSSION QUESTIONS

1. What are the issues upon which there is general agreement among business managers and business critics? What is the major issue on which they disagree?
2. How do you answer for yourself each of the seven questions under "Basic Beliefs Support an Ethic"?
3. What are the strengths and limitations of a democracy in meeting new social needs (such as pollution control or energy policy)?
4. What is the role of "mediating structures" in economic planning?
5. Outline the techniques for future forecasting, so that the information can be used in corporate strategic planning.
6. Do you think that each of the broad forecasts under "Future Business Values" is likely to come about? If they do, what significance would each have for the organization in which you are presently employed?
7. If these same projections do come about, would it bring a better or a poorer quality of life? How so?
8. Upon what basic values might it be possible to build a public policy consensus for the future? Will religion have any role in spelling out these values and articulating this consensus?

Exam Oct 1, '85   Kinkos / Scan-tron sheets ②
200 TF   #2 pencil

INDEX